THE COMPLETE CRITICAL GUIDE TO

THOMAS

Geoffrey Harvey

Routledge
Taylor & Francis Group

LONDON AND NEW YORK

First published 2003
by Routledge
11 New Fetter Lane, London EC4P 4EE

Simultaneously published in the USA and Canada
by Routledge
29 West 35th Street, New York, NY 10001

Routledge is an imprint of the Taylor & Francis Group

© 2003 Geoffrey Harvey

Typeset in Schneidler by
HWA Text and Data Management, Tunbridge Wells
Printed and bound in Great Britain by
TJ International Ltd, Padstow, Cornwall

British Library Cataloguing in Publication Data
A catalogue record for this book is available from the British Library

Library of Congress Cataloging in Publication Data
Harvey, Geoffrey, 1943–
The complete critical guide to Thomas Hardy / Geoffrey Harvey.
p. cm.
Includes bibliographical references and index.
1. Hardy, Thomas, 1840–1928 – Criticism and interpretation –
Handbooks, manuals, etc. 2. Wessex (England) – In literature –
Handbooks, manuals, etc. I. Title
PR4754 .H28 2003
823´.8–dc21   2002014228

ISBN 0–415–23491–3 (hbk)
ISBN 0–415–23492–1 (pbk)

For Lynne

CONTENTS

Series editors' preface   ix
Acknowledgements   xi
Abbreviations and referencing   xii

Introduction   1

Part I   LIFE AND CONTEXTS   3
(a)   Rural childhood   5
(b)   Architect and autodidact   8
(c)   Young man in London   13
(d)   Apprentice novelist: Cornwall and love   16
(e)   *Far From the Madding Crowd*: fame and marriage   21
(f)   Nomadic novelist   24
(g)   Dorchester, *The Mayor of Casterbridge*, and high society   30
(h)   *Tess of the d'Urbervilles, Jude the Obscure*, and
      the abandonment of fiction   34
(i)   Emergence of the poet   40
(j)   Emma's death; marriage to Florence   45
(k)   *Moments of Vision* and writing *The Life of Thomas Hardy*   49
(l)   Final years   50

Part II   WORK   55
      Hardy's categorisation of his fiction   57
(a)   Major novels   58
      Under the Greenwood Tree   58
      Far from the Madding Crowd   61
      The Return of the Native   66
      The Mayor of Casterbridge   71
      The Woodlanders   77

	Tess of the d'Urbervilles	82
	Jude the Obscure	88
(b)	Lesser novels	94
	Desperate Remedies	94
	A Pair of Blue Eyes	96
	The Hand of Ethelberta	98
	The Trumpet-Major	101
	A Laodicean	105
	Two on a Tower	107
	The Well-Beloved	110
(c)	Short stories	114
(d)	Poetry	119
(e)	*The Dynasts*	136
(f)	*The Life and Work of Thomas Hardy*	139
Part III	CRITICISM	143
(a)	Tragedy	146
(b)	Wessex	152
(c)	Humanist formalism	158
(d)	Structuralism and deconstruction	164
(e)	Psychoanalytic approaches	167
(f)	Marxist criticism	175
(g)	Feminist and gender studies	182
(h)	Poetry	190
(i)	Other topics and issues	197
Chronology		205
Bibliography		209
Index		219

SERIES EDITORS' PREFACE

The Complete Critical Guide to English Literature is a ground-breaking collection of one-volume introductions to the work of the major writers in the English literary canon. Each volume in the series offers the reader a comprehensive account of the featured author's life, of his or her writing and of the ways in which his or her works have been interpreted by literary critics. The series is both explanatory and stimulating; it reflects the achievements of state-of-the-art literary-historical research and yet manages to be intellectually accessible for the reader who may be encountering a canonical author's work for the first time. It will be useful for students and teachers of literature at all levels, as well as for the general reader. Each book can be read through, or consulted in a companion-style fashion.

The aim of *The Complete Critical Guide to English Literature* is to adopt an approach that is as factual, objective and non-partisan as possible, in order to provide the 'full picture' for readers and allow them to form their own judgements. At the same time, however, the books engage the reader in a discussion of the most demanding questions involved in each author's life and work. Did Pope's physical condition affect his treatment of matters of gender and sexuality? Does a feminist reading of *Middlemarch* enlighten us regarding the book's presentation of nineteenth-century British society? Do we deconstruct Beckett's work, or does he do so himself? Contributors to this series address such crucial questions, offer potential solutions and recommend further reading for independent study. In doing so, they equip the reader for an informed and confident examination of the life and work of key canonical figures and of the critical controversies surrounding them.

The aims of the series are reflected in the structure of the books. Part I, 'Life and Contexts', offers a compact biography of the featured author against the background of his or her epoch. In Part II, 'Work', the focus is on the author's most important works, discussed from a non-partisan, literary-historical perspective; the section provides an account of the works, reflecting a consensus of critical opinion on them, and indicating, where appropriate, areas of controversy. These and other issues are taken up again in Part III, 'Criticism', which offers an account of the critical responses generated by the author's work. Contemporaneous reviews and debates are considered, along with opinions inspired by more recent theoretical approaches, such as New Criticism, feminism, Marxism, psychoanalytic criticism, deconstruction and New Historicism.

The volumes in this series will together constitute a comprehensive reference work, offering an up-to-date, user-friendly and reliable account of the heritage of English literature from the Middle Ages to the twentieth century. We hope that *The Complete Critical Guide to English Literature* will become for its readers, academic and non-academic alike, an indispensable source of information and inspiration.

RICHARD BRADFORD
JAN JEDRZEJEWSKI

ACKNOWLEDGEMENTS

I would like to thank my colleagues in the School of English and American Literature at The University of Reading for their support, and in particular Carole Robb for her secretarial assistance. The staff of the University Library have also been most helpful. I am grateful to the series editors, Richard Bradford and Jan Jedrzejewski, and to Liz Thompson, the development editor at Routledge, for their encouragement, advice and patience during the preparation of this book.

ABBREVIATIONS AND REFERENCING

Since there are many editions of Hardy's texts available to the reader, reference is made to chapters. Where the novels are divided into parts, the part and chapter numbers are indicated. In the case of *The Dynasts*, the part, act and scene are given. The dates of composition of the poems, where this is known, is given, together with the title of the volume in which they were later published.

References to individual texts are abbreviated as follows:

AL	*A Laodicean*
D	*The Dynasts*
DR	*Desperate Remedies*
FFMC	*Far from the Madding Crowd*
HE	*The Hand of Ethelberta*
JO	*Jude the Obscure*
MC	*The Mayor of Casterbridge*
PBE	*A Pair of Blue Eyes*
RN	*The Return of the Native*
TDU	*Tess of the d'Urbervilles*
TM	*The Trumpet-Major*
TT	*Two on a Tower*
UGT	*Under the Greenwood Tree*
W	*The Woodlanders*
WB	*The Well-Beloved*

Other abbreviations are :

CP	*Collected Poems* (London: Macmillan, 1930)
L	*Letters. The Collected Letters of Thomas Hardy*, ed. R.L. Purdy and M. Millgate, 7 volumes (Oxford: Clarendon Press, 1978–88)
LN	*Literary Notebooks. The Literary Notebooks of Thomas Hardy*, ed. Lennart A. Björk, 2 volumes (London: Macmillan, 1985)
LW	*Life and Work. The Life and Work of Thomas Hardy*, by Thomas Hardy, ed. Michael Millgate (London: Macmillan, 1984)

Cross-referencing between sections is one of the features of this series. Such references are to relevant page numbers and appear in bold type and square brackets e.g. **[37]**.

INTRODUCTION

This book describes the literary career, writings and critical reception of a singular writer, Thomas Hardy (1840–1928), who achieved the status of both major novelist and major poet. His long life, beginning when Victoria was still a young queen and ending a decade after the First World War, saw many revolutionary social and intellectual changes that are refracted in complex ways in his writing. Hardy rose from rural obscurity in Dorset to scale the social heights, declining a knighthood but accepting the Order of Merit, and being accorded the honour of burial in Westminster Abbey.

Part I, 'Life and Contexts', provides a straightforward biographical foundation for the subsequent account of Hardy's writings and commentary on the vast body of criticism, which reveal the extraordinarily complex relation between his life and his work. Hardy's career is given detailed exposition, from his early years in the village of Higher Bockhampton, through his apprenticeship to a Dorchester architect, a profession that took him to London and later Cornwall where he met his wife, Emma Gifford, fame with *Far from the Madding Crowd* and his subsequent development as a novelist. Hardy's poetic career is also charted. He had produced a body of poetry in the 1860s, and he took up poetry again in the 1890s, after he had stopped writing fiction, following savage reviews of *Jude the Obscure*. This virtually new career as a poet is described, together with his growing stature as a public figure, and the vicissitudes of his private life, including Emma's death and his marriage to Florence Dugdale. Part II, 'Work', offers close readings of his major and lesser novels, his poetry, his verse epic, *The Dynasts*, his short stories, and his ghosted autobiography. Recent trends in Hardy studies are reflected in the more extensive treatment given to the lesser fiction and to the poetry. In Part III, 'Criticism', major contributions are selected from the vast output of writing on Hardy, for detailed commentary within a framework of clearly identified theoretical and other approaches, which are contextualised and explained. Areas of controversy, such as the nature of Hardy's tragedy, his treatment of women, Wessex and regionalism, and his philosophy of life, are fully discussed.

The Complete Critical Guide to Thomas Hardy permits the reader to consult the text on individual texts or topics, pursue connections between them, or read the book as a comprehensive account of his life, work and the current state of Hardy studies.

PART I

LIFE AND CONTEXTS

Thomas Hardy was born when the young Queen Victoria had been on the throne only three years, and he died when the 1920s were drawing to a close. He rose from lower-class rural obscurity to rank as the foremost writer of the age. His funeral drew large crowds, the Prime Minister, Stanley Baldwin, led the nation's mourning, and his ashes were laid to rest in Westminster Abbey. Since Hardy's death, his reputation both as a novelist and as a major poet has grown; his short stories and his minor novels are being revalued, while developments in literary theory and criticism continue to reveal fresh aspects of a writer whose modernity continually surprises.

Intensely private, evasive and ironic, Hardy has proved an elusive subject for biographers. His public life and career were relatively uneventful, and his personal life was marked by the absence of drama. Much of Hardy's life, as he observed, is present in his novels, poems and short stories, and the complex strands of relationship between his life and his writings. These encompass, uniquely, his adoption of the topography of Dorset, where he was born and grew up, for his fictional county of Wessex, and his exploration of its society and history. Further contexts are intellectual and social. In his writing Hardy engages with the ideas and trends of his age: developments in science, new philosophies that sought to fill the vacuum left by the loss of religious faith, the growth of a radical politics that gave expression to the striving of the working class for social equality and democracy, the struggle for a new status for women, and the effects of the First World War. Another important context is the literary market place in which his work was published, especially since the majority of his novels and some of his short stories first appeared as serials in the popular magazines of the day. The Victorian writer's relationship with editors and publishers was difficult. Hardy in particular, the scourge of established values, had to run the gauntlet of Mrs Grundy, the mythical prudish censor who scrutinised magazines and books for their immoral content. (Mrs Grundy, a character in Thomas Morton's comedy, *Speed the Plough*, 1798, was a neighbour who represented convention, propriety and prudery. Grundyism came to signify a narrow and rigid morality.)

(a) RURAL CHILDHOOD

In 1918, ten years before his death, Hardy observed, in his ghosted autobiography, first published in two volumes, in 1928 and 1930: 'It bridges over the years to think that Gray might have seen Wordsworth in his cradle, and Wordsworth might have seen me in mine' (*LW*, 417).

Hardy's cradle was filled, but only by chance, on 2 June 1840, because the midwife had noticed signs of life in the baby that had been pronounced dead. His had been a difficult birth, he was not a robust child, and his anxious parents did not expect him to reach maturity.

The first child of Jemima and Thomas Hardy, he was born in the family cottage, situated on the edge of heath land, up a lane in the hamlet of Higher Bockhampton in the parish of Stinsford, some two miles east of Dorchester. His powerfully influential mother Jemima, *née* Hand, from Melbury Osmond in the north of Dorset, had endured early hardship, gone into service, and attained the position of cook to the vicar of Stinsford. Her husband was an easy-going, handsome and courteous man, popular with women, and it is likely that his marriage to Jemima was precipitated by her pregnancy. The early courtship of Hardy's parents is recorded in the poem, 'A Church Romance' (prompted by the death of his mother in 1904), while Hardy employed his father's journey to Melbury Osmond for his wedding in the story, 'Interlopers at the Knap' (1884). The marriage produced further children. Hardy was very close to his sister Mary, who was born in 1841; he maintained a warm relationship with his brother Henry, born when Hardy was ten; and a second sister Katherine was born when Hardy was sixteen. The sisters entered the teaching profession, and Henry followed his father into the building trade.

The passionate interests of his parents profoundly influenced a child of acute sensibility. Jemima was a determined reader, with a fund of stories embodying local lore, while her husband loved nature and music. As Hardy's biographer, Robert Gittings has said: 'His father's enjoyment of nature was matched by his mother's extraordinary store of local legend and story. Together they filled Hardy's world with landscape and human dealing, the special blend that was to mark his poems and novels' (Gittings 1975:17). By the time Hardy was ten, his mother had introduced him to John Dryden's *Works of Virgil* (1697), Samuel Johnson's *Rasselas* (1759), and a translation of Bernardin de Saint-Pierre's *Paul et Virginie* (1788), while his father had imbued in him a love of music. Like his own father and grandfather, Thomas Hardy senior played the violin, and taught his son to accompany him when he was engaged at local parties and social events. Young Hardy was extraordinarily sensitive to melody, and the effects of this are evoked superbly in the poem, 'The Self-Unseeing', which captures a memory of dancing enraptured to the music of his father's violin.

Hardy also assimilated something of his parents' fatalism. From his father it was a straightforward acceptance of what life offered, but from his mother came a strong vein of pessimism. An entry in Hardy's

Notebook for 30 October 1870 reads: 'Mother's notion, & also mine: That a figure stands in our van with arm uplifted, to knock us back from any pleasant prospect we indulge in as probable' (Taylor 1978: 6–7). Hardy fondly describes his father, in his *Life*, as cheerful and energetic; but it was his mother who fashioned his character. His poem, 'In Tenebris III' reveals his dependence on her. Hardy was reserved, and not physically strong, and it was Jemima's combination of stern rectitude and social ambition that inculcated in him his steely determination to achieve. A further strong influence was Hardy's paternal grandmother, Mary Hardy, celebrated in the poem, 'One We Knew', who lived in the family home. To the family's stock of folk tales, she added anecdotes about the period in 1804 particularly, when coastal Dorset was on alert for Napoleon's invasion, her husband's enrollment in the Puddletown Volunteer Light Infantry, and the maintenance of a warning beacon on nearby Rainbarrow. These stories aroused Hardy's lifelong interest in the Napoleonic era that later was to find expression in his writing **[28, 101, 115, 136]**. And his grandmother's youthful memories of the cottage at Higher Bockhampton awakened in him an awareness of its extreme solitude, and a profound love of nature, as his first poem, 'Domicilium' reveals, written when he was eighteen or so.

Social class was an extremely significant influence on Hardy. In the Victorian period, gradations of social class were rigid, and to Hardy it mattered intensely that his family was a degree above its neighbours in the social scale. His father was a master mason, who employed a few men, and although in the 1851 census he had been described as a 'bricklayer', this was altered to 'mason' when in later life Hardy constructed his family tree. The business prospered when his competent brother Henry took it over, but during Hardy's childhood income was uncertain, and they relied on the produce from their smallholding. His father had occasional work from the Kingston Maurward estate, and a strong emotional attachment developed between Julia Augusta Martin, the wife of its owner, who was childless, and young Hardy. This relationship afforded a glimpse of a sphere of elegance that provided the class theme for his first attempt at fiction, *The Poor Man and the Lady*, and it became a subject to which he returned obsessively.

Although at Higher Bockhampton Hardy did not encounter directly the lives of the farm labourers, or 'workfolk' as he called them, he was acutely aware that they lived on the verge of dire poverty, in overcrowded, unsanitary cottages, and at the mercy of the farmers who hired them. Hardy remembered that the post-mortem on a shepherd-boy, who had died of want, discovered only the remnants of raw turnip in his stomach. And he later testified to Rider Haggard, the public servant, former colonial administrator, and author of *King Solomon's Mines*, who was investigating rural poverty, that in the period up to 1850–5, the condition of the agricultural labourer in Dorset was one of considerable hardship. This darker side of rural life is recorded with scrupulous fidelity in *Far from the Madding Crowd*, *The Mayor of Casterbridge*, and *Tess of the d'Urbervilles*, and embraces the agricultural depression of the 1880s, as well as the social disruption brought about by more general economic and social change **[153, 178]**.

The Church also played a central role in Hardy's early life. His grandfather and father had been involved with the Stinsford choir, until in about 1841 the vicar, Arthur Shirley, a High Churchman, secured its removal and replacement by an organ, an event that provided the kernel of *Under the Greenwood Tree*, set in fictional Mellstock, which was based on Stinsford. The Mellstock choir also features in several poems, including 'A Choirmaster's Burial'. Hardy loved the church music, attended services regularly, and taught for a while in the Sunday school. His nostalgia for those days is recorded in the poem, 'Afternoon Service at Mellstock', and he reveals his distress at his subsequent loss of religious faith in another much-anthologised poem, 'The Oxen'.

In 1850 Jemima's removal of her son from the village National School in Lower Bockhampton, built at Mrs Martin's expense, to the British School in Dorchester led to the withdrawal of estate business from her husband. In the interval between schools, Hardy accompanied his mother on a visit to Hatfield to her younger sister Martha Sharpe, elements of whose character inform Bathsheba Everdene in *Far from the Madding Crowd*, while her husband John, an agricultural bailiff and former soldier, suggested the figure of Sergeant Troy. On Hardy's return, in September 1850, he found himself walking the three miles each way to a new school in Dorchester.

(b) ARCHITECT AND AUTODIDACT

Until the Education Act of 1870 made the provision of elementary education the state's responsibility, this had been the task of the National Schools, created earlier in the century for promoting the education of the poor in the principles of the established Church. The Church also supervised the Teacher Training Colleges, from which the first trained teachers emerged in 1853, products of a strenuous process of examination, who inculcated in their pupils the rote learning of facts that Dickens satirised in his novel *Hard Times*. The dominant influence of the Church in education also extended to the universities.

While education in the nineteenth century responded to rapid social and economic change, aiming in 1870 for universal literacy, it also perpetuated social divisions, and for Hardy was inevitably bound up with class issues. He was ambivalent and defensive about his self-education, and was bitter about his exclusion from the universities, which were for the financially secure middle class. In the nineteenth century, university admission depended on competence in classical languages, and residence in a college required considerable independent means, so undergraduates came mainly from the public schools. Education is a significant preoccupation in Hardy's fiction. School teaching is seen as the focus of idealism, and for women a route to independence, but Hardy also examines how increased social mobility may blight individual lives by educating people out of their class, and how on the other hand exclusion from education may result in tragically wasted lives.

Jemima Hardy's removal of her son from the National School was a sound educational decision. From Isaac Last, the headmaster of the British School, and from 1853 of his own 'commercial academy' in Dorchester, Hardy received grounding in French and Latin, and also mathematics and mechanics. Prompted by an acute sense of social and academic inferiority, Hardy began a life-long programme of intellectual self-improvement. He hoped for a university degree, followed by ordination and a mode of life in a country parish that included the writing of poetry. However, although the lack both of a classical education and financial support made this a forlorn dream, there remained a local route into the middle class through architecture. On 11 June 1856, shortly after his sixteenth birthday, prodded by his mother, Hardy was articled for three years to John Hicks, a Dorchester architect specialising in church restoration. The perceived enormity of the lower-class Hardys overreaching themselves resulted in the Reverend Arthur Shirley's denouncing the sin of social ambition from the pulpit of Stinsford Church, in the presence of Hardy and Jemima. This searing experience, unmitigated by time or success, fostered in Hardy a bitter anger at the tyranny of class that finds perhaps its most powerful expression in his final major novel, *Jude the Obscure*, when Jude, a 'working-man', is advised by the Master of Biblioll College to remain 'in your own sphere' (*JO*, 2: 6).

John Hicks was an educated man, who ran a congenial office in South Street, next door to the school kept by the poet William Barnes, whose interest in the language and dialect of Dorset, and in poetic technique, was later to influence Hardy's own work. But a more immediate impact on Hardy's intellectual development was made by Henry Bastow. Bastow's strongly held Baptist beliefs challenged Hardy's somewhat relaxed Anglican faith, and many hours were devoted to strenuous debate about infant baptism. While Hardy was labouring at Latin and Greek, Bastow's interest in the Greek New Testament prompted Hardy to switch from Homeric to Biblical Greek. However, Hardy resisted his friend's efforts to convert him, and remained regular in his attendance at Anglican worship.

Hardy's emotional life was hampered by his shyness and evident immaturity. Like Jocelyn Pierston, the hero of his fantasy, *The Well-Beloved*, the adolescent Hardy pursued ideal beauty in girls, but in his case girls to whom he was too shy to speak, such as Elizabeth Bishop, a local gamekeeper's daughter and the subject of the poem, 'To Lizbie Browne', or Louisa Harding, a farmer's daughter to whom he never confessed his infatuation, but who is the subject of the poem, 'To Louisa in the Lane', written on her death in 1913 **[38, 45, 52, 111, 118, 127]**. Although he felt more at ease with his cousin Martha Sparks of Puddletown, who was six years his senior (and there seems to have been strong feeling on both sides), these infatuations established a life-long pattern of hesitant, idealised but sexually charged and problematic relationships with women.

By his own admission, Hardy had remained a child until he reached sixteen. Because of his continued lack of confidence and his relative immaturity, Jemima and John Hicks agreed to an extension of his articles for a further year. This enabled him to broaden his experience of life in Dorchester, a bustling county town that offered diverse entertainments for a young man, including lectures, concerts, hiring fairs and circuses. The equestrian troupe of Cooke's Circus, which presented battle scenes from the Crimean War when they visited Dorchester in 1856, was used for the circus performance of Sergeant Troy in *Far from the Madding Crowd*, while in the same year the celebration of the conclusion of the Crimean War, which was combined with the annual commemoration of Queen Victoria's coronation, provided street scenes later used in *The Mayor of Casterbridge*.

Dorchester life also had its grimmer aspects. On 9 August 1856 the public execution took place of Martha Browne for the murder of her husband. Hardy was among the large crowd near the gallows outside the prison, and in later life he recalled the shape of the woman's figure in her black silk gown hanging against the sky, and the way that, when it began to rain, her features came through the cloth that had been put over her face. Two years later, he observed from the heath near the cottage, through the family telescope, the hanging of a local man, James Seale. The effect of the telescope made it a disturbingly intimate experience. It was knowledge of this kind that Hardy drew upon in his story, 'The Withered Arm', and in *Tess of the d'Urbervilles*.

In the *Life*, Hardy offers an insight into the complex routine that shaped his experience at this period:

> To these externals may be added the peculiarities of his inner life, which might almost have been called academic – a triple existence unusual for a young man – what he used to call, in looking back, a life twisted of three strands – the professional life, the scholar's life, and the rustic life, combined in the twenty-four hours of one day, as it was with him through these years. He would be reading the *Iliad*, the *Aeneid*, or the Greek Testament from six to eight in the morning, would work at Gothic architecture all day, and then in the evening rush off with his fiddle under his arm – sometimes in the company of his father as first violin and uncle as 'celloist – to play country-dances, reels, and hornpipes at an agriculturalist's wedding, christening, or Christmas party in a remote dwelling among the fallow fields, not returning sometimes until nearly dawn.
>
> (*LW*, 36)

By far the most powerful source of intellectual stimulation for Hardy was Horace Moule **[23, 96]**, the fourth son of the Reverend Henry Moule, the energetic vicar of Fordington, a village on the outskirts of Dorchester. Hardy greatly admired the remarkable Moule family, but he was particularly close to Horace, a brilliant classical scholar, whose interests encompassed music and poetry, and who also wrote philosophical and literary articles, published books on theology and Roman history, and contributed literary reviews to major national periodicals such as the *Saturday Review*, in which he was later to review Hardy. It is not known precisely when he and Hardy first met, but they developed a deep bond. Eight years Hardy's senior, Moule possessed a fine intellect, charm, social standing, and culture that won Hardy's admiration and love. Hardy had gained as his mentor a genuinely liberal thinker.

The mid-Victorian period (1840–70) was characterised by a battle between science and religion, which found its most potent symbol in the great debate at Oxford in 1860 between Bishop Wilberforce and Charles Darwin's disciple T.H. Huxley (who coined the term 'agnostic'). Up to then, the ancient concept of the Great Chain of Being, the idea of a universe created and ordered by a loving God, had held sway. The eighteenth-century Catholic poet, Alexander Pope, in his philosophical poem, *An Essay on Man* (1733–4), describes how all living organisms have their fixed place in an immutable order. However, this view had not been unchallenged. Erasmus Darwin, Charles Darwin's grandfather, at the turn of the century had mooted the possibility of the development of species, in *Zoonomia* (1794–6). But it was during the middle years of the nineteenth century that the scientific climate changed, with a series of discoveries and inventions in technology and medicine, such as electro-magnetism, chloroform, ether, the analytic engine (forerunner of the computer), photography, steel, reinforced concrete, and the establishment of science degrees at the University of London. The beginning of the scientific and technological age bred an openmindedness, which permitted the serious consideration of new ideas. Some discoveries directly challenged religious beliefs, most significantly Sir Charles Lyell's *Principles of Geology* (1830), which posited a great antiquity for the earth and a very long period of gradual and regular change that called into question the literal truth of the Biblical account of Creation in Genesis. And in the field of biology, Robert Chambers, in his popular book *Vestiges of the Natural History of Creation* (1844), maintained a theory of biological evolution through the operation of natural law. All this culminated in Charles Darwin's epoch-making book of evolutionary theory, *On the Origin of Species* (1859) **[77, 81, 121, 201]**. Orthodox Christian belief was devastated by Darwin's theory of natural selection, because its notion of randomness, wastefulness and cruelty could not be reconciled with faith in a divinely ordered creation. There can be little doubt that Hardy and Moule discussed Darwin's book, since according to Hardy, when it was published he was 'among the earliest acclaimers' (*LW*, 58). The evolutionary struggle for existence described by Darwin chimed with Hardy's fatalistic temperament, and undermined his religious faith, as it did that of so many Victorians. Hardy's notebooks record his lifelong interest in Darwin, and his fiction and poetry explore the tragic implications of humanity's diminished place in an empty and imperfect universe. Moule also loaned Hardy Gideon Algernon Mantell's *The Wonders of Geology* (1838), introduced him to other scientific works, including Jabez Hogg's *Elements of Experimental and Natural Philosophy* (1847), and brought to his notice the controversial *Essays and Reviews* of 1860, a collection of essays on religious subjects, which was denounced by a meeting of the bishops for its liberalism.

Apart from encouraging Hardy's immersion in the intellectual debate, Moule gave further impetus to Hardy's already intense programme of self-improvement, emphasising at the same time the gulf between his dreams and their fulfilment. Through him Hardy glimpsed the intellectually exciting world of the universities, while recognising that it was closed to young men from his social background. The more specific influence of Moule on Hardy's fiction can be seen in the person of Henry Knight, mentor to the young architect, Stephen Smith in *A Pair of Blue Eyes*; but more significantly perhaps in *Tess of the d'Urbervilles*. The relationship between Moule and his doctrinaire father, who was wounded by his son's independence of mind, was uneasy, and Hardy made the occasion of an argument between them over Horace's purchase of some books that his father regarded as theologically unsound into a dispute between Angel Clare and his father. Horace's brothers, of whom two subsequently became Anglican bishops, also served as models for Angel Clare's clerical brothers.

(c) YOUNG MAN IN LONDON

After the completion of his articles, Hardy remained with Hicks as an assistant at fifteen shillings per week, staying at Dorchester and visiting his family at Higher Bockhampton at the weekends. However, in April 1862, at the age of twenty-one, in a bold assertion of independence and ambition – though with the insurance of a return railway ticket – Hardy embarked on a career in London, where he was to live until 1867. An emotional entanglement in Dorchester may have prompted his sudden decision, but his main motive was probably professional. A letter of introduction secured a position as an assistant architect and draughtsman with Arthur Blomfield, whose thriving firm specialised in ecclesiastical architecture, where Hardy showed promise. Elected to the Architectural Association in 1862, he won one of its prizes for his design for a country mansion, and in the same year he was awarded the Silver Medal of the Royal Institute of British Architects for an essay, 'On the Application of Coloured Bricks and Terra Cotta to Modern Architecture'. Architects and architecture were to figure prominently in Hardy's fiction, most notably in *A Laodicean*.

London was a booming and exciting city. In 1863 the Thames Embankment, a huge project creating the raised stone structure that forms the banks of the River Thames, was in the process of being built, and also the Charing Cross Railway Bridge, which Hardy observed from the window of his office in Adelphi Terrace. Although Hardy felt himself to be very much the provincial, he threw himself into the life of the capital. He heard Charles Dickens lecture, attended dances, saw the great actor Charles Kean and his wife in Shakespeare, and also frequently visited the opera.

In spite of the opportunities for dissipation in the capital, Hardy's life seems to have remained disciplined and devoted to self-improvement. He visited the International Exhibition at South Kensington (later the Victoria and Albert Museum) for its architectural artefacts and paintings, studied the great masters at the National Gallery during his lunch period, and enrolled for French classes at King's College. Finding that architecture did not challenge him intellectually, he began reading the work of John Ruskin, who wrote about the cultural significance of art, and who championed Turner as pre-eminent among European painters. In 1863 Hardy commenced keeping a notebook about 'Schools of Painting', in the hope of becoming an art critic. This was the beginning of a life-long interest, and references to painters and painting occur with striking frequency in his novels **[58, 80, 199–200]**. He also considered journalism as a way of financing his ultimate goal of going to university and entering the Church. However, this aim receded as under Moule's mentorship Hardy was introduced to the writings of a wide range of contemporary thinkers, including the work of John Henry Newman, the leader of the Oxford Movement, who left the Anglican Church for Roman Catholicism, and whose *Apologia pro Vita Sua* was published in 1864, on which Hardy made quite extensive notes. But Hardy also read John Stuart Mill **[85, 121]**, a seminal philosopher and economist, who formed the Utilitarian Society, wrote *On Liberty* (1859), a comprehensive defence of individual freedom, and *Utilitarianism* (1861) and who, in contrast to Newman, regarded the ideal of Christianity as negative and passive. Hardy later estimated Mill, by whom he was strongly influenced, as 'one of the profoundest thinkers of the last century' (*LW*, 355). Indeed Hardy claimed to know *On Liberty* almost by heart. Mill weaned Hardy away from a Wordsworthian reliance on nature as a moral guide (Hardy turns on Wordsworth with some bitterness in *Tess of the d'Urbervilles*, in which he explicitly rejects the comforting vision of his ode, 'Intimations of Immortality'). Hardy also studied J.M.R. M'Culloch's popularising book on economics, *Principles of Political Economy* (1825) and the 1865 translation of Auguste Comte's *A General View of Positivism* (1848) **[23, 68, 108, 121]**, a gift from Moule. Comte urged the need to complete the final, positive stage of the development of humanity through education and science. Since there was no after life, conventional religion must be replaced by a 'religion of humanity', complete with its own rituals. This would offer an alternative moral and ethical system to that of Christianity, combining service to others, compromise, and loving-kindness (Hardy's phrase). Though Hardy could not entirely share Comte's evolutionary optimism, during this idealistic phase of his life Comte was a special influence upon him, and probably assisted the gradual erosion of his religious belief.

By 1865 Hardy had begun to think of himself as a potential writer. A humorous prose sketch, 'How I Built Myself a House', was published anonymously in *Chambers's Journal* and brought his first income from writing. But rather than build on this Hardy turned to poetry, and in the same year he bought several volumes to study. Determined and methodical, he began keeping a notebook headed 'Studies, Specimens etc.', in which he listed quotations, attempted to develop a vocabulary of his own, and recorded observations of people and scenes for possible poems.

Hardy noted that 'in verse was concentrated the essence of all imaginative and emotional literature' (*LW*, 51), and in these early years he was influenced by the Romantics' conception of poetry; by the visionary power of the imagination, the moral influence of nature, and the ideal of transcendence. When Swinburne's *Poems and Ballads* came out in 1866, Hardy responded with enthusiasm, particularly to Swinburne's recognition of mutability as the essential condition of life, and his pursuit of intense experience. A similar Romantic preoccupation with the life of the senses and the importance of the moment is found in the early poetry of Tennyson and in Hardy's contemporary, Browning. Hardy's continued admiration for Swinburne is evident in his novels.

Hardy's earliest poems were written in 1865 and 1866, though for reasons that remain obscure, these remained unpublished for years. Some clearly draw on his relationship with Eliza Bright Nicholls, to whom, according to his biographer, Michael Millgate, it appears that he was 'more or less formally engaged from about 1863 until 1867' (Millgate 1982: 84). Hardy had moved his lodgings from Kilburn to 16 Westbourne Park Villas, close to Paddington Station and within walking distance of Eliza, who was employed as a lady's maid. They may have met when her father was a coastguard at Kimmeridge on the Dorset coast, or equally, because of their proximity, in London. Eliza was a deeply religious and bookish girl, and in due course Hardy's attention strayed to her more interesting younger sister, Mary Jane. His relationship with Eliza gave rise to the 'She, to Him' series of poems, and in the *Wessex Poems* volume in which they appear, on the opposite page is printed Hardy's drawing of two figures climbing the path that runs up to Clavel Tower overlooking Kimmeridge Bay. The end of the relationship is recorded in the poem, 'Neutral Tones'.

Several factors led to Hardy's decision to leave London. It was an unhealthy city for someone with his physical constitution, and his bouts of ill health were exacerbated by overwork. His loneliness often resulted in periods of depression. By 1866 he had finally realised that the Church was closed to him as a career. A university education was beyond his means. Moreover, his belief in the Church's doctrines had been gradually undermined by his innate scepticism. It had been further eroded by the rationalist, scientific climate of the age, represented not only by the great advances in science and technology, but also by the profoundly influential writings of Sir Charles Lyell, Charles Darwin, John Stuart Mill and Auguste Comte. What remained was essentially an emotional attachment to the history of the Church, and to its rituals and music. On top of all this was the breaking off of his engagement to Eliza Nicholls. Physically and emotionally exhausted, Hardy resigned his post with Blomfield and returned to Dorset.

(d) APPRENTICE NOVELIST: CORNWALL AND LOVE

In July 1867 Hardy was at home at Higher Bockhampton, and he remained in Dorset for the next three years, working for John Hicks, and then for G.R. Crickmay, a Weymouth architect, who took over Hicks's contracts on his death. Hardy enjoyed church restoration, although he was later to lament its excesses and lack of respect for tradition. Most important, he also found time to write. However, no independent career was to be made as a poet, and Hardy began to regard fiction, which had brought fame and wealth to a number of contemporary novelists, such as Charles Dickens, Wilkie Collins, George Eliot and Anthony Trollope, as offering a second-best option: 'Thus, under the stress of necessity he had set about that kind of literature in which he had hitherto taken but little interest – prose fiction' (*LW*, 58).

Hardy regarded a novel as 'an impression, not an argument', as he wrote much later in his Preface to the 1892 edition of *Tess of the d'Urbervilles*. Although he described aspects of his first novel, *The Poor Man and the Lady*, which he began in the autumn of 1867, as 'socialistic' (*LW*, 63), by 'socialistic' he meant not an ideological work, but the political radicalism of the poor man Will Strong, and also the sweeping nature of the novel's social satire. The following summer he submitted it to Alexander Macmillan, but while both Macmillan and his reader, John Morley, were impressed by its power and insight, it was felt to be defective in form and composition, lacking in plausibility, and unremitting in its satirical assault on upper-class London society. The reader at Chapman & Hall, the novelist George Meredith, recommended that Hardy should tone down the satire, or write a fresh novel with a more developed plot. Eventually Tinsley Brothers offered to publish it, but their request that Hardy should guarantee the project against financial loss was felt to be excessive, and so it lapsed and the work was never published, though Hardy drew on scenes from it for subsequent novels, *Under the Greenwood Tree* and *A Pair of Blue Eyes*, with some echoes also occurring in *Desperate Remedies*. More direct and substantial indebtedness is evident in Hardy's novella, *An Indiscretion in the Life of an Heiress*, and in the poem, 'A Poor Man and a Lady'.

During Hardy's time at Higher Bockhampton, he found himself frequently in the company of his sixteen-year-old cousin, Tryphena Sparks. A pupil-teacher in the village school at Puddletown, she was intelligent and vivacious, and she and Hardy developed a warm relationship. This is the subject of a book, *Providence and Mr Hardy* (1966), by Louis Deacon and Terry Coleman, which speculates that she had a son by him, but that a marriage was not possible because they were in fact uncle and niece. Robert Gittings and Michael Millgate have both investigated this hypothesis and dismissed it. Although the Hardy family thought that there was a serious understanding between them, this is unlikely because around the end of the 1860s and possibly into the 1870s Hardy had been involved with an attractive if rather dull local girl, Catherine ('Cassie') Pole. In any case, Tryphena vanished from Hardy's life when she went away to study as a teacher at Stockwell Normal College in London, though she retained his affection and esteem. However, after her death evidence of a degree of romantic attraction, at least on Hardy's part, is recorded in his poem, 'Thoughts of Phena, at News of her Death', in which he recalls 'the laughter in her eyes' and speaks of her as his 'lost prize'.

In the summer of 1869, Hardy agreed to spend three months in Weymouth, principally supervising the rebuilding of Turnworth church, near Blandford Forum. Poems such as 'At a Seaside Town in 1869', and 'On the Esplanade', testify to his indulgence in the pleasures that Weymouth afforded. It was still a fashionable resort, made famous by the patronage of George III, and now connected to London by the railway. As well as availing himself of the opportunity that the sea afforded for swimming and rowing, Hardy also enjoyed the social life of the town, and attended a quadrille class. The summer of 1869 also saw the end of Hardy's relationship with Mary Jane Nicholls.

His work at Weymouth completed, Hardy was at home in Higher Bockhampton when he received a request from Crickmay that was to transform his life. He agreed to fulfill Hicks's last uncompleted job, the restoration of a church in St Juliot, a tiny hamlet in Cornwall. Hardy arrived at the rectory on the evening of 7 March 1870, to be met by the rector's sister-in-law, Emma Gifford, her sister being occupied in caring for her husband, the Reverend Caddell Holder, who was suffering from gout. Emma noted in *Some Recollections*:

> I thought him much older than he was. He had a beard and a rather shabby great coat, and had quite a business appearance. Afterwards he seemed younger, and by daylight especially ... the 'blue paper' [sticking out of his pocket] proved to be the MS. of a poem, and not a plan of the Church, he informed me, to my surprise.
>
> (Hardy and Gittings 1979: 33–4)

If Hardy looked older than he was, Emma gave her age as less than it was. At the 1871 Census her age was recorded as twenty-five instead of thirty. In spite of Hardy's unprepossessing appearance, his arrival was fortuitous. Emma's life was relatively isolated, and it seems likely, as Michael Millgate suggests, that 'Hardy's engagement and eventual marriage to Emma Gifford were in some measure the calculated outcome of a conspiracy – if only of discretion – involving the entire rectory household' (Millgate 1982: 123). The romance was probably mainly on Hardy's side, although Emma's later recollections were of a joyful time. He and Emma discussed literature, there was music one evening, and on 10 March they visited Beeny Cliff, Emma on horseback. Hardy was deeply attracted to Emma because, as he recorded in the *Life*: 'She was so *living* ... Though her features were not regular her complexion at this date was perfect in hue, her figure and movement graceful, and her corn-coloured hair abundant in its coils' (*LW*, 76). Emma later served as the model for Elfride Swancourt in *A Pair of Blue Eyes*, and was the inspiration for 'Poems of 1912–13'. The magical effect of this sudden passion, nurtured by the romantic isolation of the Cornish landscape, is captured in the breathlessly joyful poem, 'When I Set out for Lyonnesse' (Cornwall). Emma was lively and flirtatious, and in those few short days succeeded in bewitching Hardy, as he captures in the poem, 'At the Word "Farewell"':

> Even then the scale might have been turned
>   Against love by a feather,
> – But crimson one cheek of hers burned
>   When we came in together.
>
> (*CP*, 406)

Having completed his survey of St Juliot Church, Hardy took lodgings in Weymouth, where he finished the drawings. During this stay at Weymouth in 1869, Hardy responded to Meredith's advice to produce a novel more strongly plotted than *The Poor Man and the Lady*. The autobiographical element of *Desperate Remedies* **[94–6]** is unmistakable, despite Hardy's claim that its hero, Edward Springrove, was based on a new assistant who arrived at Crickmay's office in the summer of 1869. The young architect of humble origin falls in love with a lady, Cytherea Graye, bearing a close physical resemblance to Emma, who after extraordinary obstacles have been overcome, he eventually marries.

Hardy completed *Desperate Remedies* in the spring of 1870, and it was sent to Alexander Macmillan two days before Hardy's first visit to St Juliot. He had attempted a sensation novel in the manner of the highly successful Wilkie Collins. It includes impersonation, illegitimacy, and murder, and is concerned with barriers of social class. Macmillan rejected the novel as being too sensational and sexually charged. During the autumn Emma copied out the revised manuscript and on 25 March 1871 Tinsley Brothers published it anonymously, Hardy having agreed to contribute £75 towards the production costs. The reviews included a measure of praise, but the influential *Spectator*'s attack on its sensational plot was damning, although it spoke warmly of the author's treatment of its rural characters. Hardy's overreaction to this review – he wished he were dead – was to characterise his extreme sensitivity to criticism throughout his life. Horace Moule's later positive comments in the *Saturday Review* failed to boost its poor sales.

Hardy's next novel, *Under the Greenwood Tree* **[58–60]**, was his response to the positive critical reception of the rustic characters in *Desperate Remedies*. It too had been started in Weymouth, and was continued at Higher Bockhampton during the spring and summer of 1871. Although it was offered to Alexander Macmillan on 7 August 1871, there was some confusion about his intentions, and Tinsley Brothers published it anonymously in two volumes in June 1872. A comedy of courtship, involving the pursuit of the young schoolmistress, Fancy Day, by three rival suitors, Dick Dewy, Farmer Shiner, and the vicar Mr Maybold, it is permeated by Hardy's recollections of the seasonal rhythm, church music, country dances, and community life. Running parallel to the courtship is the conflict over Mr Maybold's wish to replace the church choir with an organ. Mellstock is Bock-hampton, and the Mellstock Choir is based on the Stinsford church choir of the days of Hardy's grandfather. Among the favourable reviews were Horace Moule's praise in the *Saturday Review*, and the endorsement of Hardy's new vein of writing in the *Athenaeum*.

By the time *Under the Greenwood Tree* was published, Hardy had returned to London to assist T. Roger Smith in the preparation of submissions for the design of new schools for the London School Board. It was here, in response to Tinsley's request for a serial for the first number of *Tinsleys' Magazine*, that he wrote *A Pair of Blue Eyes* **[96–8]**, working rapidly to meet the publication deadlines. He produced the first instalment in London and the second at Emma's home in Cornwall. The serial ran from September 1872 to July 1873. It was published as a three-volume edition in May 1873. This time Hardy wisely retained the copyright and received £200.

During the nineteenth century the copyright laws were in disarray. The Act of 1842 did not specifically cover newspapers or magazines, and the respective rights of authors and publishers were tested in a series of court cases until a Royal Commission in the 1870s sought to define authors' rights over their contributions to periodicals. Hardy's publishing experience is typical of successful nineteenth-century novelists. The market for fiction was dominated by Mudie's Library, a circulating library to which largely middle- and upper-class readers subscribed, and which purchased new novels in bulk. The standard form of publication was the high-priced three-volume novel, known as the 'three-decker'. By the middle of the century the publication of fiction in serial form in magazines had also become popular, and was the main method by which the novels, for instance of Charles Dickens and Anthony Trollope, were made available cheaply to a growing readership. There was a division between those magazines that appealed to a middle-class readership, such as *Macmillan's Magazine*, and those such as the *Graphic*, in which Hardy published *Tess of the d'Urbervilles*, which was made up of informative essays, bits and pieces of news and comment, and articles about personalities. Hardy's experience of the frustrations of striving not only to suit his writing to the demands of the serial instalment for narrative suspense, but also to cater for the expectations and sensibilities of a particular readership, was characteristic of the publication of fiction in this period. Again typically, after the novel had been published in a magazine, or occasionally during the appearance of its final instalments, it would be published in three volumes.

In spite of Hardy's persistent avowal that he had conceived the story before his first trip to Cornwall, *A Pair of Blue Eyes* possesses a strongly autobiographical element. As in *Desperate Remedies* and *Under the Greenwood Tree*, its theme is a variation on *The Poor Man and the*

Lady, Hardy's first attempt at fiction, and in it appear thinly disguised versions of Hardy, Emma, and Horace Moule, while Mr Swancourt seems to be drawn from elements of John Gifford and Caddell Holder. Stephen Smith, a young architectural assistant, and son of a master mason, visits Endelstow vicarage (changed to 'rectory' in the 1900 edition at Hardy's request) in Cornwall, to make drawings in preparation for the restoration of the church. He falls in love with the vicar's daughter, Elfride Swancourt, whose father is offended by Stephen's lower-class status, while the rival suitor Henry Knight, is Stephen's cultured mentor. The novel is a psychological study of a woman torn between the conflicting claims of two men, and an examination of the inhibiting effects of contemporary sexual mores. On the whole, the critical reception was favourable, even from the *Spectator*. Reviewers drew attention, in particular, to its shrewd analysis of character, moral instinct, and treatment of landscape. Even the melodramatic life-and-death incident on the cliff-top was praised, together with Hardy's treatment of rural figures.

Hardy corresponded regularly with Emma and had spent three weeks in Cornwall in August 1870. They met again in 1871 and in August 1872, when Hardy formally requested Emma's hand in marriage. Her father John Gifford, a retired Plymouth solicitor, spurned Hardy's humble origins, and Jemima was also hostile, feeling the intense solidarity of the Hardy family threatened by Emma's middle-class pretensions. It was in August 1872, while Hardy was staying in Cornwall writing *A Pair of Blue Eyes*, that he received an invitation from T. Roger Smith to return to work in London, since one of Hardy's school designs had been accepted. As Hardy recognised, a point of decision had been reached, and Emma's support was crucial. She gave it willingly; Hardy declined Smith's offer and embarked boldly on a new career as a writer.

(e) *FAR FROM THE MADDING CROWD*: FAME AND MARRIAGE

Hardy and Emma continued to meet, but delayed their marriage because so far he had not made a name for himself as a novelist, nor established himself financially. That was to change in 1874 with the publication of *Far from the Madding Crowd* **[61–6]**. Leslie Stephen, the editor of the *Cornhill*, one of the foremost magazines of the day, had discovered Hardy's identity as the author of *Under the Greenwood Tree* and in 1872 had invited him to contribute a serial. Hardy began the new novel at

Higher Bockhampton, completing it in July 1874. The situation was propitious for writing. He was living in comfort, looked after by his mother, and he relished helping his father with the autumnal cider-pressing. As he told Leslie Stephen in a letter, he was living 'within a walk of the district in which the incidents are supposed to occur', and he explained that it was 'a great advantage to be actually among the people described at the time of describing them' (*L*, I, 27). Weatherbury in the novel was nearby Puddletown, and Greenhill Fair was based on Woodbury Hill Fair, near Bere Regis.

He had written to Leslie Stephen in 1872 that his tale would deal with 'a young woman-farmer, a shepherd, and a sergeant of cavalry' (*LW*, 97), but the conception expanded to include, among other things, his creation of the county of Wessex, which originally approximated to Dorset, but later grew into a much larger and more varied region. His presentation of Wessex has given rise to critical debate about the relation between fiction and history in Hardy's novels **[152–8]**. This is the first novel in which Hardy attempts to present an entire rural community, with its shared culture and human solidarity, set in a landscape he knows well. Elements of his father's personality are evident in the stoic, fatalistic shepherd, Gabriel Oak, he draws on his aunt and uncle Sharpe from Hatfield for Bathsheba Everdene and Sergeant Troy, employs his memories of circuses at Dorchester, and mines his store of folk tales. Hardy's intimate knowledge of country matters allows him to combine the novel's pastoral elements with a detailed treatment, not only of sheep farming, but also of the poverty and insecurity of farm workers. Hardy asked his illustrator, Helen Paterson, for precise detail for the agricultural dress and implements depicted, and he wished the labourers to be portrayed as intelligent, rather than as stereotypically boorish.

In his dealings with Leslie Stephen, who was afraid of offending his conservative upper-middle-class *Cornhill* readers, Hardy ran up against the timidity of Victorian magazine editors. Stephen expressed anxiety about the way in which Fanny Robin died, and suggested the omission of her baby from the coffin, at least for the serial. This established the pattern for the future, Hardy bending to accommodate the prudery of serial readers, and restoring the editorial excisions for later volume publication. At this stage in his career, Hardy was making his way, and as he wrote to Leslie Stephen, he was content 'merely to be considered a good hand at a serial' (*L*, I, 28).

Although, as an editor, Stephen gave Hardy some trouble, they remained close friends, and Hardy respected Stephen both as a critic and also as 'the man whose philosophy was to influence his own for many years, indeed, more than that of any other contemporary' (LW, 102). Like Stephen, Hardy had become a free thinker. Their conversations ranged over intellectual issues, such as the origin of the universe and contemporary challenges to religious faith, and they both found intellectual liberation in the rejection of Biblical narratives as representing literally revealed truth. Although Hardy's agnosticism was less forceful than Stephen's, significantly it was Hardy whom he chose to witness his renunciation of Holy Orders on 23 March 1875. Stephen's *An Agnostic's Apology* followed this in 1876.

Two events took place during the writing of *Far from the Madding Crowd* that had a profound emotional effect on Hardy. He fell in love with his illustrator, Helen Paterson, an attractive woman in her mid-twenties, whom much later Hardy described as the woman he should have married, 'but for a stupid blunder of God Almighty' (Millgate 1982: 159). Hardy's courtship of Emma was prolonged, they were separated by distance, and he succumbed to his predilection for intelligent and beautiful women, with whom he formed intense relationships. The other shocking event was Horace Moule's suicide. Moule was a depressive, periodically dependent on alcohol and opium, and the trigger may have been the breaking off, at her request, of his engagement to a highly cultivated governess. A few months after Hardy had visited him at Queens' College Cambridge, during the summer of 1873, Moule **[11–13, 96]** cut his throat in his rooms. Hardy's grief found expression in verse, as had that of his contemporary, the poet Tennyson, at the loss of his close friend Arthur Hallam in 1833. In 1880, visiting Queens' College Hardy wrote in his copy of *In Memoriam*, against the stanza, 'Another name was on the door', '(Cambridge H.M.M.)', and a poem based on their friendship, 'Standing by the Mantlepiece', subtitled 'H.M.M., 1873', was reserved for posthumous publication in *Winter Words*. Hardy kept his friend's earlier Christmas gift of *The Thoughts of the Emperor M. Aurelius Antoninus* by his bedside until his death.

The first instalment of *Far from the Madding Crowd* was published in the January 1874 *Cornhill*, a copy of which Hardy bought on New Year's Eve on Plymouth railway station, while he was returning from St Juliot. It appeared anonymously from January to December, and was published in two volumes by Smith, Elder & Co. on 23 November 1874. It sold well. However, Hardy's writing had become so permeated by the language of Comte that several reviewers identified the author as George Eliot, who for a time had become associated with the ideas of Comte and the Positivists **[14, 68, 108, 121]**. Indeed, the first instalment was enough to convince the *Spectator* reviewer. The *Westminster Review*, pursuing a parallel between Hardy's career and that

23

of George Eliot, compared the achievement of *Far from the Madding Crowd* with the place of *Adam Bede* among the fiction of the middle years of the century. Although this praise pleased Hardy, he felt that aspects of his art were superior to that of Eliot, that she was 'not a born storyteller by any means' and that she 'had never touched the life of the fields' (*LW*,100). The fact remained that *Far from the Madding Crowd* was a great success, and Hardy was famous.

Marriage was now possible. The wedding, which was conducted at St Peter's Church, Paddington by Emma's uncle, Dr Edwin Hamilton Gifford, the headmaster of King Edward's School, Birmingham (later Archdeacon of London), was attended only by Hardy and Emma, and two witnesses. Hardy reported the marriage in the *Dorset County Chronicle* in words that give weight to the social status of the Giffords at the expense of his own humble father:

> HARDY-GIFFORD. Sept. 17, at St Peter's Church, Paddington, by the Rev. E. H. Gifford, D. D., hon. canon of Worcester, uncle of the bride, Thomas Hardy, of Celbridge-place, Westbourne Park, London, son of Mr T. Hardy, of Bockhampton, to Emma Lavinia, younger daughter of J. A. Gifford, Esq., of Kirland, Cornwall.

> (Millgate 1982: 164)

The honeymoon took place in Paris.

(f) NOMADIC NOVELIST

On return from honeymoon, the Hardys rented a house in Surbiton (probably the period of the poem, 'Snow in the Surburbs'). It was here that Hardy realised his sudden fame and he did not know quite how to cope with it. He had successfully established himself in the middle class, but he was aware that his new status was fragile. He was a countryman at heart, yet London was the centre of intellectual and cultural life. It was the obvious place for a successful novelist to live. He still hankered after the life of a poet, but commercial success lay in fiction. And he now had a wife to support.

Far from the Madding Crowd had created a demand for Hardy's fiction. The delighted Stephen asked him for another *Cornhill* serial, to commence in April 1875. Although Hardy was aware that *Cornhill* readers wanted another pastoral novel, his choice of subject was again dictated by his oversensitive response to reviewers. Annoyed by comparisons with George Eliot, he determined to establish his own voice, and made 'a plunge in a new and untried direction', because he 'had not the slightest intention of writing for ever about sheepfarming' (*LW*, 105). Although his next novel, *The Hand of Ethelberta* **[98–101]**, begins in the new fictional county of 'Wessex', it quickly moves to London. Subtitled 'A Comedy in Three Acts', its satirical attack on the aristocracy exposes the endemic snobbery of the English class system as Ethelberta Petherwin, a woman of startling independence, brought up in rural poverty, enters aristocratic society through marriage and eventually triumphs over its decadence. Hardy's publishers were not pleased by his change of direction; especially in view of the £700 they had paid him for the serial rights and the first volume edition. *The Hand of Ethelberta* appeared in the *Cornhill* from July 1875 to May 1876, and was published by Smith, Elder & Co in two volumes on 3 April 1876. It did not attract warm reviews.

Even so, Hardy was now established as a novelist and a public figure. He joined The Copyright Association and made up part of a deputation to the Prime Minister, Benjamin Disraeli, in pursuit of improvements to copyright laws, both British and international. However, poetry remained very important to him. With an epic poem about Europe already in mind, some thirty years before *The Dynasts*, June 1874 found Hardy pursuing stories of the battle of Waterloo from among its remaining survivors at the Chelsea Hospital, and in November 1875 'The Fire at Tranter Sweatley's' was published in *The Gentleman's Magazine*.

Hardy had completed *The Hand of Ethelberta* in Swanage, to which he and Emma had moved in July 1875. Their lodgings were very similar to those taken by Ethelberta in Knollsea, where Captain Flower is based on Captain Masters, Hardy's lodging-house keeper at West End Cottage. On their way to Swanage, Hardy and Emma stayed in Bournemouth (the Sandbourne of *Tess of the d'Urbervilles*), which Hardy greatly disliked. There on a wet St Swithin's Day they quarrelled, as his poem, 'We Sat at the Window', dated 'Bournemouth 1875', records. However, a later poem, 'Once at Swanage' reveals the resumption of a happy relationship. Hardy's sisters Mary and Kate visited them and picnicked at Corfe Castle, although mutual antagonism prevented normal intercourse between Emma and Jemima Hardy.

In March 1876, while Hardy and Emma looked for somewhere more permanent to live, they took lodgings in Yeovil. May of the same year found them on the continent again for a second holiday, the main reason for which was Hardy's desire to visit the battlefield of Waterloo. This was a brief fallow period in Hardy's writing career, and as Lennart Björk has suggested, in his edition of *The Literary Notebooks of Thomas*

Hardy, he needed a period of reflection. Such was Hardy's intellectual insecurity that he immersed himself in philosophy, history, sociology, aesthetics and literary criticism, jotting down in his notebooks his reading in, for instance, psychological and social authors, and also passages from writers critical of Christianity. In addition he recorded ideas that reflected his own aesthetic of anti-realism, and observations used for incidental details in his work, as well as copying out erudite passages that might provide material for his novels and support their structure of ideas (*LN*, xx–xxi).

On 3 July 1876, Hardy and Emma moved to Sturminster Newton in north Dorset, in the Vale of Blackmoor (the 'Valley of the Little Dairies' of *Tess of the d'Urbervilles*). They rented Riverside Villa, by the Stour, a setting described in the poem 'Overlooking the River Stour'. They entered into the town's social life and, as the poem 'Two-Years' Idyll' testifies, this was to prove one of the happiest periods of their married life. It was at Sturminster Newton during the winter months of 1876–7 that Hardy began writing *The Return of the Native* **[66–71]**, which is set in the immediate environs of the family home at Higher Bockhampton. Characteristically, however, he felt obliged to bolster his powerful evocation of this heath land and his tragic treatment of its inhabitants with some twenty literary notes from his notebooks.

Hardy sent part of the manuscript to Leslie Stephen, who turned it down, Hardy noted, because 'he feared that the relations between Eustacia, Wildeve, and Thomasin might develop into something "dangerous" for a family magazine, and he refused to have anything to do with it unless he could see the whole. This I never sent him; and the matter fell through' (Millgate 1982: 188). It finally appeared in *Belgravia* from January to December 1878, and was published by Smith, Elder & Co in three volumes on 4 November 1878.

After *The Hand of Ethelberta*, Stephen had shrewdly advised Hardy to sustain his own originality. Among other things, this meant elaborating the fictional county of Wessex. The sketch map that Hardy published as a frontispiece to the volume edition of *The Return of the Native* is a map of the heath land around the cottage at Higher Bockhampton, which becomes Bloom's End. Like most of Hardy's best writing, this novel is informed by childhood memories of landscape, nature, the isolated rural community, and also by the exploration of human relationships, including the Freudian love between Clym Yeobright and his dominant, socially ambitious mother.

Although these autobiographical strands energise the narrative, Hardy was concerned to dissociate himself from his hero: 'I think he is the nicest of all my heroes, and *not a bit* like me' (*LW*, 520). As Michael

Millgate has suggested, most interesting is Hardy's hypothetical examination of a course he had not taken – he did not go home to the heath, like the perverse idealist Clym – and through this analysis, says Millgate, Hardy could 'see more plainly, and perhaps justify to himself, the course he had in fact chosen to follow' (Millgate 1982: 201).

Once again the demands of the magazine-reading public affected the structure of Hardy's narrative. As he remarked in a footnote to the Preface of the 1912 Wessex edition of *The Return of the Native*, the marriage of Thomasin and Diggory Venn was required by 'certain circumstances of serial publication', the original intention being for Thomasin to remain a widow, while Venn mysteriously disappears, having 'retained his isolated and weird character to the last'. Even with this concluding marriage, however, reviewers regarded *The Return of the Native* as gloomy and intellectual. The *Spectator* critic (doubtless Richard Holt Hutton) thought that the novel was influenced by the philosophy of Arthur Schopenhauer, the author of a pessimistic philosophy propounded in *The World as Will and Idea* (1819), though Hardy had not read him at this stage **[43, 121, 126, 138]**. Schopenhauer argued that Will, manifested in man as the self-conscious ego and in nature as unconscious forces, is the only reality, creating and sustaining a malignant world, in which the concepts of a divinely ordered universe and free will are illusions. Hutton felt that in this novel Hardy's fatalistic view of life undermines the 'ethical system' based on the Positivist values of Comte that Clym Yeobright brings back from Paris.

Hardy felt that for professional reasons he needed to live near London, so he and Emma moved to Tooting, where they leased a large house, on 18 March 1878. Hardy dated the beginning of their marital difficulties from this time. Emma may have begun to resent Hardy's professional preoccupation and success. She may also have started to display in middle age symptoms of the mental instability that was to develop later. Their continuing childlessness had been poignantly underlined during their stay at Sturminster Newton by the pregnancy of their maid and the early death of her illegitimate infant.

In London Hardy enjoyed his status as a major novelist. He was elected to the Savile Club, the foremost literary club, and made friends in literature and publishing, lunching with Tennyson and his family, and meeting the publisher, Alexander Macmillan. But in February 1879 he was called back to Dorset by his mother's illness, and while there visited Weymouth, Portland, and Sutton Poyntz for material for his next novel, *The Trumpet-Major* **[101–4]**, described by Hardy as 'a cheerful, lively story' (*L*, I, 65), which after unsuccessful efforts, he eventually placed with *Good Words*, where it appeared from January to

December 1880. Smith, Elder & Co later published it in three volumes on 26 October 1880.

Against the background of the preparation for Napoleon's invasion three men, two of them brothers, court a young woman. For the readers of *Good Words*, the rejected suitor, the honourable Trumpet-Major, John Loveday, simply leaves for Spain, but for the readers of the volume edition, Hardy altered the final paragraph to reveal that he is destined to die there in battle, thus giving weight to the historical context. In spite of the elements of romance, *The Trumpet-Major* is a historical novel. The context for the years 1804–8, was supplied by research in the British Museum Library during the spring and summer of 1879, and by Hutchins's *History and Antiquities of the County of Dorset*, from which Hardy compiled '*The Trumpet-Major* Notebook'. Of course, he knew Weymouth well, and the house where Nelson's Admiral Hardy was born at Portisham, and he also drew on his grandmother's memories of the atmosphere of panic, the drilling of volunteers, the signal fires in readiness, and the grand coming of George III to Weymouth **[7, 101, 115, 136]**. Reviewers praised John Loveday, were divided over Anne Garland, enjoyed the relief from the gloom of *The Return of the Native*, and warmed to the evocation of a past world.

At this stage of his career, Hardy was well known to a discerning readership, and his reputation was enhanced further by the publication of two excellent short stories in the *New Quarterly Magazine*, edited by his friend, Charles Kegan Paul. 'The Distracted Preacher', which appeared in April 1879, was based on tales of smuggling along the Dorset coast that he had heard, possibly from Eliza Nicholls's father, or from Captain Masters at Swanage, or from his father's accounts of contraband hidden in former years in the cottage in Higher Bockhampton. The following April he published 'Fellow-Townsmen'. Hardy's serials and short stories were gaining admirers in America, and his American publisher Harper invited him to write a serial for the European edition of *Harper's New Monthly Magazine*. *A Laodicean* **[105–7]**, subtitled 'A Story of Today', is a love story following the comic pattern of obstacles overcome, but it is also an exploration of the conflict between ancient and modern, focused through a young London architect, Charles Somerset, and Paula Power, the daughter of a railway magnate and heir to a medieval castle. The idea for the novel's theme seems to have arisen from a meeting with the poet and critic, Matthew Arnold **[85, 89, 106, 121]**, in February 1860 at a dinner in London. Hardy's notebook summarises a passage on the relationship between 'the modern spirit' and 'the imaginative reason' from Arnold's essay, 'Pagan and Medieval Religious Sentiment', a central issue in this novel.

Inevitably, there is an interweaving of autobiography. As Hardy's biographer, James Gibson has pointed out, 'in 1900 Hardy told an American visitor *"A Laodicean* contained more of the facts of his own life than anything else he had ever written" ' (Gibson 1996: 84). The title, *A Laodicean* – a person lukewarm particularly in religious or political matters – relates especially to Paula Power, but also to George Somerset's embracing of various styles of architecture. Of course it represents, too, the bent of Hardy's own temperament and intellect.

Hardy had completed the novel during a painful illness caused by inflammation of the bladder, dictating it to Emma who nursed him devotedly throughout. The doctor advised months of rest in order to avoid an operation. Hardy did not venture out until May 1881, when *A Laodicean* was finished. (His experience is recorded in the poem 'A Wasted Illness'.) The serial appeared in *Harper's New Monthly Magazine* between December 1880 and December 1881, and Samson Low published the first British volume edition in December 1881. Most reviewers were disappointed by Hardy's movement of the novel's setting away from Wessex, and apart from Havelock Ellis, writing in the *Westminster Review*, they did not recognise his experimental treatment of the modern; the way he employs his characters' determined allegiance to the principle of intellectual flexibility to explore and question the rigid nature of ideology, tradition, and social roles.

In September 1880, on a visit to Dorset, Hardy had consulted his brother Henry about buying a plot of land near Dorchester on which to build a house. He wanted to be nearer his aging parents, felt sufficiently secure to avoid London, and was less inclined to pander to Emma's social aspirations. Moreover, he was now known as the novelist of the fictional county of Wessex, and his best novels had been written while living in Dorset. He left London and settled into a house in Wimborne Minster, a small, bustling market town, with a fine old minster, situated on the river Stour, some twenty miles from Dorchester. Hardy's established social position was recognised by the invitation he and Emma received from Lord and Lady Wimborne to a ball at Canford Manor in December 1881.

While living in Wimborne, Hardy wrote his next novel, *Two on a Tower* [107–10], in response to a request for a serial for the *Atlantic Monthly* magazine. He did some research for it at the Royal Observatory at Greenwich (the Transit of Venus, the apparent passage of the planet across meridian of place, which allowed observers to measure the distance of the sun from the earth, took place in December 1882, so Hardy's choice of astronomy as his subject was topical). The novel also develops the theme of *The Poor Man and the Lady*. It is, as Hardy called it, a romance. It involves a secret marriage, later found to be invalid, an illegitimate child, and the death of the heroine. It was serialised in the *Atlantic Monthly* from May to December 1882, and published in Britain by Samson Low in three volumes at the end of October 1882. Its scientific bias made it uncomfortably modern, and the reviews were largely unfavourable. Only Havelock Ellis, writing in the *Westminster Review,* championed Hardy's art. The *Saturday Review* critic was repelled by it, while the reviewer in the *St James's Gazette* lamented its ridiculing of a bishop of the Church of England. However, in spite of the novel's poor reception, sales were quite strong.

Hardy was busy planning his move to Dorchester, but before he left Wimborne he was invited by *Longman's Magazine* to contribute an essay on 'The Dorsetshire Labourer'. Although Hardy includes in it a warm endorsement of the activities of Joseph Arch, the agricultural labourers' champion, he also preserves an element of detachment, treating the problems of the rural poor from a historical perspective. On the one hand, he defends the labourer from the Hodge stereotype (agricultural workers were regarded as boorish and went under the general name of Hodge), and writes movingly about past oppression, but on the other hand he records improvements in the standard of life. He also minimises the effects of the agricultural depression of the 1880s, which was brought about by a fall in the price of wheat and the extension of cheap food imports, resulting in a hundred thousand agricultural workers leaving the countryside during the decade. However, Hardy sees this as affecting Dorset somewhat less than other areas of the country because of its greater reliance on livestock farming. He laments the depopulation of the countryside and the disappearance of rural tradesmen and craftsmen, but this nostalgia is tempered by approval of technological and economic change. Hardy also continued with shorter fiction while at Wimborne, writing a novella, 'The Romantic Adventures of a Milkmaid' **[118]**, published in the *Graphic* on 25 June 1883, and one of his best short stories, 'The Three Strangers' **[115]**, which appeared in *Longman's Magazine* in March 1883.

(g) DORCHESTER, *THE MAYOR OF CASTERBRIDGE*, AND HIGH SOCIETY

Wimborne had failed to satisfy Emma's desire for social distinction, while she and Hardy also suffered from the damp air of the river Stour, so they decided to move to Dorchester, where they rented Shire-Hall Place in Shire-Hall Lane in June 1883. In November work began preparing the site of a new house a mile outside Dorchester, close to the road to Wareham. The house was to be built by Hardy's father and brother Henry. Hardy prepared the drawings, meticulously oversaw all aspects of the building, and planted between two and three thousand Austrian pines, both as a windbreak and to ensure privacy. The house was humorously named Max Gate, after a nearby tollgate known as 'Mack's Gate'. A comfortable house with one and a half acres, in an elevated position with fine views, it was designed around the require-ments of its inhabitants. It made a statement about Hardy's status as a successful professional man, and it offered Emma the standard of life she felt due to her rank. Hardy made his upstairs study an inviolable retreat, in which he worked habitually for most of each day. From a family point of view, the house was sufficiently close to Higher Bockhampton for Hardy to walk over to see his parents every Sunday, but not too close to permit the danger of Emma and Jemima crossing each other's paths, although Thomas and Jemima did visit Max Gate occasionally. The plot on which the house stood had originally been leased from the Duchy of Cornwall, but in September 1886 Hardy purchased the freehold, subsequently adding rooms and extending the gardens. He entered into local society, becoming a justice of the peace and a member of the Dorset County Museum. He would remain at Max Gate until the end of his life. There he felt more in touch with the past; both the distant past represented by the Romano-British remains uncovered during the building of the foundations, and more recent history, including his childhood. He also felt increasingly that the centre of his interest was the fictional county of Wessex, with Casterbridge (Dorchester) at the hub of its agricultural community. Hardy recognised that his unique position in contemporary fiction depended on his ability to connect rural Dorset and the great urban readership.

The return to Dorchester and Hardy's renewed interest in history were the impulses behind his next novel, *The Mayor of Casterbridge* **[71–6]**. Composed during his residence in Dorchester, and continued during the building of Max Gate, it was completed on 17 April 1885. It made good commercial sense to emphasise *The Mayor of Casterbridge* as a 'Wessex' novel, recalling for potential readers his earlier successes with *Far from the Madding Crowd* and *The Trumpet-Major*. In the writing of the novel, he was preoccupied by the need to attain historical accuracy in his presentation of the market town of Casterbridge, now fully conceived for the first time as the centre of a tightly knit Wessex community. He wanted to record a vanishing way of life. Set in the years of Hardy's childhood, the story draws on his memories of Dorchester, and also on his own researching in the files of the *Dorset*

County Chronicle from January 1882 onwards. There he came across incidents such as a wife selling in Somerset, information about fluctuations in the corn trade in Dorset during the early years of the century, and an account of the fleeting visit to Dorchester of Prince Albert in July 1849. Hardy explores the forces of historical change and their impact on a rural community in his treatment of the conflict between Henchard and his *protégé*, the young Scotsman, Donald Farfrae, but the subtitle, 'A Story of a Man of Character', draws attention to the psychological complexity of Michael Henchard, a young unemployed hay-trusser, who gets drunk at a country fair and sells his wife to a sailor, and years later as mayor of Casterbridge suffers at the hands of retributive justice.

The Mayor of Casterbridge appeared first as a serial in the *Graphic* from 2 January to 15 May 1886. Hardy felt that the necessity of including an incident in each weekly part was damaging to the novel's artistic integrity, though he also asserted that the plot was 'quite coherent and organic, in spite of its complication' (*LW*, 186). Several significant revisions were made to the text that was published in two volumes by Smith, Elder & Co on 10 May 1886. So far as the reviewers were concerned, this novel seems to have suffered by comparison with other less gloomy Wessex fictions, and apart from Richard Holt Hutton's *Spectator* review of 5 June 1886, praising the psychological realism of Henchard's characterisation, the novel's reception was disappointing.

From this period until the early years of the twentieth century Hardy's life oscillated between Dorchester and London, where he took Emma annually away from the claustrophobia of Max Gate and the tension of their increasingly difficult marriage. These visits also kept Hardy in touch with his urban readership, to which he alludes in his essay, 'The Profitable Reading of Fiction' (1888). Hardy's London connections are given a significant amount of space in his *Life*. Among the writers he encountered were Henry James, George Meredith, whom he had met earlier, Walter Pater and George Gissing. He also relished discussions with eminent politicians. Hardy was rather conservative politically. He opposed William Gladstone's first Irish Home Rule Bill, designed to give Ireland a legislative responsibility for domestic affairs. Like Matthew Arnold, he feared democracy, which he saw as democratic privilege, although he supported the Liberal Party's proposed extension of the franchise to agricultural workers. He also suspected that idle labour would demand financial support from the worthy members of society. It is unsurprising that Hardy counted many Conservative politicians among his acquaintance. In London aristocratic ladies, such as

Lady Portsmouth, invited him to their parties and dinners, while in Dorset his fame began to attract to Max Gate numerous visitors, many of them literary figures, such as Robert Louis Stevenson and his wife in August 1885.

Towards the end of 1885, work began on a new novel, *The Wood-landers* **[77–82]**. Some years later, Hardy confessed that he liked this story best of all his novels because of its geographical location and scenery. It is set in the wooded area in the vicinity of Melbury Osmond, north-west of Dorchester, where his grandmother, Betty Swetman had brought up her family in conditions of poverty, and where his parents, Thomas and Jemima, had been married.

The writing of *The Woodlanders* was hampered by a bout of depression. Hardy felt the pressure of writing for serialisation, which had commenced nine months earlier, in May 1886 in *Macmillan's Magazine*, where the novel ran until April 1887. Macmillan published it in three volumes on 15 March 1887, when a number of excisions, mainly to do with Fitzpiers's sexual encounter with the working-class girl Suke Damson, forced on Hardy for serialisation, were reinstated in the first volume edition. On the whole this novel was well received. Edmund Gosse's praise of its 'richness and humanity' in the *Saturday Review*, is typical of the appreciative responses. The *Academy* went so far as to call it 'the best and most powerful work Hardy has produced since *Far from the Madding Crowd'*. However, some reviewers, such as Coventry Patmore in the *St James's Gazette*, and Richard Holt Hutton in the *Spectator*, worried about its morality.

While this elegy for a rural past was being written, the other cele-brant of Dorset life, the poet William Barnes, died on 5 October 1886. Barnes had been the special voice of Wessex for Hardy and his poem, 'The Last Signal' registers a symbolic gesture of benediction from the older man, as the gleam of sunlight on his coffin lid seems to be 'a farewell ... signaled on his grave-way, / As with a wave of his hand' (*CP*, 444). And the responsibility for speaking for Wessex is transferred to the younger author.

On 14 March 1887, Hardy and Emma began a liberating holiday in Italy. Literary visits were mandatory and included the graves of Shelley and Keats in Rome, the site of a Napoleonic triumph at the bridge at Lodi in Milan; and in Venice places associated with Byron. Returning to London in April, Hardy attended various social functions, and he and Emma stayed on in London during the summer to watch Queen Victoria's Golden Jubilee celebrations.

Back at Max Gate at the end of July, Hardy found himself responding to magazine editors' pleas for stories. Hardy's *Life* reveals how he was noting tales of local superstition, such as gave rise to 'The Withered Arm' [116–17], which Hardy published in *Wessex Tales* [114], the first of his four books of short stories, enhancing his position as a historian of Wessex culture. Macmillan published this volume, which includes some of his best stories: 'The Three Strangers' [115], 'Fellow-Townsmen' [119], 'Interlopers at the Knap' [119], and 'The Distracted Preacher' [119], in May 1888. Osgood, McIlvaine & Co published, in 1891, Hardy's second volume of short stories, a group entitled *A Group of Noble Dames* [114], produced for the *Graphic* in the interlude between writing the two halves of *Tess of the d'Urbervilles*.

(h) *TESS OF THE D'URBERVILLES, JUDE THE OBSCURE,* AND THE ABANDONMENT OF FICTION

The Victorian middle class image of women was culturally controlled. They were denied political and economic power, and were expected to conform to the idea of separate spheres for men and women, which finds expression in the poet, Coventry Patmore's vision of domesticity, expressed in a series of poems endorsing married love in *The Angel in the House* (1854–63). Women were also denied any sexual feelings. And they were doubly victims of idealisation and abuse, particularly of the double standard in sexual morality, which branded liberated women as 'fallen' while condoning their lovers. As the nineteenth century progressed, influenced by such thinkers as John Stuart Mill and Harriet Martineau, the women's movement gained momentum, until just after the turn of the century the coining of the term 'New Woman' denoted the achievement of a measure of independence. Hardy's intelligent and sympathetic portrayal of women is informed by his perception of the inextricable entanglement of gender and class issues, particularly the importance of education and marriage as offering upward social mobility. His early efforts in fiction to undermine Victorian attitudes were hampered by censorship, but as an established novelist he championed the struggle of the strong, intelligent, sexual woman to achieve selfhood and social freedom.

Tess of the d'Urbervilles [82–8] is a deeply personal novel. Indeed, Hardy said that had it not been too revealing, he would have called it *Tess of the Hardys*. In 1885 Hardy had visited the Manor House at Wool and heard a paper about the Turberville family buried at nearby Bere Regis. The decline of a noble family was brought to mind by a visit early that autumn to the remains of Woolcombe, an estate once owned by some of the Dorset Hardys. The landscape of the novel was suggested by his visit in the autumn of 1888 to the areas of the 'Valley of the Great Dairies' and the 'Valley of the Little Dairies'. One of the sources of Tess was a young milkmaid, Augusta Way, who worked on the Kingston Maurward Estate. The midnight baptism of Tess's baby, Sorrow, was based on the experience of their maid, Jane Phillips at Sturminster Newton, and on that of Hardy's maternal grandmother, Kate. Tess's hanging for murder recalls that of Martha Browne, while the character and attitudes of Angel Clare are reminiscent of Horace Moule. Hardy struggled with the title. There were false starts: 'The Body and Soul of Sue', 'Too Late, Beloved', then the same title without the comma. Finally he settled on *Tess of the d'Urbervilles*, Tess's name having been altered from Rose-Mary.

W.F. Tillotson of Bolton offered 1,000 guineas for the new novel, a comparatively large sum considering that at the turn of the century the annual income of a rising professional man was approximately £700. Writing commenced in the autumn of 1888, but Hardy soon found himself renewing battle with the tyranny of the market place. His story of violation, illegitimacy, unauthorised baptism, and murder, with its challenge to patriarchal authority and sexual hypocrisy, frightened his Christian publisher, as he must have known it would. Hardy's frustration at the censorship exercised by squeamish editors erupted in his fierce essay, 'Candour in English Fiction', published in the *New Review* in January 1890. In it he complained of the way in which the truths of realism and the integrity of the writer's conscience and imagination are traduced by the compulsion to produce a *dénouement* 'dear to the Grundyist'.

Hardy and Tillotson agreed to cancel their contract. The proposed novel was then turned down successively by *Murray's Magazine* and *Macmillan's Magazine*, and was sent eventually to Arthur Locker of the *Graphic*, as Hardy describes in the *Life*:

> [The plan] was not to offer the novel intact to the third editor on his list ... but to send it up with some chapters or parts of chapters cut out, and instead of destroying these to publish them, or much of them, elsewhere, if practicable, as episodic adventures of anonymous personages ... till they could be put back in their places at the printing of the whole in volume form.
>
> (*LW*, 232)

Thus in the *Graphic* serialisation, the scene of Tess's violation was replaced by a mock-marriage with Alec d'Urberville, and the baptism and burial of Tess's baby were excised from the manuscript. These appeared as 'Saturday Night in Arcady' in the *National Observer* on 14 November 1891, and 'The Midnight Baptism: A Study in Christianity' in the *Fortnightly Review* in May 1891. They were reinstated in the volume edition. Hardy thus sought to reconcile his disgust at the hypocrisy of magazine editors, his scrupulous artistic integrity, and his commercial interests. He concealed his anger behind a mask of cynicism, claiming in his autobiography that in mutilating his novel, 'he carried out this unceremonious concession to conventionality without compunction and with cynical amusement, knowing the novel was moral enough and to spare' (*LW*, 232).

Tess of the d'Urbervilles appeared in weekly instalments in the *Graphic* from 4 July to 26 December 1891, and was published by Osgood, McIlvaine & Co in three volumes in December 1891, with much of the original manuscript restored, though still omitting the scene of the dance at Chaseborough, which was not included until the Wessex edition of 1912. Hardy also added the defiant subtitle, 'A Pure Woman Faithfully Presented by Thomas Hardy'. In a sense, this work was never really completed, and as with his other novels he continued to revise it in subsequent editions.

Tess of the d'Urbervilles was a huge success and the first printing sold out within a month. The *Westminster Review* described it as one of the greatest novels of the century, and made the usual flattering comparison with George Eliot. The *Athenaeum* pronounced it a great novel, and the *Star* and the *Illustrated London News* similarly lauded it. However, characteristically Hardy chose to attend to the negative reviews, such as that in the *Saturday Review*, which bridled at Hardy's presentation of Tess's sexuality, or Richard Holt Hutton's questioning of her purity in the *Spectator*. After reading Mowbray Morris's comment in the *Quarterly Review*, that Hardy had told 'a disagreeable story in a coarse and disagreeable manner' he commented, 'Well, if this sort of thing continues no more novel-writing for me. A man must be a fool to deliberately stand up to be shot at' (*LW*, 259).

Tess of the d'Urbervilles was controversial and provoked furious arguments. The Duchess of Abercorn told Hardy that she had to separate those dinner guests who loved the novel from those that abominated it. However, the author of *Tess of the d'Urbervilles* was in even greater demand than before for dinners and parties. The spring of 1892 found Hardy, having shaved off his beard, as a mark his second wife believed of his success, but leaving the familiar moustache of later photographs, attending social functions, staying at Lady Jeune's, and writing affectionate letters to Emma at Max Gate. Down in Dorset, pilgrims flocked to explore Wessex, and even perhaps to encounter the famous author in the environs of Max Gate.

By this point in their married lives, Hardy and Emma had grown apart. A number of things contributed to their difficulties. Emma did not understand the demands of a famous writer's life. His literary distinction had secured his election, in 1891, to the exclusive Athenaeum Club, a club reserved for persons of 'distinguished merit' in their field, and he took the opportunity to spend part of the year in London, often in the company of beautiful aristocratic women. But perhaps more important was the fact that Emma's religiosity had become eccentric. She found her husband's agnosticism increasingly offensive. It was from this period that she began keeping secret diaries, recording her resentments at Hardy's behaviour. However, it was his father's death on 20 July 1892 that seems to have widened the breach. His widowed mother took up more of Hardy's time, the enmity between Jemima and Emma, no longer checked by Thomas Hardy senior, broke out afresh, and until Emma's death in 1912 his sisters Mary and Kate were forbidden to visit Max Gate. Hardy managed to maintain his obligations to both wife and family by frequently walking over from Max Gate to Higher Bockhampton.

The death of Hardy's cousin, Tryphena Sparks, his 'lost prize', would have given rise to regretful reflection on an alternative marriage. In the *Life* he refers to the curious telepathic occurrence when he began work on the poem, 'Not a line of her writing have I', later published as 'Thoughts of Phena, at News of her Death', in a train to London, while unknown to him she was dying. Hardy was so moved by her death that, together with his brother Henry, he made the long cycle ride to Exeter, in order to visit her grave at nearby Topsham.

Late in 1891, while *Tess of the d'Urbervilles* was appearing in the *Graphic*, Hardy had commenced work on a new novel, *The Well-Beloved* [110–14], the result of Tillotson's request for another serial. He was at pains to explain to Tillotson its use of scenes from London society, as well as others from a remote area of the country. He also stressed its modernity, adding defensively the remarkable reassurance that it was suitable reading for fastidious readers of all ages. It was serialised weekly in the *Illustrated London News* between 1 October and 17 December 1892, under the title, *The Pursuit of the Well-Beloved: A Sketch of a Temperament*, which was altered to *The Well-Beloved* for volume publication in 1897, after *Jude the Obscure*.

Hardy's story owes something to the influence of Shelley's presentation of Platonic love in his poem, 'Epipsychidion', particularly Hardy's account of the young London sculptor, Jocelyn Pierston's Platonic pursuit of ideal feminine beauty as it migrates through three generations of the same family. Finally in old age the impulse leaves him, and he marries and settles in the community of the Isle of Slingers (Portland in Dorset), whence his family originated. Hardy described the story as experimental and revised it heavily for publication in volume form, where he treated Pierston's infatuation with greater candour. It is strongly autobiographical, especially in Hardy's concern with the relationship between lack of sexual fulfilment and artistic creativity. On the whole this novel was favourably received.

Hardy's own pursuit of the well-beloved led him to fall in love with Florence Henniker, the wife of a senior army officer and sister of Lord Houghton, the Lord-Lieutenant of Ireland. Hardy met her in May 1893 at the Vice-Regal Lodge in Dublin. Attractive and intuitive, as Hardy described her, she was independent and intellectually ambitious. Hardy fell under her spell, advising her on her efforts at fiction, writing her many letters, and although on a visit they made to Winchester in August 1892 she made plain the futility of his passion, they remained friends until her death in 1923. The emotional summer of 1893 gave rise to the short story, 'An Imaginative Woman' **[118]**, published in the *Pall Mall Magazine* in April 1894. His involvement with Florence Henniker is also recorded in a number of poems, including 'At an Inn', 'A Thunderstorm in Town', 'In Death Divided', 'The Division', 'A Broken Appointment', and 'Wessex Heights', in which she is described as 'one rare fair woman' **[10, 45, 52, 111, 118, 127]**.

In October 1893, Hardy brought together some short stories for publication by Osgood, McIlvaine & Co, entitled *Life's Little Ironies* **[114]**; among them 'A Tradition of Eighteen Hundred and Four' **[115–16]**, 'On the Western Circuit' **[117–18]**, 'The Melancholy Hussar of the German Legion' **[116]** and one of his finest stories, the superbly daring 'The Fiddler of the Reels' **[117]**. Several of the stories in this volume, published on 22 February 1894, move away from Wessex, anticipating *Jude the Obscure* in their treatment of middle-class life and issues to do with sexuality, marriage, social class, and education.

Hardy's final, great tragic novel, *Jude the Obscure* **[88–94]**, bears the mark of Florence Henniker in the characterisation of its heroine, Sue Bridehead, whose full name is Susanna Florence Mary Bridehead. Sue's sexual unresponsiveness, ecclesiastical interests, and intellectual gifts all point to Florence Henniker as a model. For Sue's experience as a trainee teacher at the Training College at Melchester, Hardy was indebted to his sisters Mary and Kate, both of whom attended a similar college at Salisbury. Like Sue, Kate in particular chafed under the disciplined regime. And while work was progressing on *Jude the Obscure*, Hardy visited Tryphena Sparks's old college at Stockwell.

For the geographical background, and significant elements of character and situation in *Jude the Obscure*, Hardy drew on family history. In September 1892 he had visited Fawley in Berkshire, the village from which his maternal grandmother, Mary Head, had come, and which features in the novel as Marygreen. Sue's name echoes her surname, while Jude's surname is Fawley. Hardy's conception of Jude owes a debt to his uncle John Antell, a Puddletown shoemaker and a brilliant autodidact, who bitterly resented his exclusion from formal education. Jude's trade of stonemason came naturally to mind because during the gestation of this novel from a jotted outline to a completed manuscript, between 1890 and 1894, Hardy had spent some time restoring St Peter's Church in West Knighton. Among the many disparate experiences that feed into *Jude the Obscure* were his debates about the topical issue of the liberated 'New Woman' with his London hostess Lady Jeune, whose husband, a divorce-court judge, also provided him with the opportunity to discuss the divorce laws **[79, 92]**. All these elements are given narrative shape by Hardy's desire to criticise, more explicitly than before, society's oppressive structure and attitudes; especially its hypocritical treatment of women, the divorce laws, the failure of the education system, and the increasing irrelevance of a rigid and exclusive Church.

Hardy was aware that his new novel strayed considerably from the family magazine story that Harper & Brothers had requested, but they refused to release him from the contract. He was forced to produce a bowdlerised version in *Harper's New Monthly Magazine*, which ran from December 1894 to November 1895. The first instalment bore the title, *The Simpletons*. The second and subsequent issues were published under the title *Hearts Insurgent*, to avoid confusion with Charles Reade's *A Simpleton*, published earlier by Harper.

Osgood, McIlvaine & Co published the re-titled *Jude the Obscure* in volume form on 1 November 1895. Reviews were polarised. The *Pall Mall Gazette* called it 'Jude the Obscene'. W.W. How, Bishop of Wakefield, claimed to have burnt his copy. He also managed to persuade W.H. Smith's popular circulating library, which like Mudie's Library was a culturally influential force for opinion-forming, to ban it. However, an anonymous reviewer for the *Saturday Review* commented in remarkably modern terms that Jude's is 'the voice of the educated proletarian, speaking more distinctly than it has ever spoken before in English literature'. But it was the damning reviews that Hardy remembered, 'the experience completely curing me of further interest in novel-writing', as he noted in his 1912 postscript to the Preface. He was tired of being misread. He had also been thinking for some time about devoting considerably more attention to the writing of poetry. Hardy's decision to abandon fiction was confirmed by a review of the volume edition of *The Well-Beloved*, published after *Jude the Obscure* in 1897. The reviewer in *The World* proclaimed: 'Of all forms of sex-mania in fiction we have no hesitation in pronouncing the most unpleasant to be the Wessex-mania of Thomas Hardy'. Hardy was disgusted.

(i) EMERGENCE OF THE POET

The phenomenal sales of *Tess of the d'Urbervilles* gave Hardy the financial security that allowed him to concentrate on poetry. Moreover, the 'impressionism' he had employed in his fiction, and which had been misunderstood, now seemed to be more appropriate to poetry. His view of the function of his poetry was clear; it was to communicate unconventional ideas and powerful feelings: 'Perhaps I can express more fully in verse ideas and emotions which run counter to the inert crystallized opinion – hard as a rock – which the vast body of men have vested interests in supporting' (*LW*, 302), and quoting Leslie Stephen: 'The ultimate aim of the poet should be to touch our hearts by showing his own' (*LW*, 131).

Hardy alludes to the intensely personal nature of his verse in his Preface to his first volume, *Wessex Poems*, published by Harper & Brothers in 1898. It is evident, too, in the sketches he included in the volume, and in his veiled references to various women: his cousin, Tryphena Sparks in 'Thoughts of Phena, at News of her Death', written in March 1890; his sister Mary Hardy, in 'Middle-Age Enthusiasms', inscribed 'to M.H.'; Emma in 'Ditty' '(E.L.G.)'; and Florence Henniker in 'At an Inn'. It was a characteristic of successive volumes of Hardy's poetry that they also included poems written in the 1860s. *Wessex Poems* includes 'Neutral Tones', written in 1867, which deals with his parting from Eliza Nicholls. The references to women in the volume, particularly Florence Henniker, Mary Jeune, and Agnes Grove, whom he had met in 1895, fuelled Emma's jealousy.

Wessex Poems clearly aimed to benefit from Hardy's association with the county of his fiction. It is an uneven volume, comprising a variety of subjects including history (the Napoleonic Wars), love, loss of religious faith ('The Impercipient [At a Cathedral Service]'); aging ('I Look into My Glass'); bereavement (the poem about Tryphena Sparks and also 'Friends Beyond'); and the comic poem, 'The Fire at Tranter

Sweatley's'. Hardy kept to traditional poetic forms, but experimented with language. The volume was widely reviewed, but not well received, and the edition of 500 copies sold very slowly. The general perception was of a major novelist dabbling in poetry.

Although Hardy and Emma visited London during 1898, when he did some research at the British Museum for *The Dynasts*, and indulged in the new craze of cycling, around the Dorset lanes, they grew steadily further apart. For his fifty-ninth birthday, she pointedly gave him a Bible. She also wrote to his friend Edward Clodd, a banker and rationalist author, about his godlessness. And she embarrassed visitors with her ramblings about his immorality. Emma also became increasingly jealous of his fame, thinking of herself as a writer, and wishing they were like the poets, Robert and Elizabeth Browning. She even began to tell visitors that she had written her husband's novels. Emma's complex tragedy lay in her being yoked to so unconventional a writer, in her professional jealousy of him, for she regarded herself as an aspiring writer herself, and as Michael Millgate (1982) has noted, in her gradual losing touch with reality. Her innate warmth and generosity had been replaced by rancour, as increasingly she clung for solace to religion and to her social superiority. A letter to Elspeth Grahame, wife of Kenneth Grahame, the author of *The Wind in the Willows* (1908), is typical of her complaining:

> Keeping separate a good deal is a wise plan in crises – and being both free – & *expecting little* neither gratitude, nor attentions, love, nor *justice* … If he belongs to the public in any way, years of devotion count for nothing.
>
> (Millgate 1982: 397)

A war in which Florence Henniker's husband was to be involved was impending in South Africa, as the result of the rebellion of the Boers, or Afrikaners, against British rule. Hardy's feelings were deeply ambivalent. His interest in military adventure prompted his cycling excitedly to Southampton to witness the departure of the troopships in October. In November he watched the artillery battery leaving Dorchester barracks. Yet war was abhorrent to him and this outbreak engendered extreme pessimism about humanity's lack of moral progress. Hardy deplored mindless jingoism, and the Boer War gave rise to some fine poems, including 'The Going of the Battery', written on 2 November 1899, and those extraordinary poems about the casualties, 'Drummer Hodge' and 'The Souls of the Slain' **[48–9, 128–30]**.

The arrival of the new century gave Hardy something of an emotional lift, as his superbly achieved poem, 'By the Century's Deathbed' (better known by its revised title, 'The Darkling Thrush') reveals. It was written on 31 December 1900 and was included in Hardy's second volume of verse, *Poems of the Past and the Present*, published by Harper & Brothers in November 1901. Almost twice the size of *Wessex Poems*, this volume included, in its first section entitled 'War Poems', several poems written in response to the outbreak of the Boer War. Of the 'Poems of Pilgrimage' section, 'Shelley's Skylark', written in 'The neighbourhood of Leghorn: March 1887', recalls Hardy's interest in the Romantics, while the final sequence, 'Miscellaneous Poems' includes a number of poems, such as 'To an Unborn Pauper Child', first published in the *Academy*, 23 November 1901, that reflect on the nature of a universe inhabited by vulnerable humanity. Other poems that stand out are: 'In Tenebris I', 'A Broken Appointment', 'Tess's Lament', 'The Self-Unseeing' **[123–4]**, and 'The Ruined Maid', written in 1866, during Hardy's early period in London.

Hardy's war verse had begun to attract attention and the *Saturday Review*, which had panned *Wessex Poems*, now decided that Hardy was 'a profoundly interesting poet', though 'without a singing voice'. But although the reviews generally were more favourable, the *Athenaeum* sounded a note that was to re-echo in critical comment on Hardy's poetic output – that it was clumsy, and worse, pessimistic. Hardy called himself a meliorist, believing in the doctrine that the world may be improved by human endeavour. In 'In Tenebris II' he identifies himself as one, 'Who holds that if way to the Better there be, it exacts a full look at the Worst'. In January 1902 he noted, 'Pessimism (or rather what is called such) is, in brief, playing the sure game. You cannot lose at it; you may gain. It is the only view of life in which you can never be disappointed' (*LW*, 333). Hardy had stated plainly enough in an interview with William Archer in 1901: 'But my pessimism, if pessimism it be, does not involve the assumption that the world is going to the dogs. ... On the contrary, my practical philosophy is distinctly meliorist. What are my books but one plea against "man's inhumanity to man" – to woman – and to the lower animals?' (Gibson 1996: 147–8). Nevertheless, Hardy found himself continually having to mount a defence against the charge of pessimism.

While Hardy celebrated the ending of the Boer War, Emma was suffering from depression, and since London was likely to be crowded in a year that would see the coronation of King Edward VII, they forwent their annual visit, staying instead in Dorset and visiting Bath and Bristol. In September the first part of *The Dynasts* **[136–9]**, which he regarded as the major work of his life, was completed and was published on 13 January 1904 by Hardy's new publisher, Macmillan. *The Dynasts* was, Hardy claimed in a letter to Frederick Macmillan, 'the longest English drama in existence' (*L*, III, 277). It was an epic dramatisation of European history from 1805, when Napoleon rose to power, up to his defeat at Waterloo in 1815. Hardy had been thinking about this work since the 1870s, and had researched it assiduously for so long that he almost felt that he had lived through the Napoleonic years.

In addition to Napoleon and a range of historical figures, the poem employs a variety of Spirits who comment on the action. Hardy's patriotism led him to include several English heroes, notably Nelson. But the controlling philosophy of the work echoing, as has been mentioned, Arthur Schopenhauer's *The World as Will and Idea*, is the Immanent Will [27, 121, 126, 138], which renders our notions of free will illusory. The first reviews in 1904 had been on the whole negative. The epic drama form baffled some critics, while others complained that it was unpoetic. However, reviews of Part 2, which appeared in 1906, were warmer, while Part 3, published in 1908, was acclaimed and sold well. When in 1921 Hardy received a birthday address signed by 106 younger writers, it included the significant sentence: 'We thank you, Sir, for all you have written ... but most of all, perhaps, for *The Dynasts*' (Millgate 1984: 446).

The early stages of the writing of *The Dynasts* had been accompanied by anxiety and depression. By 1903 Emma had become more eccentric, and she took her niece, Lilian Gifford, who was staying with them, on a jaunt to Calais, the first of several such trips. And 1904 brought a series of deaths. On Easter Sunday, Hardy's mother Jemima died at the age of ninety. She left a considerable gap. But she had been in failing health, and Hardy's deeply ambivalent emotion is honestly presented in his poem 'After the Last Breath', written in 1904 and published in *Time's Laughingstocks* in 1909. Emma did not attend the funeral. In the same year Hardy also lost his old friends Leslie Stephen and Horace Moule's brother Henry.

The first of many honours to be bestowed on Hardy was the conferment of an honorary Doctor of Laws by Aberdeen University in 1905, to be followed by several universities, including Oxford and Cambridge. In that year and the following Hardy was in London, following his regular round of dinners, literary gossip, theatre, and concerts, and visits to the British Museum, while when at Max Gate, he pursued his hobby of cycling.

The earliest record of Hardy's relationship with Florence Dugdale is a letter he wrote to her on 2 January 1906, thanking her for a box of flowers that she had sent him following a visit to Max Gate. How they first met is not known. Florence gave various accounts of it, and Hardy himself is evasive in his *Life*, where he records that one of the visitors to Max Gate in the autumn of 1910 was 'Miss Dugdale, a literary friend of Mrs Hardy's at the Lyceum Club, whose paternal ancestors were Dorset people dwelling near the Hardys, and had intermarried with them some 130 years earlier' (*LW*, 378). That Hardy's relationship with Florence had developed considerably by that date, is revealed in the poem, 'After the Visit', which celebrates a visit to Max Gate by Florence in 1910. It was printed in the *Spectator*, 13 August 1910, and subsequently published in *Satires of Circumstance* in 1914. After Emma's death Hardy added, below the title, '(To F.E.D.)'. Hardy was attracted to this shy headmaster's daughter, who was twenty-seven and involved in journalism and the writing of children's stories. By the end of 1906 Hardy had enlisted her help with his research for *The Dynasts* at the British Museum. They met frequently in London and at the Aldeburgh home of Edward Clodd. Florence also helped Emma by typing up the manuscripts of her stories. Hardy's relationship with Florence intensified as his marriage declined. Florence, who had become part of the household, was aware of this and felt sorry for both Emma and Hardy.

The rift in the marriage was deepened by Hardy's fame and wealth, which increased with the large sales of his works, in particular Macmillan's Pocket Edition. He was sought out by younger writers, such as H.G. Wells, George Bernard Shaw; and also by Joseph Conrad, whom he met in 1907. In 1908 his eminence brought him the offer of a knighthood, which to Emma's disgust he rejected. His feeling was, he records in the *Life*, 'that any writer who has expressed unpalatable or possibly subversive views on society, religious dogma, current morals ... must feel hampered by accepting honours from any government' (*LW*, 352). However, he accepted the Order of Merit from the new King, George V, on 19 July 1910, when he was accompanied by Florence, because Emma had a severe cold. Belated local recognition came with the Freedom of the Borough of Dorchester in November of the same year.

Poetry and drama largely occupied 1908 and 1909. In 1908 the final part of *The Dynasts* appeared. Hardy had also written a gracious and perceptive Preface to his edition of the *Select Poems of William Barnes*, which was published on 24 November 1908, and the local Hardy Players produced a performance of *The Trumpet-Major*. For Hardy the major literary event of 1909 was the publication of his third volume of poetry,

Time's Laughingstocks, in December, but the year had also been marked by significant losses. The poet Swinburne had died in April and Hardy, angered by the hypocritical reaction of the press, celebrated him with the poem, 'A Singer Asleep', written at Bonchurch in 1910 and later published in *Satires of Circumstance*. In the following year Hardy made a pilgrimage to Swinburne's grave on the Isle of Wight. Also in 1909, his old acquaintance George Meredith died, leaving Hardy as the foremost living writer.

Hardy was anxious about *Time's Laughingstocks*. He had not had a volume of verse published since 1901. He was doubtful about the inclusion of 'A Trampwoman's Tragedy', which had appeared in the *North American Review* in November 1903, and 'A Sunday Morning Tragedy', which had been published in the *English Review* in December 1908. Both of these poems had previously been declined by magazine editors as likely to give moral offence. Hardy's publisher, Sir Frederick Macmillan, had to make up his mind for him about 'Panthera', which drew on a legend that Christ was possibly fathered by a Roman centurion. In his Preface Hardy noted the 'lack of concord in pieces written at widely severed dates, and in contrasting moods and circumstances'. Seven poems in this volume were written during his early years in London, between 1865 and 1867, with some from his time in Weymouth in 1869, while others date from the 1890s. His mother's death in 1904 prompted 'A Church Romance', first published in the *Saturday Review*, 8 September 1906, and 'After the Last Breath', among others. His grandmother is recalled in 'One We Knew', written on 20 May 1902, together with other reminiscences of his family; several poems are based on Wessex life, while love poems include 'On the Departure Platform' (Florence Dugdale) and 'The Division' (Florence Henniker), which was written in 1893 **[10, 38, 52, 111, 118, 127]**. There are narrative poems, including 'A Trampwoman's Tragedy', which in spite of editors' objections, Hardy placed high among his verse and 'A Sunday Morning Tragedy'. Also included were philosophical poems, such as 'God's Education'. It was a sound collection of 94 poems, signalling Hardy's status as a major poet. It was well reviewed, and sold out the print-run of 2,000 copies in one year.

(j) EMMA'S DEATH; MARRIAGE TO FLORENCE

In 1911 Hardy began the daunting task of revising his work for the definitive Wessex Edition proposed by Alexander Macmillan for publication in 1912. He could not resist the temptation to make further extensive revisions to the language of his texts, as well as to his prefaces, adding a General Preface to the edition. He also categorised his fiction, which as he anticipated led to considerable debate [57]. And he gave Macmillan his own map of Wessex. During 1911 and 1912, Hardy continued to see a good deal of Florence Dugdale. Emma meanwhile was in poor health and increasingly unstable, so much so that when the representatives of the Royal Society of Literature, W.B. Yeats and Henry Newbold, visited Max Gate to present Hardy with its gold medal on his seventy-second birthday, in spite of their protests, Emma was excluded from the little ceremony. Her health continued to deteriorate, and while entertaining visitors to tea on 25 November 1912, she became unwell. The next day a doctor was summoned. On 27 November she died of impacted gallstones and heart failure. Hardy's biographers differ sharply over his alleged immediate response to her death. James Gibson defends Hardy against Robert Gittings's imputation of possible callousness because, according to the maid Dolly Gale, he paused to criticise her for having a crooked collar when she reported her mistress's final illness (Gittings 1978: 149). Hardy was by nature punctilious, he may have been unconsciously delaying out of fear of what he would encounter upstairs; but most likely his lack of urgency stemmed from an ignorance, shared by Emma's doctor, of the seriousness of her condition, which had continued over a period .

Emma's funeral took place on the following Saturday. She was buried at Stinsford alongside the Hardy family. Hardy's grief was unexpected and overwhelming. His wreath bore the words, 'From her Lonely Husband, with the Old Affection'. He was consumed by guilt about his years of neglect, also by the bitter comments that he discovered in her diaries. Especially poignant was her account of the joyful days of their first meeting, recorded in *Some Recollections*. Hardy's immediate feeling of remorse pervades such poems as 'The Walk', published in *Satires of Circumstance*.

The culmination of this emotional turmoil was a visit, with his brother Henry, to St Juliot on 6 March 1913, over forty years after his first journey to inspect the church there. He visited Boscastle again, and also Beeny Cliff. This pursuit of the past gave rise to some of Hardy's greatest verse. Emma is the 'voiceless ghost' he seeks in 'After a Journey'; she is the young 'ghost-girl-rider' in 'The Phantom Horsewoman', written in 1913; she calls to him in 'The Voice', written in December 1912; while 'Beeny Cliff', written in March 1913, is the destination of their rambles. These poems, which were collected as 'Poems of 1912–13' in *Satires of Circumstance*, represent a period of remarkable creativity, which also saw his notable public poem on the occasion of the loss of the *Titanic*, 'The Convergence of the Twain'. This was first printed in The Souvenir Programme of the 'Dramatic and Operatic Matinée in Aid of the "Titanic" Disaster Fund' at Covent Garden, 14 May 1912. In the following year, 24 October saw the publication of Hardy's fourth and last collection of short stories, *A Changed Man and Other Tales* **[115]**.

Florence remained at Max Gate in anticipation of her marriage to Hardy, which had become an assumed fact, in the company of either Kate Hardy, who acted for a time as her brother's housekeeper, or Lilian Gifford, Emma's niece. Thus a veneer of respectability was preserved. Astonishingly, in 1913 Hardy received a visit from his former *fiancée* Eliza Nicholls, who had never married, in the forlorn hope that their relationship might be revived. Hardy and Florence were married quietly at Enfield Parish Church on 10 February 1914 at eight o'clock in the morning in the presence of Hardy's brother Henry, and Florence's father and youngest sister. To Hardy the marriage seemed a wise course, though he acknowledged that both he and his new wife possessed temperaments inclined to melancholy. He was seventy-four and she was thirty-five.

Florence found living with a writer, whose work transcended personal embarrassments, affected her spirits. When Hardy's volume, *Satires of Circumstance* was published on 17 November 1914, with its magnificent poems celebrating Emma in the section 'Poems of 1912–13', she was desolate. Like Emma before her, she had written confidential letters of complaint to Hardy's old friend, Lady Hoare, and on this occasion she wrote:

> It seems to me ... that I am an utter failure if my husband can publish such a *sad sad* book. He tells me that he has written *no* despondent poem for the last eighteen months, & yet I cannot get rid of the feeling that the man who wrote some of those poems is utterly weary of life – & cares for nothing in this world. If I had been a different sort of woman, & better fitted to be his wife – would he, I wonder, have published that volume?
>
> (Millgate 1982: 499)

The title of the volume derives from a series of poems printed in the *Fortnightly Review* in 1911, many of them offering jaundiced views of marriage, and of human frailty, which reflected Hardy's mood at the time. As well as the great elegiac poems written after Emma's death, there is a section called 'Lyrics and Reveries', which includes 'Channel

Firing', written in April 1914 and published in the following month in the *Fortnightly Review*, a poem about the gunnery practice Hardy could hear from his study at Max Gate. Also included are 'A Singer Asleep', 'The Convergence of the Twain', and poems of human concern, such as 'Beyond the Last Lamp', which appeared in *Harper's Monthly Magazine* in December 1911, or the unsentimental, 'Ah, are you Digging on my Grave?', which was first published in the *Saturday Review* of 27 September 1913. There is the cynical poem, 'God's Funeral', and in a section called 'Miscellaneous Poems' is 'In the Servants' Quarters', a striking poem about Peter's denial of Christ. Among the 107 poems are a number of great poems. Unfortunately, reviewers tended to pay attention to 'Satires of Circumstance'. They disliked their bitterly ironic tone, and there were the usual references to Hardy's technical awkwardness. Virginia Woolf, however, wrote to Hardy expressing her view that it was the most remarkable volume of poetry published during her lifetime.

In the background had been the inevitable war that Hardy dreaded **[41, 128–30]**, anticipating that it would be horrific and prolonged. When it was declared on 4 August 1914, he said that: 'It was seldom he had felt so heavy at heart as in seeing his old view of the gradual bettering of human nature … completely shattered by the events of 1914 and onwards' (*LW*, 395). He was overwhelmed by a sense of futility and waste, and regretted ending *The Dynasts* with hope for the progressive ennoblement of humankind. Hardy's faith in human progress persisted, but at a very low ebb, in his own histories of obscure rural folk, as in 'In Time of "The Breaking of Nations" ', written in 1915 and published in the *Saturday Review*, 29 January 1916. Although implacably opposed to war, and suspicious of Britain's lingering imperial ambitions, Hardy put his weight behind the war effort. In common with contemporary writers, such as G.K. Chesterton, Rudyard Kipling, John Galsworthy, Arnold Bennett, Arthur Conan Doyle, and H.G. Wells, he was called upon to work for the War Propaganda Bureau. Although his war poems in general have more in common with the pity of Wilfred Owen and the anger of Siegfried Sassoon, he wrote a somewhat jingoistic poem called ' "Men Who March Away" ' on 5 September 1914, for publication in the *Times* a few days later on 9 September. He also joined appeals for refugees. Hardy gave permission for a performance of *The Dynasts*, directed by Harley Granville Barker, in November 1914, as a way of raising public consciousness about the principles underlying the conflict. In 1916 he gave letters and manuscripts to the Red Cross sale, and in 1918 he contributed the manuscript of *Far from the Madding Crowd*. However, at the same time, Hardy's singularly compassionate nature expressed itself in his visits to German prisoners of war held near Dorchester. He also sent them copies of his books, and employed some of them in his gardens.

There were further more immediate sources of distress. During 1915, Florence had been unwell, and had undergone a minor operation in London. There was the shocking news of the loss in battle of a young cousin, Frank George Hardy, of whom Hardy had become fond, and had settled on as the heir to Max Gate. And on 24 November 1915 there occurred the death from emphysema of Hardy's beloved sister Mary, a loss which, according to his other sister Kate, aged him considerably.

(k) *MOMENTS OF VISION* AND WRITING *THE LIFE OF THOMAS HARDY*

Throughout 1916 Hardy remained at Max Gate, apart from a brief visit to Cornwall. His daily routine centred on his work. On 30 November 1917 his largest body of verse appeared, *Moments of Vision*, a collection of 159 poems. Astonishingly, with few exceptions, they were written during the previous three years, which constitute Hardy's most creative period as a poet.

This highly personal book is suffused by memories of Emma, but also of his sister Mary, in 'Logs on the Hearth', written in December 1915, and the family home in the visionary poem, 'Old Furniture'. Hardy's preoccupation with the family may be seen in 'Heredity', while the magnificent 'During Wind and Rain', based on Emma's recollections of her early years at Plymouth, celebrates past friendships. Some poems, for instance 'Afternoon Service at Mellstock', or 'The Oxen', printed in the *Times* on 24 December 1915, record his loss of religious faith. This volume also includes some impressive war poems, such as 'In Time of "The Breaking of Nations" ', 'I Looked Up from My Writing', and 'The Pity of It', first published in the *Fortnighty Review*, April 1915. In this volume Hardy's restless pursuit of variety in subject, form and tone is undiminished. Disappointingly, it was moderately received.

Just as so many of the poems published in *Moments of Vision* look back over Hardy's life, so too did his next project, his autobiography (though he forbade the use of that word). It appeared after his death in two volumes, as *The Early Life of Thomas Hardy* in 1928 and *The Later Years of Thomas Hardy* in 1930 **[139–41]**. It announces itself as having been written by Florence Emily Hardy, but it was ghosted by Hardy. His motives were complex but perfectly understandable. He had long

and unfortunate experience of literary critics and hunters of biographical material. He wished to be the first in presenting his own
account of his life and work. Finding that the writing of biographies
was becoming inevitable, he endeavoured to present an image of
himself, through his wife's 'biography' of him, as a major author and
public figure. With Florence's assistance, Hardy systematically prevented any sign of his intervention appearing. An intensely sensitive
and evasive man, Hardy sought to conceal his private self from public
inspection. Robert Gittings has called the whole process deceitful and
stupid. He also objects to Hardy's vanity in parading the names of his
famous society acquaintances. James Gibson, however, views this as
part of the richness of a book which includes 'comments on life, current
affairs and literary matters ... memories of the past and wealth of
anecdote and reminiscence' (Gibson 1996: 175), and he regards the *Life*
as 'one of Hardy's greatest works' (Gibson 1996: 175). After Hardy's
death, Florence deleted some of the references to the rich and famous;
she cut out several references to Emma, and also excised Hardy's more
vehement comments on those reviewers at whose hands he had
suffered.

(1) FINAL YEARS

The period up to Hardy's eightieth year was marked by the presentation
to him by his new young friend, the poet Siegfried Sassoon, of a volume
of forty manuscript poems by contemporary poets, to mark his seventy-
ninth birthday; by the end of the war, which Hardy greeted gloomily
as an unsatisfactory settlement; and by the publication of his *Collected
Poems* [119–36] in 1919. He was also working on the de luxe Mellstock
edition of his works. Typically, he continued to work most of the day
in his study, but roused himself at tea-time to entertain what had by
this time become a stream of visitors. Fame also meant that by now
Hardy was used to having honours conferred upon him. In 1920 he
was awarded an honorary Doctor of Letters degree from Oxford University, and witnessed *The Dynasts* being performed by the University
Dramatic Society. On his eighty-first birthday he received an address
by 106 younger writers, accompanied by the gift of a first edition of a
volume of Keats's poetry.

Late Lyrics and Earlier was published on 23 May 1922, in an edition
of 3,200 copies, and reprinted twice by the end of the year. As its title
suggests, music has a strong influence on the volume, which includes
several 'songs'. Poems about Emma appear again, as well as those about

other women, such as Helen Paterson in 'The Opportunity', and poems about ghosts (inhabiting Max Gate in the year 2000) in 'The Strange House', and 'Voices from Things Growing in a Churchyard', which appeared in the *London Mercury* in December 1921. Hardy's father's life is celebrated once more in 'On One Who Lived and Died Where He Was Born'. There are also familiar Hardyean themes of old age, love, and animals, in for instance, 'Last Words to a Dumb Friend', written on 2 October 1904. The volume consists of 151 poems from the period between 1866 and 1921. It is unusual in covering every decade in his poetic career. It is introduced by a long 'Apology', in which Hardy rounds on those critics who have labelled his work pessimistic, defending it as simply 'questionings' of reality, and asserting his belief in the amelioration of suffering through loving-kindness and scientific knowledge. He also attacks the supernaturalism of established religion, stressing the importance of continual change in literature and religious belief. For good measure, he castigates those reviewers not alert enough to register the mixture of humour and gravity in his verse.

The same year saw the publication of his poetic drama, *The Famous Tragedy of the Queen of Cornwall*, an undistinguished work based on legends associated with Tintagel and the romantic landscape of Cornwall, which was performed by the Hardy Players in 1923. Also in 1923, through the poet Robert Graves, Hardy struck up a friendship with T.E. Lawrence (Lawrence of Arabia), who was stationed as a soldier in Dorset. But 1923 was particularly notable for a luncheon visit to Max Gate on 20 July by the Prince of Wales, which represented the British establishment's endorsement of Hardy as the grand old man of English letters.

The relationship between Hardy and Florence by now had come under some strain. Florence was gloomy by nature, did not enjoy good health, and had an operation in 1924 for a lump in her throat. She was also intensely possessive. When Hardy found Tess Durbeyfield brought to life by a young local amateur actress, Gertrude Bugler, the daughter of Augusta Way, the 'original' Tess, in the Hardy Players' production of *Tess of the d'Urbervilles*, Florence intervened to prevent her professional engagement for the part on the London stage. Through it all, shielded from tourists by his wife and secretary, Hardy continued his disciplined routine, and on 20 November 1925 another book of poetry, *Human Shows, Far Phantasies, Songs and Trifles*, was published. These 152 poems, a few from his earliest period of composition in the 1860s, are miscellaneous. They include the well-known 'Waiting Both', first published in the *London Mercury* in November 1924, 'A Sheep Fair', and 'Snow in the Suburbs'. Emma's death again features, there are poems on nature and the seasons, and reflections on time, concluding with 'Why Do I?', an endeavour to explain his principle for living.

Hardy's final year was characterised by unrelenting activity. His last important public appearance was at the laying of the foundation stone for the Dorchester Grammar School in July, and his eighty-seventh birthday was spent in Devon with his friend Harley Granville Barker, a dramatist, producer and critic, whose naturalistic presentation influenced twentieth-century theatre. In the autumn Hardy was present at a meeting at the Dorset County Museum. He continued to work on *Winter Words*, a volume of poems planned for publication on his ninetieth birthday. This eighth and final volume of verse was published posthumously on 2 October 1928. Most of the 125 poems had been written since *Human Shows* appeared in 1925, but as usual some date back to the 1860s. It is a varied volume, including several poems that had recently been published in the *Daily Telegraph*. There are songs and ballads, memories of women he had loved, such as 'Concerning Agnes' (21 May 1928) or reaching further back, 'To Louisa in the Lane' (26 April 1928) **[10, 38, 45, 111, 118, 127]**. There are observations of nature in 'Proud Songsters' (9 April 1928), or 'I Watched a Blackbird' (2 July 1928). Some poems deal with earlier traumas, such as the suicide of his friend Horace Moule, which is explored obliquely in 'Standing by the Mantlepiece (H.M.M., 1873)', and some with memories of his family, for instance, 'Family Portraits', which had been published in *Nash's and Pall Mall Magazine* in December 1924. Poems such as 'Christmas in the Elgin Room', written in 1905 and 1926 and printed in *The Times*, 24 December 1927, and 'Drinking Song', which appeared in the *Daily Telegraph* on 14 June 1928, deal with the inevitable death of beliefs as they are replaced by new systems of faith. A number of poems that also appeared in the *Daily Telegraph* focus on Hardy's private self, as in 'Childhood among the Ferns' (29 March 1928), or 'He Never Expected Much' (19 March 1928); and others on his preparation for death, such as 'The New Dawn's Business' (20 March 1928), or 'A Wish for Unconsciousness' (5 July 1928). The final poem, also published in the *Daily Telegraph*, on 18 September 1928, gestures towards silence – 'He Resolves to Say No More'.

After a short illness, characterised by progressive weakness, Hardy died on 11 January 1928. He had seemed better on that morning, but suffered a heart attack in the evening. The news was announced on the radio. A public funeral was deemed appropriate for so distinguished a writer, in spite of the Dean of Westminster's anxiety about burying an agnostic in the Abbey. His literary executor, Sir Sydney Cockerell, and Sir James Barrie, who were present to support Florence, pressed for a public ceremony, against Hardy's own wish to be interred with his family in his beloved Stinsford churchyard. In a macabre compromise, it was decided that his body would be cremated for burial in the Abbey, but that his heart would be removed for interment at Stinsford. Both funerals took place on 16 January, Florence leading the public mourning, and Henry Hardy the private ceremony. Hardy's pallbearers included some of the foremost writers of the age; Sir James Barrie, John Galsworthy, Sir Edmund Gosse, A.E. Housman, Rudyard Kipling, George Bernard Shaw, as well as the Prime Minister, Stanley Baldwin, and Ramsay MacDonald. The occasion drew large crowds. Among the many tributes that appeared, that by his old friend Edmund Gosse has a particular resonance: 'the throne is vacant, and Literature is greatly bereaved … His modesty, his serenity, his equipoise of taste, combined with the extraordinary persistence of his sympathy and curiosity, made him an object of affectionate respect to young and old alike' (Gibson 1996: 193).

FURTHER READING

The essential starting-point is Hardy's disguised autobiography, in Michael Millgate's restored edition (1984), which reveals Hardy's endeavour to establish his literary reputation. Robert Gittings (1975) describes the secret collaboration of Hardy and Florence in producing the ghosted autobiography as deceitful, and focusing on Hardy's alleged snobbery about his social background, he seeks to uncover the truth behind the deception. Gittings remains unsympathetic in his study of Hardy's later years (1978), in which he castigates Hardy for his supposedly cruel treatment of Emma in the years before her death, and among another things, for his elusiveness, his meanness and his morbid temperament. Michael Millgate's biography (1982), though not always entirely comfortable with its subject, is the definitive biography. It is an extraordinarily detailed and judicious work of scholarship, and very informative about influences on Hardy's writing. Martin Seymour-Smith (1994) challenges earlier biographers' perceptions of Hardy's snobbery, misogyny and pessimism, and explores the positive aspects of his sexual relationships, approaching them through psychoanalytic theory. Paul Turner (1998) is valuable primarily for his examination of Hardy's reading and his use of it in his work. Among briefer biographies, F.B. Pinion (1992) has written a scholarly, somewhat conservative book, with some illuminating discussion of Hardy's friends, while James Gibson (1996) offers a lucid, appreciative and perceptive account of

Hardy's literary life. Two readable books that offer a context for the period are the collection of essays edited by Boris Ford (1958, revised 1982), and J.A.V. Chapple's general book on documentary and imaginative literature from 1880 to 1920 (1970). The publishing background to Hardy's fiction is provided by N.N. Feltes (1986) and J.A. Sutherland (1976).

PART II

WORK

HARDY'S CATEGORISATION OF HIS FICTION

In the 1912 General Preface to the collected 'Wessex' edition of his work, Hardy divides his fictions into groups **[46]**. He notes that 'the first group is called "Novels of Character and Environment"; and contains those which approach most nearly to uninfluenced works; also one or two which, whatever their quality in some few of their episodes, may claim a verisimilitude in general treatment and details'. In spite of Hardy's typically ambiguous statement, it seems clear that he regarded these novels as dealing with human concerns in the realist tradition. They include: *Under the Greenwood Tree, Far from the Madding Crowd, The Return of the Native, The Mayor of Casterbridge, The Woodlanders, Tess of the d'Urbervilles, Jude the Obscure, Wessex Tales* (short stories), and *Life's Little Ironies* (short stories).

Hardy identifies a second group as 'Romances and Fantasies', a definition which he calls, unhelpfully, 'sufficiently descriptive'. These include: *A Pair of Blue Eyes, The Trumpet-Major, Two on a Tower, The Well-Beloved,* and *A Group of Noble Dames* (short stories). Hardy explains the third group (*Desperate Remedies, The Hand of Ethelberta, A Laodicean,* and *A Changed Man and other Tales* (short stories) in the following terms:

> The third class – 'Novels of Ingenuity' – show a not infrequent disregard of the probable in the chain of events, and depend for their interest mainly on the incidents themselves. They might also be characterized as 'Experimental', and were written for the nonce simply; though despite the artificiality of their fable some of the scenes are not without fidelity to life.

For most of the twentieth century Hardy's 'Novels of Character and Environment' were regarded as his major fiction. In spite of its slightness, *Under the Greenwood Tree* is discussed here as belonging to the group of major novels, partly because it obviously belongs among the humanist realist fiction, but also because of its assured artistry. More recently, a process of revaluation of Hardy's lesser novels, his 'Romances and Fantasies' and 'Novels of Ingenuity', has been under way, based on the anti-realist strategies that they deploy.

(a) MAJOR NOVELS

Under the Greenwood Tree

The novel's original title, *Under the Greenwood Tree or the Mellstock Choir: A Rural Painting of the Dutch School* **[19–20]**, signalled three main artistic aims. The first part of the title, which comes from a song in Shakespeare's *As You Like It*, suggests a secluded pastoral world characterised by harmony with nature, music and the celebration of love. For his portrayal of the Mellstock choir, Hardy drew on the experiences of his father, grandfather and uncle at Stinsford, where the choir had been removed in about 1841 **[8]**. As the writing progressed, Hardy shifted the interest from the choir to the courtship of Fancy Day the new schoolmistress by three suitors; Dick Dewy the tranter's son, Farmer Shiner and the new young vicar Mr Maybold, though he preserved a link between the two strands of the narrative. The third part of the title alludes to the detailed portraits of ordinary cottage life in Dutch art **[14, 80, 199–200]**. For instance, the shoemaker, Mr Penny, framed by his window as he works, is portrayed as being represented by 'some modern Moroni' (*UGT*, 2: 2).

The term 'pastoral' is inadequate to register the density of this slight but superbly achieved novel. Hardy foregrounds daily occupations, with detailed descriptions of shoe making, bee keeping, and the tapping of a cider barrel. Collectively these portraits build up a picture of communal solidarity in a village where the idiosyncratic inhabitants are a source of collective wisdom, and where even the eccentric Mrs Day and the simpleton Thomas Leaf have an acknowledged place. Hardy's concern to portray this world with scrupulous fidelity involves recording the forces of change, symbolised by the replacement of the church choir by a fashionable cabinet organ. This minor change, common in churches elsewhere, creates a sense of loss, suggested by the way the musicians, now scattered throughout the body of the church, feel not only redundant, but also out of place.

Fancy Day, the organist who replaces them, and the focus of the novel's love interest, also represents change. An *ingénue*, she is coquettish, and self-absorbed. Although the daughter of a rural worker and a governess, she is an upwardly mobile trained teacher. Fancy and her socially ambitious father, Geoffrey Day, who turns down Dick Dewy as her suitor, anticipate Grace Melbury and her father in *The Woodlanders* **[77–82]**. Fancy's choice is between Dick Dewy and the vicar, a bourgeois interloper who tempts her with the prospect of a shared culture, for which her education has prepared her. Although engaged to Dick Dewy, she accepts Mr Maybold, but retracts her promise the next day. Fancy's decisions are highly significant in revealing her character and Hardy's values. Her confession to Mr Maybold of her true nature indicates a redeeming self-awareness, and her choice of the morally superior Dick Dewy, whose magnanimity links him to his grandfather William Dewy, reveals her capacity to make a proper evaluation of his worth.

The contrast between the natures of Fancy and Dick, which Dick maturely recognises, is symbolised economically on the morning of the harvest Thanksgiving and Fancy's *début* at the new organ. It is a schematic opposition of vanity and selflessness. While she dresses audaciously in blue, with her curls showing and a hat and feather in order to be the centre of attraction in the church, Dick is wearing his funeral clothes, on his way to carry out a long-standing promise to his dying friend John Dunford to be a pall bearer at his funeral in neighbouring Charmley. Dick's pursuit of Fancy Day is believable. He has received an education and is a respected tradesman; while she is still very much part of village life. And in the end it is these communal values, represented by Dick, that secure her for him; not unrealistically, however, as the narrator makes clear in the references to 'those beautiful eyes of hers – too refined and beautiful for a tranter's wife, but perhaps not too good' (*UGT*, 5: 1).

Continuity and harmony are central values in *Under the Greenwood Tree*. Hardy's interest in heredity is given visual and symbolic force when Mr Penny the shoemaker identifies a likeness between Fancy's boot and the last on which her father's footwear is made. Music, the most obvious symbol of harmony, is introduced in the opening pages as the choir assembles in the dark lanes on Christmas Eve to visit the houses in the village. Another traditional symbol of communal solidarity is the dance at the Tranter's party, which is enhanced by the two extremes of society that stand outside it; Enoch the trapper and the vicar Mr Maybold. The most obvious unifying force is the rhythm of the seasons. The time span of the novel runs from winter through to a second spring, which embodies the idea of renewal. Its parallel with the marriage of Fancy and Dick symbolises hope for the future of the community, and also for the agriculture on which it depends.

Hardy's version of pastoral in *Under the Greenwood Tree* is given significance by his realism. The economic basis of the village, and people's consequent relative social status are emphasised, for instance when Dick delays his arrival at the church for his wedding in order to hive a swarm of bees. There are hints at the end of the novel that Fancy's destiny will embrace motherhood and domesticity. A sense of loss is also present in the narrative; there is the removal of Fancy's furniture from her father's house, while Enoch has mysteriously left the village. And always in the background is death; the funeral of Dick's friend and the knowledge that Mrs Brownjohn has buried three children. However, such realistic observation forms the basis of Hardy's quiet symbolism. His use of a greenwood tree at the end of the novel is anticipated in the opening pages, in which Dick traversing the dark lanes instinctively distinguishes the various species of tree from the sounds they make. The tree represents a society in harmony with nature and with itself, apart from the bustle of the urban world, but not timeless, nor immune to change. In this novel, which Hardy places among 'Novels of Character and Environment', his fidelity is to environment in the widest sense; evident in his minute delineations of nature and rural occupations, his ear for the natural rhythms of dialogue and dialect, his alertness to humour, and his detailed descriptions of interiors of houses, the church, and the gallery where the choir sits. Such places, subject to repeated human activity, achieve value as the site of ritual.

Further reading

This novel has not attracted as much attention as one might expect. Early studies treated it uncritically as a pastoral idyll. However, for Danby (1959) time threatens the traditional community and undermines the novel's comic resolution, foreshadowing the pessimism of Hardy's later work. Draffan (1973) reads this text as a somewhat jaundiced study of village life, arguing moreover that Hardy reveals no sense of loss at the removal of the choir, as his interest switches to the love story. Toliver (1962) focuses on the social tension in the courtship of Dick Dewy and Fancy Day, and suggests that the relationship between them at the conclusion of the novel is an unstable compromise. In a discriminating essay, Page (1975) examines Hardy's wide-ranging use of pictorial traditions in his combination of a realistic evocation of community with pastoral romance. From a historical perspective, Howard (1977) endorses the accuracy of Hardy's portrayal of the stratified community of Mellstock (Stinsford) from her research of the 1841 census, and argues that the novel reveals a tension between history and pastoral. This text has also received some attention from materialist critics. Wotton (1985) suggests that the dance is a way in which the workfolk degrade the civilised through ritual; while Goode (1988) argues that the self-conscious pastoral is used to manipulate the contemporary reader, but 'what the text does is to subvert the moral prison of Victorian sentimentality by a trace of real earthiness' (Goode 1988: 13).

Far from the Madding Crowd

Far from the Madding Crowd is strongly influenced by the world of the ballad, but as its title – a line from Gray's 'Elegy Written in a Country Churchyard' – suggests, it also celebrates the removed rural life. Hardy described *Far from the Madding Crowd* **[21–2]** as a 'pastoral tale' (*LW*, 98). He underlined this by allusions to Milton's *Lycidas* and Virgil's *Georgics*, and by having in his hero Gabriel Oak, a shepherd who could play his flute with 'Arcadian sweetness' (*FFMC*, 6). This romantic, patient lover of Bathsheba Everdene is the chief representative of Hardy's pastoral ideal, a 'pastoral king' (*FFMC*, 6) as he calls him, whose 'Pastoral Tragedy' (*FFMC*, 5), the loss of his sheep, has reduced his status to that of a hired man on Bathsheba's farm. Oak retains a quiet authority partly through his associations with the values of an idyllic pastoral world. He naturally courts Bathsheba by taking her a present of an orphaned lamb. However, the elements of pastoral are rooted with compelling realism in the rituals of the farming calendar, such as sheep shearing and harvesting, and in the social events that structure and give meaning to the life of the agricultural community. Hardy gives a voice to the community through the workfolk who meet at Warren's Malthouse; Poorgrass, Coggan, Tall, Fray and others. They are presented without condescension, speaking in authentic dialect, and they are a source of gossip and humour. As a repository of traditional rural wisdom, they also provide a sense of a living culture, against which the main characters are judged.

The symbolic centre and spiritual heart of *Far from the Madding Crowd* is the Great Barn, a grand medieval structure in which the sheep shearing takes place. Hardy is at pains to emphasise the harmony between the shearers and the barn, and the continued relevance of the building to the life of the community. Unlike the other medieval buildings, the church and the castle, 'the old barn embodied practices which had suffered no mutilation at the hands of time' (*FFMC*, 22). By extension, as Hardy suggests of the sheep shearing, 'This picture of to-day in its frame of four hundred years ago' stands for the village of Weatherbury, which in comparison with cities was 'immutable' (*FFMC*, 22).

The even-tenored life of the rural community is disturbed by the arrival of a woman farmer in Bathsheba, who has inherited her uncle's farm, and who is placed in a traditionally masculine role. This is challenged by the dramatic appearance of Frank Troy, a figure from the world of ballad; a dashing sergeant of cavalry, of good family and education, who is also a mercurial, sexually predatory scapegrace. Troy's sexual awakening of Bathsheba is achieved in the famous scene of his

THOMAS HARDY

sword drill (which Hardy researched), with its erotic symbolism of penetration, in 'the hollow amid the ferns' (*FFMC*, 28), as he fascinates and dominates her, enforcing his sexual mastery. His rootless modernity is also a disruptive element in Weatherbury. He has no feeling of responsibility to the farming community. Stupified by drink after the harvest supper, he is oblivious to the vulnerability of the ricks to the coming storm. He also lacks the countryman's sense of continuity and time (symbolically he offers his watch to Bathsheba), and has no feeling either for the rhythms of nature. One of Troy's functions in the narrative is to upset the ordered pattern of rural life.

Hardy gave no hint to Leslie Stephen, in his original suggestion for the novel, that Bathsheba would occupy its central role. It is evident that Hardy was interested in the complexity of her psychology, particularly in relation to her own sense of identity. An intelligent, capable woman, she almost ruins her life by her sexual responses to the men who pursue her. She seems to fear the moral power bestowed on Oak by virtue of his critical observation of her; she is almost beaten down by the social expectation of marriage following Farmer Boldwood's receipt of her Valentine; but she feels sinful in the sexual abandon of her surrender to Troy. Yet in this relationship she succumbs to her fundamental desire to have her independent spirit tamed in a way that she knows Oak could never do.

The narrative seeks to emphasise the conflictual condition of her mind. Initially, she is presented from the point of view of Gabriel Oak, who is observing her as she sits on a waggon, narcissistically regarding her own extraordinary beauty in a small looking glass, conjecturally dreaming of triumphs over men. She uses her sexuality as a form of defence and control. Hardy describes her as a woman whose independence of men is necessary to her sense of identity, and who regards marriage as literally a degrading sacrifice of self. Her experience with Sergeant Troy is profoundly de-stabilising, when she finally realises how her selfhood is bound up with her passion for him at the moment he kisses the dead Fanny Robin, his wife, as he says, in the sight of heaven because of their previous sexual relationship. After the shooting of Troy, the proud Bathsheba is brought to utter prostration. The complexity of Bathsheba's presentation is a source of critical debate, particularly among feminist critics of the novel **[185, 186, 188]**.

Hardy uses the social ritual of the Valentine to complex effect. It symbolises that combination of character, accident, and social convention that characterises the operation of the world of Hardy's novels. For Bathsheba, sending the Valentine is a whimsical freak, originating with Liddy. The working of chance is symbolised by the tossing of a hymn book to decide whether the recipient is to be little Teddy Coggan or William Boldwood. Boldwood is transfixed by it, 'till the large red seal became as a blot of blood on the retina of his eye' (*FFMC*,14). This imagery is proleptic of sex and death. The solitude of his home has been penetrated, and the regular pattern of his life is about to be tragically disrupted by an overwhelming obsession.

Evidence from the manuscript of the novel suggests that William Boldwood was introduced at a later stage of composition. His entry into the text provided Hardy with a powerful contrast between Troy's instinctive understanding of women and Boldwood's sexual obtuseness. Boldwood is a penetrating study of an obsessive personality, whose sexual desires, sublimated in the successful running of Little Weatherbury Farm, once awakened dominate him. Boldwood's courtship, subtly understood by Gabriel Oak, although superficially social and doggedly persistent, is also pathologically sexual. His life subsequently adopts the pattern of tragic drama. His pursuit of Bathsheba is thwarted, on the point of her yielding to the sheer pressure of his presence, by the sudden arrival of Frank Troy. Boldwood's ignominious public collapse on the occasion of Bathsheba's marriage to Troy has serious social consequences when he fails to secure his ricks against the great storm. Baffled again by Troy's reappearance to claim his wife at the Christmas party at which Boldwood has just coerced her into a promise of their future engagement, he acknowledges Troy's authority over his wife, but her cry when she is touched by him releases the rage that prompts him to shoot the soldier dead.

The full tragic implication of this act Hardy reserves for the discovery in a locked closet in Boldwood's home of expensive lady's dresses, and a case of jewelry, accumulated secretly, labelled 'Bathsheba Boldwood', each dated six years in advance. This fetishism and obsessive ferocity for possession produces sympathy for Boldwood and makes acceptable his reprieve from the gallows after his failed suicide attempt. However, he is thwarted yet again in his surrender to the police and his desire for the oblivion of death, and he is forced to live out his obsession to the end.

The melodramatic climax to the narrative of the two rivals clears the way for Gabriel Oak, who has channelled his love into devotion and service, and who earns his reward through trials of his merit. The eventual union of Oak and Bathsheba is foreshadowed from the beginning by her evident disturbance at his proposal of marriage in a scene that carries a strong undercurrent of sexual tension. Also proleptic is the intensely visual, symbolic scene in which Gabriel and Bathsheba work together to thatch the rick – the harvest on which the community depends – before the rain comes, silhouetted by lightning – in which each acknowledges the other's true worth.

The novel's closing scenes inversely parallel Gabriel's early courtship. Again Bathsheba pursues him, but this time prompts him to renew his offer. Both have matured through experience. Gabriel Oak represents the stoical endurance of a man who has learnt to work with the unpredictability of nature, the volatility of women, and to discipline his own feelings and conduct. Bathsheba represents the achievement of a true sense of self-worth, and the clear-sighted recognition of human values. Now that Oak is taking the tenure of Boldwood's farm they are social equals, who between them will maintain the village community. Low-key domestic realism at the conclusion supports the symbolism of the continuity of rural values and a profounder love deepened by friendship that supplants mere passion. They walk to their wedding on a damp and misty morning.

The narrative of *Far from the Madding Crowd* is designed to suit publication in serial form. As well as the contrast established between Bathsheba's three suitors, there is a deliberate contrast between the fate of Bathsheba and that of Fanny Robin. They are linked through Fanny's meeting with Gabriel Oak on the road to Warren's Malthouse, through Fanny's employment by Bathsheba, and through her relationship with Troy. The traditional ballad tale of the young rural servant girl seduced and betrayed by a soldier tactfully counterpoints the main story. The height of Bathsheba's success as a new woman farmer – introducing herself with authority as the mistress of Weatherbury Upper Farm, and entering the male world of the Casterbridge corn market – frame Fanny Robin's pleading in the snow outside Troy's barracks from across the river. Bathsheba's marriage to Troy at Bath is matched by Fanny's death in the Union at Casterbridge. Her death also signals the death of Bathsheba's marriage. Although the chapter in which Bathsheba discovers the baby in Fanny's coffin is entitled 'Fanny's Revenge', Hardy avoids melodrama. It is an emotionally powerful scene in which both Troy and Bathsheba are forced to be true to their own natures in confronting the past. It is a richly visual, deeply ironic and symbolic tableau, as husband and wife bend over the coffin of his mistress and child. It is symbolic both of sexual compulsion and the power of social class, with their attendant patterns of betrayal.

Far from the Madding Crowd is an intensely visual novel. Its more striking scenes include the startling image of Gabriel Oak and Bathsheba Everdene perilously defying the cosmos on the rick in the storm, the lantern illuminating Troy's uniform when his spur is symbolically

entangled with Bathsheba's skirt in the fir plantation, and Troy's performance as Dick Turpin at Greenhill Fair. As so often in Hardy's novels,
such scenes involve an observer. Gabriel Oak watches Bathsheba
through a hole in the hut where she is tending two cows with her
aunt, while Troy observes Bathsheba talking with Boldwood through
a slash in the tent at Greenhill Fair. As well as its visual effects, *Far from
the Madding Crowd* displays Hardy's narrative skills in his use of
melodrama, ballad stories and psychological exploration. These are
fused and held together by a detailed realism that relies not only upon
descriptions of agricultural life, but on the evocation of a traditional
community whose continuity Hardy cherishes.

Further reading

As part of his existential humanist approach, Morrell (1965) argues for
the value of Gabriel Oak's realistic accommodation to the forces of
Nature. He 'neither evades [reality] nor resigns himself to it; he makes
something out of it' (Morrell 1965: 63). From a Lacanian perspective,
Garson (1991) similarly regards Oak as the novel's only integrated
character because he submits to the Other (Lacan's theories are
discussed in Part III). Also from a psychoanalytic point of view, Sumner
(1981) reveals how Hardy's treatment of William Boldwood
corresponds to Freud's account of repression; D.H. Lawrence (1936)
summarises his view of sexual psychology in his assertion that Troy is
the only man who understands Bathsheba; while Wright (1989) places
Bathsheba among Hardy's erotic women who exercise power through
their sexual fascination. From a feminist angle, Garson also sees Hardy's
treatment of Bathsheba's narcissism as his way of controlling an
independent woman; while Morgan (1988) represents a number of
feminist critics who regard the novel as revealing the power of male
ideology to subdue and discipline the female. She regards Oak as Hardy's
spy and censor, policing Bathsheba in an 'insidious form of subjugation'
(Morgan 1988: 44), which succeeds in devitalising her. Focussing on
the isssue of gender, Shires (Higonnet 1993) registers the 'growing
uncertainty at the end of the nineteenth century about: what is a
woman?' (Higonnet 1993: 64), for conventional representations of
masculinity and femininity are called into question by the simultaneous
sexual power and powerlessness of both Oak and Bathsheba. Marxist
criticism from Williams (1970) onwards has engaged with the novel's
pastoralism. Williams focuses on Hardy's creation of a modern society
and deconstructs the humanist pastoral of Wessex, insisting that Oak's
experiences mirror the typical risks undertaken by small-capital

farming. Wotton (1985) sees the Great Barn as representing the proletarianisation of the labour force existing alongside pockets of pre-capitalist modes of production. Goode (1988) also focuses on the barn episode, which he regards as 'truly an organic image, drained of its ideological medium, but it is violated by the historical actuality of the novel' (Goode 1988: 17–18). From a formal point of view, Kramer (1975) finds in the novel elements of Hardy's tragic concerns, including the irresolvable dichotomy between free will and determinism, which is analysed through Boldwood; and Casagrande (1982) sees Hardy's tragic pattern as preventing the complete transformation of Bathsheba Everdene. Gatrell (Falck-Yi 1993) discusses the evolution of Hardy's conception of Bathsheba and explores her psychological complexity in the context of Victorian notions of sexuality and marriage. Particularly illuminating are his treatment of the novel's intertextual relation with Goldsmith's *The Vicar of Wakefield* and his allusions to John Schlesinger's film (*Far from the Madding Crowd*).

The Return of the Native

The opening of *The Return of the Native* **[26–7]**, devoted to the description of a wild tract of unenclosed heath land, is unique in Hardy's fiction. The initial description of Egdon, given from the point of view of the narrator in the central valley of the heath, is of a vast bowl claustrophobically blocking out the outside world. Hardy's reference to the changeless nature of Egdon, which encompasses all time from pre-history to the present, which acknowledges only the rhythm of the sun and the seasons, and in which clock time is meaningless, introduces a destabilising vision as space and time expand dizzyingly. Humanity is reduced to a historical footnote. Yet Hardy's is not a nihilistic vision, for landscape is given significance by human presence, and here on the white surface of the Roman road is the reddleman's van. Houses have been established on the heath, often identified as tiny points of light in the great darkness, and the novel's tragic drama is localised in places named Blooms-End, Mistover Knap, and the Quiet Woman. The heath's tragic dimension is alluded to in Hardy's association of the heath with 'that traditionary King of Wessex', in the Preface to the 1895 edition, and in his reference to the heath's omnipresent, anthropomorphic face, 'suggesting tragical possibilities' (*RN*, 1: 1).

Hardy defines his characters and concerns against the heath. It represents one term of the dialectic between the ineluctably material and permanent, and the state of flux of the modern mind. Clym Yeobright, who is brought back to his native heath, is the example of the modern type, for whom the inviolate heath offers 'ballast to the mind adrift on change, and harassed by the irrepressible New' (RN, 1: 1). While in a chapter entitled 'My Mind to me a Kingdom is' (quoting a poem usually attributed to Sir Edward Dyer, a courtly poet who lived between 1543 and 1607), Hardy draws attention to Clym's essentially modern preoccupation with intellectual speculation. By contrast, Eustacia Vye is introduced as Queen of Night, and treated with ambivalent irony as the 'raw material of a divinity' (RN, 1: 1). In status and beauty no one on Egdon is her superior, and this affords her a kind of dignity. Her silhouetted figure on the top of Rainbarrow gives significance to the heath. She is also at one with the heath in her sensuous understanding of its dark mysteries, but this aspect of her nature is at war with that of the girl from the fashionable seaside resort of Budmouth, for whom the heath and nature are hateful. It is the power of her malevolent enemy the heath, manifested in the driving storm that hastens her towards her death (Hardy leaves it unclear whether it is an accident or suicide), that finally affords her a tragic status.

The situation Hardy has created on Egdon Heath is almost that of a social experiment, for its community is strikingly divided. The furze-cutters, whose workplace it is, appear almost to be an extension of the heath itself, while the other characters are uprooted middle-class people who are forced into encounters in a world that they find inhospitable or uncongenial. Thus the tragedy may be seen as having a powerful social cause. Eustacia, the daughter of a bandmaster from Corfu, and the granddaughter of a sea captain, is a middle-class girl who dreams of cosmopolitan pleasures. Of the two men who could offer these, Wildeve's social status is ambivalent, since he gave up a career as an engineer to be the innkeeper of the Quiet Woman; while Clym Yeobright, ironically returned dissatisfied from the material world of Paris, is stranded between his intellectual ideals and the realities of the life of the heath community. The heath enforces a reduction both of the outsiders' aspirations and of their social status: Wildeve to the level of a rural innkeeper, Clym to a furze-cutter, Eustacia to a furze-cutter's wife, Diggory Venn from a dairy farmer to a reddleman. A reddleman travelled around rural areas selling reddle, a red ochre, which was used for marking sheep. It is the major characters' unstable class positions, with their accompanying frustrations, that drive the action of the novel.

The background to the modern intellectual, social and moral pre-occupations of the novel, is formed by the lives of the heath dwellers. They represent for Hardy the valuable continuity of instinctual wisdom and an unreflective capacity for joy. There is a poignant encounter between Clym Yeobright, who has brought back from Paris Comtean ideas **[14, 23, 108, 121]** of a religion of humanity and the imperative of progress, and a group of the heath dwellers, to whom he expounds his idea of setting up a local school. Timothy Fairway immediately sees his scheme as irrelevant, while another comments on the goodness of his heart, but agrees about the futility of his impractical notions.

In the lives of the heath dwellers, Hardy records and endorses the survival of an older pagan world that had its basis in dependence on the earth. This gave rise to rituals of propitiation, primitive modes of thought, the vestiges of which may be seen in their customs and superstitions. Hardy makes explicit the pagan origins of the May-revel; while the great bonfire on Rainbarrow at the beginning of the novel is the ancient south Dorset fertility ritual of lighting midsummer fires, displaced to Guy Fawkes Day, which is suggested by the ember-dancing that follows the dying down of the fire.

Animistic beliefs are evident in Susan Nonsuch's image-magic, or in Christian Cantle's awe of the dice and fear of the devil. The deeply instinctual Eustacia Vye is also associated with paganism in several ways that enhance her status in the narrative. She is not only associated with the pre-Christian darkness of the heath, but Susan Nonsuch identifies her as a witch, and her daring cross-dressing as the Turkish Knight in the mummers' play of St George (a Christianised version of the ritual sacrifice of a human victim as representative of winter), results in her proleptic ritual death. And as Hardy makes clear, her moonlight dance with Wildeve is a Dionysian celebration of passion. Hardy endorses the vigorous paganism of Grandfer Cantle, Timothy Fairway and the others, who have long forsaken churchgoing as an outworn social custom, though they still dwell within the parish. His corresponding animus against Christianity may be seen in his presentation of Christian Cantle, a kind of caricature of a Christian man, an impotent man whom women shun, who withdraws from the dancing around the bonfire and is fearful of the heath.

If Eustacia dominates the opening of the novel, with her dramatic appearance on Rainbarrow and her provocative lighting of signal fires, Clym is prominent in the second half of the novel, particularly the ending. It has frequently been noted how the first half is dominated by classical imagery, while Biblical imagery governs the second half. But it would be too simple to invoke Arnoldian terms and see the death of the pagan Hellenic force, Eustacia, as permitting the triumph of the Hebraic ideas of Clym, or to regard her death and his survival as the crushing of female audacity in claiming a legitimate expression of her romantic self in a world dominated by men. Hardy's treatment of Clym at the end of the novel is sympathetic but severe. He has replaced the romantic symbol of Eustacia on Rainbarrow, but only in the role of a preacher of humanistic Comtean sermons on the theme of loving-kindness, which the heath dwellers listen to abstractedly out of sympathy for the tragic story of his life.

Clym Yeobright's life has been determined by two events directed by the heath; his commitment to Eustacia at the midpoint of the novel, ominously under a lunar eclipse, and the death of his broken-hearted, estranged mother from an adder bite. Mrs Yeobright objects to Eustacia on social grounds (a bandmaster's daughter), sexual grounds (she is 'voluptuous') and on moral grounds (she is 'idle') (RN, 3: 5), but what she most fears is losing her hold over Clym. And it is not difficult to see that in choosing Eustacia over his mother Clym is virtually willing his own destruction, for his love for his mother is absolute. The tragedy of Clym Yeobright may be cast in Oedipal mould, that of a young man bound to a dominant, ambitious mother who channels her thwarted aspirations through him, inculcating in him the Victorian materialist work ethic. She sends him out into the world to become wealthy and respected, and to marry a docile well born lady, who unlike the wilful and passionate Eustacia, will not threaten her relationship with him. His blindness has a symbolic link with castration. Clym's return to the house (kept as a kind of shrine to his mother) after the wedding of Thomasin and Diggory Venn reveals the tragic effect of his guilt, and his choice of the Biblical text from Kings 2, which he preaches on Rainbarrow, encapsulating a relation of filial obedience, is ironic in the light of both Solomon's and Clym's defiance of their mothers' wills. Clym's preaching on this text may be seen as part of a tragic cycle of Oedipal guilt and expiation in which he remains trapped. Clym's life and dilemmas are in important respects very close to Hardy's own; including his espousing the influential ideas of Comte and his difficulty in escaping the claims of the past.

The Return of the Native has the feeling of an experiment. It combines an autobiographical element, a sociological study of displacement, and the use of the enclosing landscape of Egdon Heath as a stage for classical drama. Hardy aimed at intensification of the tragic experience, and he was pleased with his achievement of the classical unities of place and time (the action covers a year and a day), which is unusual in fiction. He also gives the novel a five-act structure, in his five books, and throughout the text there are allusions to Greek drama.

The sixth book, 'Aftercourses', is problematic. In a footnote to the 1912 edition of *The Return of the Native* Hardy laid the marriage of Thomasin and Diggory Venn at the door of serialisation, claiming that he had wished to retain the weird and solitary character of Venn, and to allow him to disappear mysteriously, while Thomasin was to remain a widow. Hardy's dilemma is reflected in his treatment of Diggory Venn, who may be regarded either as an alienated, meddling malcontent, a destructive figure, censoring female independence and blighting two marriages; or as a patient lover, whose stoical endurance is rewarded.

Venn is rendered primarily symbolically. Indeed, at times he seems almost an extension of the heath. He and Thomasin are both intimately connected to it, and through this they have a profound affinity to each other. For neither of them does it represent either an idyllic or an imprisoning environment, but a known and benign place. In his symbolic transformation from outmoded reddleman to his former occupation of dairy farmer, and in his marriage to the 'good' heroine, as Hardy called her, Hardy seeks an accommodation between the community of the novel and the displaced characters. However, this celebratory conclusion forms a sharp contrast with the tragic destinies of those whose claims upon life were made in the face of the ultimate reality symbolised by the heath.

Further reading

Johnson (1894) regards Hardy's first attempt at tragedy as exemplifying the characteristic inexorability of his tragic vision. However, Kramer (1975) sees it as an apprentice tragedy in which Clym Yeobright is an impercipient and unsuccessful tragic hero, but which is important for the study of Hardy's development of tragic form, because of its division of interest between Clym and Eustacia Vye. More recent critics have tended to concentrate their attention on one or other of the two main protagonists. Garson (1991) offers a Lacanian and feminist reading of Eustacia, who amounts to no more than 'a catalogue of culturally coded parts' and 'As a result, she can be seen as a victim not only of her husband's misreading but of all male readings of woman as Other (including the author's)' (Garson 1991: 71). Gribble (1996) finds Eustacia a divided figure, torn between the impulse to challenge male hegemony through her independent sexuality and her adolescent perpetuation of naïve, romantic ideas. However, for Langbaum (1995) Eustacia achieves the stature of a romantic heroine seduced by notions of her tragic destiny. Both Eustacia Vye and Clym Yeobright interest Sumner (1981), who explores, from a psychoanalytic point of view, Hardy's presentation of Eustacia's neurosis and Clym's Oedipal relationship with his mother. Brown (1954) is typical of humanist critics who are concerned with the conflict between rural and urban cultures, and with Hardy's rejection of the urban way of life. Millgate (1971) takes a different humanist slant, regarding Clym's destiny as that of an ironic Christ-figure, reduced to preaching humanistic sermons. The materialist critic, Wotton (1985) finds an ideological contradiction between Hardy's presentation of the bourgeois destruction of rural tradition and the workfolk's subversion of civilised life through communal rituals. An element of critical controversy surrounds Diggory Venn. From a feminist perspective, Morgan (1988) sees Venn as 'a power-mongering bully and degrader of voluptuous womankind' (Morgan 1988: 75), and a male censor of Eustacia's splendidly assertive sexuality. Hardy's conclusion has also attracted critical attention, notably Berger (1990), who argues that the conventional comic resolution, the marriage of Thomasin and Venn, is deliberately unconvincing, in order to draw attention to the artificial constraints of closure demanded by the convention of realism. Boumelha (1999a) argues for seeing the novel as structured around a division into feminine and masculine worlds, characterised by romantic desire and ambition. 'As the novel progresses, the tragedy of Eustacia is placed precisely at the intersection of these two worlds' (Boumelha 1999a: xxv).

The Mayor of Casterbridge

In the first edition of this novel, Hardy added the subtitle *The Life and Death of a Man of Character* [31–2], expanding this in 1912, after revisions in the intervening years, to *The Life and Death of the Mayor of Casterbridge: A Story of a Man of Character*. All the terms of the deliberately chosen title are important in suggesting this novel's strongly Aristotelian tragic form [146–52], which records the rise of Michael Henchard, a hay-trusser, to a position at the apex of the community of Casterbridge, after committing the sin of 'selling' his wife at Weydon Priors Fair years before, and the subsequent decline of his fortune based on economic misjudgment and the public revelation of his past shame. The experience of the egotistical King Lear; his banishment of Cordelia, his deepening remorse, his longing for reconciliation with his family, his loss of his daughter, and his tragic death find parallels in the story of Michael Henchard.

The family group presented at the beginning of the novel, trudging across a generalised and timeless landscape, represent the age-old story of marital discontent and economic vulnerability. This narrative is dramatically refocussed and given tragic impetus at Weydon Fair. Henchard's decision to 'sell' his wife and rid himself of the wearisome responsibility of a family is the novel's crucial determining act. This choice is made believable, even understandable, by its context of physical exhaustion, alcohol, and the Babylonian fair, where buying and selling involves a degree of corruption, symbolised by the faintly sinister woman selling her adulterated furmity which was made from wheat boiled in spiced milk. However, it is a fundamental act of inhumanity and it proceeds from Henchard's complex, volatile nature, in which generosity, love, frustration and brutality are compounded. The emphasis on 'character' in the novel's title is reinforced by Hardy's quotation from Novalis (the pseudonym of the German Romantic poet and novelist, Friedrich Leopold von Hardenberg), 'Character is Fate' (*MC*, 17). Throughout the novel Henchard blames fate for his declining fortune, but signally fails to recognise that it is his character that contains the seeds of its own destruction. A crucial instance is his feeling that he is the subject of malevolent forces, when immediately after his confession to Elizabeth-Jane that he is her father, he opens a letter left for him by his dead wife. Its revelation that her father is in fact the sailor Newson destroys Henchard's happiness at the moment of its birth.

This is one of a series of coincidences and chances that contribute to the novel's air of tragic inevitability, but like Henchard's shocked recognition of his skimmity-ride effigy in the river, it proceeds from character. A skimmity-ride involved the public parading of the effigies of people who had transgressed moral and social codes. Just as his effigy is the public result of his passionate affair with Lucetta Le Sueur, so his impulsive reconciliation with his long-lost daughter arises from his compulsive need for love and restitution. His better nature emerges in his efforts to repair the damage of the past in his treatment of Susan and Elizabeth-Jane, and also Lucetta. But these efforts are thwarted, partly by chance, but mainly by his own responses to people and events.

In Henchard, Hardy presents a Faustian figure, a 'vehement, gloomy being, who had quitted the ways of vulgar men without light to guide him on a better way' (*MC*, 17). He is a fascinating psychological study of a driven, tormented character, trapped by the mores of early Victorian society and by the politics of town life. Obscured by guilt, Henchard's fundamental impulse is towards self-destruction. Perverse and stubborn, Henchard's every action works against his own best interests. He makes an enemy of his manager Jopp by his whimsical hiring of Farfrae; an enemy of Farfrae because of his jealousy; and of Jopp again whom he blames for his ignoring of the weather prophet. In the process he alienates those he most needs, including Elizabeth-Jane.

Michael Henchard is afforded moral stature through his suffering, but also through the contrast Hardy makes between him and Donald

Farfrae, a far more superficial figure. The rivalry between Henchard and Farfrae is intensified by its inclusion of sexual, economic and political components. Henchard is forced to cede to his rival his former lover, his business, and his position as mayor. Indeed, underlying this tale of the usurpation of the old rural values by the restlessly modern and urban, is a primitive narrative drawn from folktale and mythology, of ritual combat resulting in the casting out of the old king by the young hero. The relationship between Henchard and Farfrae echoes that of the Biblical story of Saul in the Book of Samuel. Henchard is alluded to at significant points as Saul, who loved the shepherd boy David, but who tried to kill him, just as Henchard seeks the life of Farfrae.

In a sense *The Mayor of Casterbridge* is a historical novel. Hardy draws on memories of Dorchester when he was a youth, but he also places the story even earlier. It opens near the beginning of the nineteenth century, and most of the action takes place nearly twenty years later. Although the railway reached Dorchester in 1847, it has not yet reached Casterbridge; in the novel the Royal Personage arrives by coach (Prince Albert visited in 1849); and the Repeal of the Corn Laws (1846) is shown to be affecting a community dependent on agriculture. Hardy also evokes a longer historical perspective in the town's Roman origins and the square pattern of its streets, and the Ring where Henchard meets his wife on her reappearance. Hardy's major preoccupation is change. Looking back from the 1880s, he recreates a world that has been radically altered; the Three Mariners Inn has been pulled down, together with part of Mixen Lane, which has led to the extinction of a social underclass involved in petty crime and vice.

The conflict between old and new is presented most vividly in the struggle between Henchard, whose brusque personal methods of dealing in corn and hay represent the old order, and the canny Scot Farfrae. His easy sentimentality about his native Scotland, which he is set on leaving, his replacement of personal business-dealings with a more formal system, his introduction of mechanisation, his disguising the impurities in the wheat, his rational shrewdness in buying and selling small volumes of corn as prices fluctuate, his estimation of Elizabeth-Jane's financial carefulness – all point to his function as an intrusive figure, who stands for the forces of modernity and change.

The community of Casterbridge is central to this novel, and its base in the economic geography of the region is given with realistic detail. Its shops are full of agricultural implements, while its relationship with the enclosing agricultural landscape, and its dependence on the corn and hay harvests, is suggested by the progress of a butterfly along the

High Street from one field to another, and the thistledown floating through the town in the autumn. Hardy's extraordinary capacity for salient detail enables the market place, the town's economic heart, to function symbolically. It is the hub of social activity, observed by Elizabeth-Jane and Lucetta from the upper window of High-Place Hall, but it is also where the hay waggons of the rivals Henchard and Farfrae collide at night.

Casterbridge has a deceptive air of changelessness, but in fact is presented unsentimentally. Hardy emphasises the conservatism that stems from its geographical remoteness. Its values are brutally mani-fested in the traditional skimmity-ride that has disastrous consequences for Lucetta Le Sueur. Realistically, the impulse to publicly shame the town's hypocritical social superiors emanates from Peter's Finger, the public house that functions satirically as the 'church' for Mixen Lane, the sordid area of Casterbridge in which social discontent festers. Collectively the minor figures provide a subversive commentary on their betters. Their discussion outside the King's Arms, where Henchard is presiding over a dinner, and the description of the social sub-divisions of Mixen Lane, connected with its several various public houses, add a vital dimension of social realism.

The Mayor of Casterbridge has a tragic inevitability. With an eye for both realism and the ironic structure of tragedy, Hardy charts the decline of Henchard and the corresponding rise of Farfrae by their exchange of dwellings and possessions, including Lucetta Le Sueur. The inexorability of Henchard's accelerating decline and fall are terrible. All the significant figures of his past, each betrayal, return to haunt him – Susan, Elizabeth-Jane, Lucetta, Newson. Each step of his decline forces him to encounter his past. Each effort at reparation and recon-ciliation fails. He is reduced to his original trade, leaving Casterbridge in the same clothes and with the same implements that he had entered it, revisiting the scene of his first act of betrayal, and finally dying alone on Egdon Heath.

However, as well as its powerful linear drive, the form of this novel also possesses the circularity implied by the symbolism of the Wheel of Fortune. Hardy makes this explicit with the reappearance of the furmity woman, who witnessed the wife-selling episode at Weydon Priors Fair, in the court at Casterbridge, presided over on that day by Henchard, at the moment when his fortunes are in the balance. Again coincidence simply reinforces character. Her revelation of his secret past and hidden sin, with its resulting social shaming, is the symbolic registering of the inescapable claims of the past. It also marks, as Hardy put it, 'the edge or turn in the incline of Henchard's fortunes' (*MC*,

31). But both the concept of moral consequences and the revolution of Fortune's Wheel are rooted in the rash choices of a frustrated, intemperate and drunken young hay-trusser twenty years before.

Hardy retains the reader's sympathy for Henchard in several ways. He ignores the gap of time between his moral crime at Weydon Priors, picking up the thread of the narrative again at the height of his social prestige and power as mayor. This enforces the idea of deeds determining inevitable consequences, but it also avoids recording the processes by which Henchard renounces strong drink, suppresses his conscience, disciplines his character, and turns his energy towards achieving economic and social status in Casterbridge. Hardy's focus is on the experience of loss and suffering, which humanises Henchard and puts him in touch with the more feminine aspects of his personality. This process is marked by Hardy's use of telling detail. In his pride as mayor, Henchard wears old-fashioned but fine clothes, with a jewel-studded shirt and a heavy gold chain. At the greeting of the Royal Personage, he emerges pathetically in battered finery waving a tattered flag. Sympathy is also produced through Henchard's generous pawning of his gold watch to pay a poor creditor, and by Abel Whittle's devotion to him in his misery, like Lear's fool. But the source of greatest sympathy is the point at which the linear impetus of Henchard's narrative is completed and at which at the same time its circular movement comes to rest, with Henchard's lonely death and his bleak testament, revealing his final achievement of tragic understanding.

There is an anti-realist current in *The Mayor of Casterbridge* that proceeds from Hardy's multi-angled vision. Interwoven with social and economic realism are melodrama, the grotesque and the absurd. This is signalled as a creative principle at the opening of the novel, when Henchard sells Susan. The fair is populated by some grotesque characters, and there is the ironic turn of events when, contrary to all expectation, Henchard's extravagant gesture finds a response in Newson, who readily takes Susan and her daughter off Henchard's hands. Melodrama often serves to figure the symbolic, for instance, when Henchard brutally subdues the bull that endangers Lucetta and Elizabeth-Jane, a visual correlative of Henchard's inner struggle with his own dangerous nature, while his secret meetings with Susan in the Ring, where in Roman times people were put to death for entertainment and more recently for their crimes, create an atmosphere of foreboding and the effect of tragic foreshadowing.

The characters of Lucetta Le Sueur and Elizabeth-Jane are presented somewhat ambiguously. Lucetta's relatively exotic background and status contribute to the melodrama of her shaming and death.

Elizabeth-Jane has a more important narrative function, dependent on her being placed naturally at the centre of a web of character relations, which enables her to observe and overhear a good deal. Somewhat priggish, she represents the bourgeois values of equanimity and endeavour. She has the sense of economic self-preservation and social ambition to accept Donald Farfrae when Lucetta dies. Some readers have seen her as a means of maintaining sympathy for Henchard, while others have regarded her as a rather cool and conventional character, suited to represent, with Farfrae her husband, the rational modernity of a new order of nineteenth-century urban life.

Further reading

Johnson (1894) first identified the novel's Aristotelian design, with its relentless pattern of retribution. King (1978) sees the inevitable form of Greek tragedy as unifying the novel. However, Kramer (1975) finds two structures in evidence, the tragedy of Michael Henchard, but also the cycle of change at work within Casterbridge society, while Brooks (1971) discovers an Absurdist element of tragi-comedy in the presentation of Henchard's experience, especially in the reappearance of the furmity woman. From a psychoanalytic approach, Meisel (1972) regards this novel as the one in which Hardy identifed for his object of study the isolated ego, recognising that 'the unconscious is the true psychic reality' (Meisel 1972: 9). The self-destructive element of Henchard's personality interests two psychoanalytic critics. Sumner (1981) sees Hardy's interest as lying in Henchard's self-destructive psychology of aggression, while Giordano (1984) studies him as an example of egotistical suicide. A striking feminist reading is offered by Showalter (1979). She charts Henchard's loss and recovery of the feminine dimension of his nature through his rise in the male world of business and politics and his subsequent fall, which coincides with the reappearance of the repressed women from his past life. Brown (1954) pursues the humanist theme of the conflict between the countryman and the alien invader (Lucetta Le Sueur as well as Donald Farfrae), while Gregor (1974) takes a broader sociological view of Hardy's exploration of the relation between Henchard's personal history and the history of the south-west of England in the 1840s. The issue of the division of Hardy's interest between tragedy and sociology is taken up by Lerner (1975). An essay by King (1992) discusses Hardy's characterisation.

The Woodlanders

The setting, concerns, and mood of *The Woodlanders* **[33]** are consonant with the Wessex of the earlier novels. There is an element of nostalgia in Hardy's treatment of the woodlands of Little Hintock. Although such rural economies were very much alive in Hardy's day, he strikes an elegiac note in his evocation of a world that will inevitably pass away. However, the woodlands do not form the backdrop to an idyllic pastoral of humanity living in tranquil harmony with nature. The trees, which are such a dominant presence in the novel, compete with each other for nourishment and light, are vulnerable to disease and damage, and are frightening in their moaning under the lash of the storm. The woodlands represent the Darwinian struggle for existence **[12, 81, 121, 201]** that Hardy sees as extending not only to the inhabitants of this little world but also beyond: 'Here, as anywhere, the Unfulfilled Intention, which makes life what it is, was as obvious as it could be among the depraved crowds of a city slum' (*W*, 7). Although the woodlands are home to Marty South and Giles Winterborne, they are also the economic foundation of their existence. The plantations are managed by and supply Mr Melbury the timber merchant. The woodland crafts on which this remote hamlet depends are recorded in such detail as to give the narrative the feel of documentary. However, the habitual association of the woodlanders with the trees has formed their values. Marty South and Giles Winterborne are custodians of woodland lore, and the quiet rhythm of the scene in which they plant trees suggests their submission to the seasons. But above all they represent fidelity to the community into which they were born.

The Woodlanders is a novel about how the collective life of the community, as well as individual lives, are disrupted by well-to-do newcomers, the young doctor Edred Fitzpiers and the wealthy Mrs Felice Charmond. Hardy's movement from the provincial town of his previous novel, *The Mayor of Casterbridge*, to Little Hintock, which lies 'outside the gates of the world' (*W*, 1) allows him to explore the effects of the intruder in a contrasting environment. Experimentally, Hardy has placed in intimate connection with each other two groups of people; the woodlanders, with their intensity of feeling, inwardness, sense of tradition, and communal solidarity; and the interlopers, with their materialism, education, manners, and superior social class. Their alien status is partly signified symbolically through their experience of the woodlands. Fitzpiers is oblivious to them as he rides through them fast asleep on his journey home, and his light burning late into the night is a discordant, unnatural feature. Mrs Charmond loses her way entirely in the woods, suggesting her even more hopeless alienation from rural values. The Hintock way of life, with its hardship, its intricate rural economic system, and its communal values, means nothing to them. They represent the wider, restless world of the nineteenth century and its rootless modernity.

Hardy's experimental interest in the impact particularly of Fitzpiers on the woodlanders is suggested by his original idea for the title, 'Fitzpiers at Hintock'. Through his professional role, the young doctor functions very much as a catalyst, bringing into close proximity the workfolk and their social superiors. Fitzpiers's fashionable interest in the intellectual currents of the age, in contemporary science and German metaphysics, are those of a dilettante. His whimsical retreat from normal life to bury himself in the countryside and in transcendental philosophy displays a self-serving egoism and lack of human sympathy that is confirmed by his insensitive approach to old John South's obsession with the tree overlooking his home, and to Grammer Oliver, whose brain he seeks to purchase for the purpose of experiments after her death. Felice Charmond, whose name like that of Fitzpiers has a foreign origin, is also a shallow egoist. A former actress, she plays the beguiling seducer in her little drama with Fitzpiers. Her falsity is rendered with comic symbolism on the occasion of Fitzpiers's visit, when she endeavours to look alluring by wearing the hair-piece made up from Marty South's hair, and tries to appear liberated by pretending to smoke a cigarette.

Hardy characterises the bourgeoisie in *The Woodlanders* by their instinct of possession. Fitzpiers's sexual domination of Grace, Felice Charmond and the local girl Suke Damson, is matched by Mrs Charmond's crude exercise of economic power. Marty South's surrender of her beautiful hair, and consequent loss of her femininity, is the result of economic blackmail, for behind the transaction is the concealed threat of eviction from her cottage. In this single action Hardy suggests the callous use of power of the landlord class, but what really threatens the fabric of the community is Mrs Charmond's seizure, on the death of Marty's father, of Giles Winterborne's houses, held on the ancient lifehold system.

Grace Melbury is situated by Hardy very precisely between the two groups of simple woodlanders and sophisticated urban interlopers. She has been left stranded by the fashionable education her father has purchased for her, and although she has not lost her deep affection for the places of her girlhood, or her love of nature, she has as Hardy remarks, 'fallen from the good old Hintock ways' (*W*, 6). Urban influences have matured her and she has become acutely conscious of social class.

Her father's obsession with social class drives the plot. It causes him to break faith with Giles Winterborne, who was promised to Grace, when Giles loses his houses. Melbury's efforts at control also play their part in Grace's marriage to the doctor, who offers the level of social intercourse and refined manners she has become used to. Hardy's recurrent interest in the problem of marrying across class boundaries involves, in this novel, Grace's learning the superficial values of the class to which she aspires, and her initiation into the compulsions of sexual attraction that transgress not only the boundaries of class but also the marriage contract. In this novel, for the first time, Hardy reveals his developing interest in the issue of adultery and divorce, which points forward to its extended treatment in *Jude the Obscure* **[39, 92]**.

The Woodlanders is also strongly influenced by Hardy's interest in aspects of human psychology, which emerges in various oblique ways; through symbolism, landscape, and narrative point of view. He explores how preoccupations with the driving forces of sex and class deepen into obsessions, intensified in the natives of Little Hintock by the isolation that fosters introspection, and reinforced among the interlopers by their feeling of apartness. Sexual obsession is manifested in Giles, Marty and Fitzpiers, while obsession with the power of class is evident in Mr Melbury and Mrs Charmond. At the centre of this web is Marty South, whose point of view is structurally important. Hardy places her in ironic situations where she can observe the increasingly complex relationships of the major figures in the community, particularly Grace's crossing of the class divide and her choice of sexual partner. Marty's narrative role also contributes to the action, when her overhearing of Grace's parents' conversation about the possibility of their daughter's marriage with Giles impels her to the shocking cropping of her hair and sets in train a sequence of significant events.

The subtlest and most realistic study of the workings of class obsession and sexual choice is Grace Melbury. Resisting her father's conventional reliance on femininity as ensuring entry into the middle class through marriage, and rejecting Giles's timid courtship, she instinctively chooses the man who offers sexual excitement and endorsement of her new social status. This results in the moment of tragi-comic recognition during Fitzpiers's illness, when she visits his bedroom in company with Mrs Charmond and Suke Damson, with the bitter jest, 'Wives all, let's enter together!' (*W*, 35). She is forced to confront the extent of Fitzpiers's sexual conquests, and the relative shallowness of her love for him. After the dashing of her hopes for divorce, Grace's reconciliation with her errant husband on her own terms seems entirely realistic. She has asserted her independence from her chastened father, her ties to Little Hintock have been loosened, and she responds with interest to Fitzpiers's new medical practice in the midlands.

A pivotal event in the plot is also contingent on obsessive behaviour. Old John South's haunting fear that the tree adjacent to his cottage will topple onto it and kill him is treated drastically by Fitzpiers, when instead of prescribing medical relief for his extreme anxiety, he orders the felling of the tree, the shock of which kills the old man. The unforeseen consequence is that economics now drives the plot. Without his property, Giles is no longer eligible as a suitor for Grace, while the pulling down of the houses and the altering of the road results in the accident that brings together Fitzpiers and Felice Charmond.

In *The Woodlanders* Hardy's fidelity to the material world provides the basis for his symbolic treatment of character. Giles Winterborne is established as an intensely realistic figure; psychologically and sexually inhibited by his sense of social inferiority, and spiritually rooted in his pursuit of the woodland crafts. However, as he emerges memorably out of the landscape bearing his cider-making equipment, he is perceived by Grace as an allegorical figure, 'Autumn's very brother' (*W*, 28). Later in the novel Grace recalls him as 'the fruit-god and the wood-god in alternation' (*W*, 38). This is given significance structurally by its being placed immediately following Grace's anxious parting with Fitzpiers, who is on his way to visit Mrs Charmond. His vanishing into the landscape is balanced by Giles's looming out of it, in a symbolic moment that registers the moral qualities of the characters in relation to nature, and also foreshadows Grace's oscillation towards Giles.

The intensely visual quality of *The Woodlanders* owes something to Hardy's immersion in the works of the Impressionists **[14, 58, 199–200]** while he was engaged in writing it. This influence had the effect of reinforcing his natural inclination to register episodes in visual terms. In the opening scene of the novel, for instance, Barber Percomb, looking into the doorway of Marty's cottage, observes her illumined by a lamp, which intensifies her hair, while leaving the rest of her body vague and obscure. This point of view, says Hardy, 'composed itself into an impression-picture of extremest type' (*W*, 2). However, in *The Woodlanders* impressionism, symbolism and realism co-exist with the melodramatic, the tragic, the comic and the elegiac. This defeats critics' attempts to discern a unifying genre, or indeed a unifying tone. However, Hardy clearly had tragedy in mind when he claimed that the remote setting of Little Hintock was appropriate to 'dramas of a grandeur and unity truly Sophoclean' (*W*, 1) **[146–52]**. No character is immune from some element of tragic experience. In addition to the varied sufferings of the lovers, Giles, Grace, Marty and Fitzpiers, there is also Mr Melbury's bewilderment at the unhappy outcome of Grace's marriage, and Suke Damson's distress at losing her doctor lover. But perhaps the closest to tragic treatment is the life of Giles Winterborne, the victim of his obsession with Grace, of the tyranny of social class, and of his timid adherence to social convention that leads to his death.

In the conclusion of the other relationship, which occupies several chapters after Giles's death, melodrama shades into bathetic comedy as Tim Tangs's man trap, set for Fitzpiers in revenge for his relationship with Tangs's fiancée, catches only Grace's dress, and the married couple retreat to a local hotel. Grace's uneasy victory over her husband is undermined by the realism of the public house conversation about the nature of marriage. This ambivalent comedy of marital reconciliation is balanced against Giles's death, elevated in the closing lines of the novel by Marty's simple devotion to 'a good man [who] did good things!' Her dumb eloquence, stoicism and faithful love do indeed strike a final tragic note. She has authority as the prime observer of the action. She is also an economic victim, a Darwinian survivor **[12, 77, 121, 201]**, the repository of Little Hintock's innate moral wisdom, and a truly elegiac figure.

Further reading

Although *The Woodlanders* contains some elements of the pastoral convention, the humanist critic, Howe (1968) points out that it also offers a realistic portrayal of the conditions of rural life, while its final chapters involve compromises that are very close to actuality. Gregor (1974), in a similar vein, sees this novel as the beginning of Hardy's examination of human relatedness – his perception of human activity as a great web, which involves possession, both sexual and economic. The absence of a clearly defined centre in this novel has occasioned persistent debate. From a formal point of view, Millgate (1971) focussing on the final chapters, with their unsettling mixture of genres, finds the novel 'a tragic-comedy of social and sexual mismatching' (Millgate 1971: 278). In somewhat different terms, Kramer (1975), in spite of Hardy's early reference to Sophocles and the potential in Little Hintock for the operation of universal tragedy, regards this novel as revealing Hardy's 'democratization of tragedy' (Kramer 1975: 136), and he locates the cause in society. In Lacanian terms, according to Garson (1991), the dispersal of interest in this text is figured in the narrative by the *corps morcelé*, and by imagery that points to the desire for both economic and demonic possession, 'the analysis of which is one of the novel's central concerns' (Garson 1991: 81). A materialist examination of the text discovers Hardy's presentation of the society of Little Hintock to be contradictory. Although Hardy is critical of the way class impairs judgement, as in Melbury's estimation of Fitzpiers, his portrayal of society as a collection of individuals affords 'no possibility for working class solidarity, knowledge and action' (Wotton 1985: 52). Brown (1954) regards this novel as representing Hardy's most profound feelings for traditional agricultural life. However, Boumelha (1982), approaching the novel as a feminist, sees it as Hardy's most radical to date. Although she notes that he draws on genres that are sometimes incompatible, he makes the issues of sexuality and divorce explicit for the first time, and shows the convention of marriage being undermined by the natural law of desire. Ingham (1989) argues for Hardy's evolution of the new feminine sign of the womanly for Grace, by which she means her frank sexual desire for both Fitzpiers and Giles Winterborne. Also feminist in its inflection is Kiely's essay (Higonnet 1993), which enlists Foucault and cinematic theory in an exploration of solitude and narrative representation. In a later essay, Ingham (1998) examines Hardy's endeavour to decode meaning by a method similar to Darwin's evaluation of data, but which involves applying a moral dimension absent in Darwin. Interpretation in this polyvalent text, Ingham argues, does not depend on the evolutionary paradigm, but employs philosophy, drama, and a concept of tragedy, while the significance of gender overshadows that of social class.

Tess of the d'Urbervilles

Although Hardy revealed in his *Life* that the world of *Tess of the d'Urbervilles* **[34–6]** was close to his own experience, as the son of a local mason, who was also a famous author and intimate of London society, his attitude to this world was ambiguous. Moreover, the publication of this novel was tortuous and painful. It was cut for serialisation and revised for the first edition, to which Hardy added the famous subtitle 'A Pure Woman Faithfully Presented by Thomas Hardy'. These may have been some of the reasons why Hardy, in this text more than in others, succumbed to his restless habit of continual revision, a major effect of which was to emphasise Tess's purity and her position as victim.

Clearly Hardy regards Tess's tragic flaw as her sexual nature. It is this that invites the unwanted attentions of the predatory Alec d'Urberville, that seduces the ascetic Angel Clare, and that attracts the narrator, who frequently calls attention to Tess's peony mouth, her eyes, neck, hair, and her curvaceous figure. This has led some psychoanalytic and feminist critics to suggest that Hardy is implicated in Tess's subjection to the voyeuristic male gaze **[171, 178, 184]**. Both Alec and Angel regard her as an object of desire, and she becomes their victim, violated by Alec and later abandoned by her husband. Alec assumes her compliance in a sexual relationship, equating her with other country conquests, while Angel fits her into his Romantic pre-conceptions of nature. It is Angel's crude application to Tess of the hypocritical Victorian double standard of sexual morality that re-engages Tess in a fresh cycle of suffering on the bleak upland farm at Flintcomb-Ash, leading to her re-encounter with Alec and to his murder.

In the opening scene of the novel, Tess's position as the potential victim of the power of her own sexuality is immediately foreshadowed. In the ancient fertility ritual of the May Day festivity, she is marked out proleptically with the red ribbon in her hair. As Tony Tanner (1968: 222–3) has noted, this initiates a pattern of imagery that runs through the novel, linking the crises of her experience; the blood pouring from the horse's side and splashing Tess, which foreshadows her loss of virginity, the sign-writer's red paint, the red threshing machine, the stains on her skin in the garden, Tess's drawing blood from Alec's mouth with a gauntlet – all these form part of a series of omens culminating in the blood-stained ace of hearts that appears on the ceiling after she stabs Alec to death.

Hardy makes clear that it is Tess's innate predisposition to passive fatalism that contributes to her destiny and implicates her in her own tragedy. She lacks the will to impose herself on life, and so with the exception of her one act of defiance in killing Alec, life chooses for her. Although guilt-stricken by her responsibility for the death of the horse Prince, and in spite of her desire to provide for her family, her quest for local work is desultory; she does nothing about Alec d'Urberville's obvious and unwelcome pursuit of her; she fails to confess her relation with Alec to Angel before their marriage; and when desperate for relief from the grim tyranny of Farmer Groby, while the other girls leave and manage to obtain better employment, Tess vaguely hopes that something will turn up.

Tess is not simply presented as a passive victim, however. Through-out the novel she is shown as experiencing tension between the intractable materiality of the social and economic world in which she has to live, and her extraordinarily vulnerable, sensitive self. Hardy is particularly interested in the nature of her consciousness, and in the intense subjectivity of her experience. Concerned to establish that her sense of guilt is the result of conventional education and not in accordance with the laws of nature, Hardy points out that 'the world is only a psychological phenomenon' (*TDU*, 13). In Tess's case this involves an extraordinary ability to merge her senses with her consciousness to an almost mystical degree of intensity. She tries to explain this phenomenon in conversation with Dairyman Crick, and Hardy graphically portrays it operating in her experience of the garden at Talbothays, when she listens to Angel playing his harp.

An important dimension of *Tess of the d'Urbervilles* is its debt to the oral tradition; to stories about wronged milkmaids, tales of superstition, and stories of love, betrayal and revenge, involving stock figures. This gives *Tess of the d'Urbervilles* an anti-realistic inflection. From the world of ballad and folktale Hardy draws such fateful coincidences as the failure of Angel to encounter Tess at the 'Club-walking' on which he intrudes with his brothers, the letter to Angel that she accidentally slips under the carpet, the loss of her shoes when she tries to visit his family, and the family portraits on the wall of their honeymoon dwelling, as well as several omens. This chimes effectively with a world in which the rural folk have a superstitious and fatalistic attitude to life.

At the same time, the early scenes of the novel serve to embed the narrative firmly in realism. Marlott is presented as a contemporary historical place. While Tess's superstitious mother belongs to the Jacobean rather than the Victorian age, Tess has been educated to the Sixth Standard by a London-trained teacher at the National School. As a result of this upbringing, we are told that she speaks two languages, standard English as well as the local dialect, and is a girl with the potential for social mobility. Hardy does not present her as a sentimentalised pastoral vision of a peasant girl, but as the late-Victorian daughter of a small-dealer and lifeholder, while her lover Alec d'Urberville is the son of a retired manufacturer from the north. Although there is a schematic quality to the presentation of Alec and Angel in the text, Hardy is not recording the simple decline of a rural way of life under the impact of alien intruders intent on cultural rape [152–8]. As *Tess of the d'Urbervilles* reveals, rural society in Dorset was complex. Old customs survive in the May Day festival, the hiring fair, and the Lady Day migrations, but the county was also home to middle-class families and attracted wealthy people seeking rural retirement. The introduction of modern farming methods is registered by Farmer Groby's use of the new mechanical threshing machine, under the supervision of its engineer, and the relation between the dairy industry of Dorset and the market in London is emphasised when Angel and Tess take the milk to the railway station. Here Hardy's characteristic combination of symbolist and realist techniques produces a complex effect. The reader views Tess from the perspective of a locomotive, which produces a distancing effect, making the ordinary rural world appear momentarily strange; but the importance of this scene lies in its use of Tess's voice, as she speculates about the anonymous London customers for their milk, which situates her within a larger economic and cultural world.

Angel Clare does not really take Tess's discourse seriously. He does not listen to her on several important occasions. His is an attempt at cultural appropriation. Hardy registers Tess's unease at Angel's attempt to dignify her, and so own her, by bestowing on her the names of classical goddesses. She asserts her right to selfhood in her pained protest, 'Call me Tess' (TDU, 20). Hardy describes Angel as that 'sample product of the last five-and-twenty years' (TDU, 39), a man who follows John Stuart Mill **[14, 121]** and Matthew Arnold **[28, 89, 106, 121]**. However, his self-contradiction emerges in the unacknowledged conflict between paganism and the residual influence of Christianity. His preference for Greek mythology over Christianity, and his idealistic, agnostic pursuit of 'Pagan pleasure' (TDU, 25) in Var Vale are neutralised by his Arnoldian inability to divorce himself from an emotional reliance on the moral imperatives of traditional Christian doctrine. The strength of this influence was stressed by Hardy in revisions to the first edition of the novel, when he introduced the description of Angel Clare's face as inflexible, and captured his naïve response to Tess by adding the ironic word 'virginal' in the memorable statement, 'What a fresh and virginal daughter of Nature that milkmaid is' (TDU, 18).

Tess of the d'Urbervilles contains a more open attack on contemporary religion than earlier novels. Although a good man, Angel's clerical father, like the Reverend Moule, on whom he is based, is dogmatic. Also trapped by doctrine is the vicar who refuses Christian burial to Tess's baby Sorrow. Angel's neo-Christianity is opposed by the paganism of Dorset. This is evident in the extensive pagan imagery used of Chaseborough – Car Darch with her Greek form, 'beautiful as some Praxitelean creation', and the Ovidian revel of 'satyrs clasping nymphs – a multiplicity of Pans whirling a multiplicity of Syrinxes' (TDU, 10). Paganism is also embodied in various aspects of sun-worship; the sun-oriented fertility ritual of the 'Club-walking' episode at Marlott, and the instinctive sun-worship that takes place at Talbothays, with its 'impassioned, summer-steeped heathens' (TDU, 25), where ironically

Angel becomes Tess's 'Apollo' (*TDU*, 57), and where submission to the power of the sun becomes inextricably entangled with love and sexuality. This pattern of reference reaches a fitting culmination with Tess's occupation of the sacrifical stone at Stonehenge, a centre of sun-worship. Although Tess, with her feelings of generalised anxiety represents what Angel rightly identifies as 'the ache of modernism' (*TDU*, 19), she is also ancient and pagan.

The bourgeois ethic and *laissez-faire* capitalism of the modern world are symbolised by the *nouveau-riche* Alec d'Urberville, the usurper of an ancient name. He is also a figure drawn from the melodrama of the contemporary stage, where his detested class was represented in a recognisable though exaggerated form. Hardy registers this economically in the text by his moustache, his cigar, his gig and spirited horse, his proprietorial address to Tess as 'my beauty' (*TDU*, 5), and his demanding a kiss. The precise nature of Alec's violation of Tess is left deliberately ambiguous. Hardy's revisions to the text strongly imply an element of coercion. Equally he makes it clear that Tess was dazzled by Alec, and for a while remained with him as his mistress. As D.H. Lawrence famously noted, Alec speaks to the female in Tess in a way that Angel is simply unable to. Although a superficial man, Alec's feelings for Tess are genuine, and he makes a genuine attempt at reparation that is rebuffed. But in Hardy's revisions to the novel, a corollary of his 'purification' of Tess is that Alec d'Urberville is progressively demonised.

The movement of the novel is rhythmical. It oscillates between Tess's consciousness and the world she inhabits; between a close observation of Tess and the distanced perspective that sees her variously as a 'fly on a billiard-table' (*TDU*, 16), or the object of attention of the winter birds that alight on the frozen landscape at Flintcomb-Ash. As Ian Gregor (1974: 280–3) has remarked, the text is structured by patterns of 'flux' and 'reflux', 'fall' and 'rally'. These testify to Tess's innate power, even after the murder of Alec, when she initates a further movement towards recovery in bestowing her sister Liza-Lu on Angel. Movement also involves journeying, and Tess's journey towards the place of sacrifice at Stonehenge is through a landscape both realistically evoked and symbolically resonant. Tess's experience is rooted in the intractable, material earth, but the phases of her experience represent stages in her spiritual development. The ordinariness of Marlott gives way to the discordant luxury of the bourgeoisie at Trantridge. The revels at debased Chaseborough give rise to Alec's opportunistic imposition of his sexual will on Tess, and the death of Sorrow. At Talbothays Tess commences a period of rallying stimulated by the fecund landscape and the heat of the sun, her traumatic rejection takes place at her ancestral home, and this is followed by a period of travail on the bleak landscape of Flintcomb-Ash. Her crime is committed in the decadent seaside town of Sandbourne, and her journey concludes with her symbolic resting on the stone of sacrifice at Stonehenge, a conclusion that affords a Sophoclean dimension to the tragedy.

In his Preface to the 1892 edition of *Tess of the d'Urbervilles* Hardy warns the reader that 'a novel is an impression, not an argument'. However, the text offers several explanations of Tess's tragedy; social, psychological, hereditary, and fatalistic, all of which proceed from the assumption that Hardy's text is in some sense determined, and that the character of Tess is somehow knowable. Indeed, the tragedy of Tess is in this sense overdetermined. But it should be remembered that the character of Tess is constructed in the text from many points of observation, including that of the ambivalent narrator; constructed that is from impressions.

Further reading

A persistent area of debate has been the tension between history and fiction in Hardy's presentation of Wessex. Among critics who explore the text in relation to the history of Dorset are Brown (1954), who sees it as a record of the decline of the agricultural community; Merryn Williams (1972) whose analysis reveals Hardy's understanding of a complex rural economy; and Kettle (1953), who from an early Marxist humanist point of view, discovers in this text 'the destruction of the English peasantry' (Kettle 1953: 45). This view is modified by Raymond Williams (1970), who emphasises Tess's education and social mobility. A later Marxist materialist, Goode (1988) finds in Tess an alienated working class woman, representative of a whole historical process. Another area of debate concerns genre. For Lawrence (1936) the novel's tragic grandeur is diminished by Tess's submission to social codes; Brooks (1971) sees Tess as a type of character interacting with fate; Morrell (1965) argues from an existential humanist position that Tess's fate is the consequence of her failure to act; while Kramer's reading (1975) reveals a text concerned with individual consciousness, and that 'within the pages of the novel Tess is tragic only to herself' (Kramer 1975: 117). Different deterministic interpretations are given by humanists influenced by New Critical procedures, including Holloway (1953), Van Ghent (1953), and Tanner (1968). Miller (1982) deconstructs the text to reveal that it is overdetermined by numerous contradictory explanations for Tess's fate. Psychoanalytic critics see Tess's tragic experience as determined in various ways. Waldoff's essay (1979) argues for the crucial importance of Angel Clare, who is subject to a Freudian split between the affectionate and the sexual currents of his feelings. Also focussing on Angel Clare, Sumner (1981) sees the tragic issue in Jungian terms, in his unconscious projection of his anima onto Tess. The Lacanian critic, Garson (1991) argues that Hardy's attempt to create a unified Tess fails because the text produces Hardy's own somatic anxieties, and reveals 'her genesis in dissolution and fragmentation' (Garson 1991: 150). Feminists also attend in different ways to Hardy's relation to Tess. Boumelha (1982) argues that Hardy's androgynous mode of narration founders because of his erotic fascination with her. Ingham (1989) notes how in Tess Hardy develops a new feminine sign for the fallen woman, who possesses spontaneous sexuality. Morgan (1988) argues for Hardy's frank presentation of Tess's mature sexual nature and fierce self-determination; while Jacobus (1976), in a textual study, shows how evidence of Tess's purity was added by Hardy to overcome the censor; and Higonnet (1993b) explores the relation between gender and theory in the problem of separating the voice of the character from that of the narrator. In a later essay, Higonnet (Dolin 1998) explores Hardy's narrative strategies, and discusses his modern understanding of realism, the discontinuity produced by his juxtapositioning of genres, his anti-realistic allusions to fairy-tale, and the double violation of readers' expectations provided by the novel's ending.

Jude the Obscure

In the story of Jude Fawley [39], the stonemason from a poor rural background, an autodidact whose dreams of a university education are thwarted, and whose love for the idealised Sue Bridehead ends in despair, Hardy was drawing to some extent on his own experience. It also gave impetus to his bitter attack on marriage and his interest in the topical issue of divorce. Another contemporary issue is that of higher education for the working class, for Jude stands at the end of a development in adult education which led to the opening of Ruskin College in Oxford in 1899. In his portrayal of Sue, Hardy also draws on the contemporary phenomenon of the New Woman, who had been denied an autonomous existence and was asserting her claim to independence of thought and action.

Hardy was aware that he had written a subversive novel, championing the oppressed working class and the Women's Movement of the day, questioning the sanctity of marriage vows, exploring the grounds of religious faith, and challenging dominant social institutions such as the universities and the Church. The original title of *Jude the Obscure*, *The Simpletons*, gestures not unfairly towards the naïve, almost child-like quality of Jude and Sue, whose unworldly idealism marks them from the beginning as vulnerable. In a defensive Preface to the 1912 edition Hardy describes the novel's subject as 'the shattered ideals of the two chief characters', as their instincts are forced by society into moulds that do not fit them. As Hardy's epigraph for the novel, 'the letter killeth' suggests, this results in tragedy.

The intellectual and spiritual turmoil described by Matthew Arnold in 'The Scholar Gypsy' as this 'strange disease of modern life' **[28, 85, 106, 121]** is registered partly by Hardy's decision to locate the action of *Jude the Obscure* in towns rather than in rural Wessex. In their wanderings his characters encounter among other places, Christminster, Melchester, Aldbrickham, and Shaston. Hardy explicitly characterises Jude's desire to enter the university as 'his form of the modern vice of unrest' (*JO*, 2: 1), and the dilemma of the uprooted, socially mobile individual is most obviously emphasised in 'At Christminster'.

In a letter to Edmund Gosse, Hardy identified as his theme the contrast between the ideal life and the squalid real life Jude is fated to lead (*L*, II, 93). This recurrent tension structures Jude's experience and organises the text. Hardy's attitude to Jude is profoundly ambivalent, veering between sympathy, mockery, and bitterness at Jude's victim-isation. The narrator's reference to Christ in the early stages of the novel suggests the spiritual nature of young Jude, who describes Christminster as 'the heavenly Jerusalem', and later identifies himself with Christminster in scriptural terms: 'I'll be her beloved son, in whom she shall be well pleased' (*JO*, 1: 6). But in the middle of this splendid spiritual reverie Jude is awakened to the reality of the claims of the flesh when Arabella, a 'complete and substantial female animal' (*JO*, 1: 6), strikes him with a pig's pizzle and years of study are abandoned. Later, when Jude returns to Marygreen, after his disillusioning experi-ence in Christminster, and sits by the well, he reflects 'what a poor Christ he made' (*JO*, 2: 7). When his obsession leads to his watching the Remembrance Day procession, there is a moment of foreboding as Sue links him to Christ going up to Jerusalem. Similarly the brutal realism of Arabella's association with pigs foreshadows her later seduction of Jude in a bedroom over her father's pork shop.

Jude's first entry into Christminster, looking for work as a stone-mason, is not heroic. Christminster, contemptuously described by Sue as the place where Jude was 'elbowed off the pavement by the millionaires' sons', a place composed of 'fetishists and ghost-seers' (*JO*,

3: 4), betrays him by its arrogance and exclusivity, represented by the advice of the Master of Biblioll College that he should keep to his trade. However, Jude's fundamental error is his rejection of a moment of realistic insight into the worthwhile nature of his labour as a stone-mason, and the opportunities afforded by town life. In any case, he is an impractical dreamer, who has not even found out how to apply for admission to a college. Instead he scrawls his anger on its walls, and in despair recites the Nicene creed in Latin in one of the town's public houses. Jude self-consciously regards himself as a symbol of the intellectual and social restlessness of the time. His speech to the crowd, raising the question whether he should attempt to cross social barriers, challenges a complacently exclusive society. It is a naïve, self-indulgent gesture, but the disillusion from which it proceeds is realised symbolically as the brutality of the social order is seen in the cruelty of the cabman kicking his horse.

Sue Bridehead occupies part of the pattern of contrasts on which Hardy revealed *Jude the Obscure* was constructed. Arabella represents the lure of the flesh, but offends Jude by her grossness; while Sue stands for sensitivity and intellect, but frustrates him by her sexual reticence. However, Hardy's attitude to Sue, who represents Jude's alternative dream, is profoundly ambiguous. Jude's first glimpse of her, like his first view of Christminster, is deeply ironic. Her work in an ecclesiastical shop conceals the fact that she is an agnostic intellectual, who among other modern writers reads the philosopher John Stuart Mill. Yet the first image turns out to be the true one, for Sue has a profoundly ambivalent attitude to authority, suggested by her fear of her landlady's discovery that her little statues are pagan, and confirmed by her decision to marry Phillotson and be a dutiful Christian wife.

Sue possesses a deeply contradictory personality. A determined indi-vidualist who fears marriage as a degrading form of social prostitution, she is deeply narcissistic and neurotically insecure, which results in a farcical vacillation. Having flirted with Jude, enjoyed the games with authority represented by her Training School, and opted for a conven-tional marriage with a man she does not love, Sue then teases Jude by living with him during the period before her wedding. She also displays her intense jealousy of Arabella's place in Jude's sexual life, and her vindictiveness in revenging herself on Jude, while at the same time tormenting herself. Her physical aversion to her husband results in her elopement with Jude. Phillotson recognises in their almost disembodied unity the kind of intensely spiritual union described by the poet Shelley, and Hardy carries the irony of this understanding further when Sue's narcissism and desire for control demand that Jude apply to her lines from Shelley's poem 'Epipsychidion' about 'A seraph of Heaven, too gentle to be human/Veiling beneath that radiant form of woman' **[111, 121, 192]**. Hardy handles the scene at the inn at Aldbrickham, where Jude had slept with Arabella, ambiguously. Underlying his respect for Jude's sensitivity lies an undercurrent of mockery at his being diverted once more from his studies, this time by a woman who denies him sexual fulfilment.

Hardy's complex treatment of Jude and Sue depends on a shifting point of view, which ranges from admiration and sympathy to mockery and anger. However, underlying this changing perspective is the novel's major ironic pattern; the way Jude and Sue exchange places. In the beginning he is conservative and religious, while she is radical and agnostic. But they are divided by the pressure of society, and when after Jude's dismissal from church restoration they have to leave Aldbrickham, Sue withdraws into her essential self, while Jude gains in independence and dignity as he relinquishes his faith.

The descent into tragedy occurs when Jude's obsession with Christminster **[146–52]** reasserts itself. This comes after the visit of Jude and Sue to the Great Wessex Agricultural Show, a point of equipoise and holiday from care. But the omens of tragedy are present. Arabella spies on the carefree couple, Physician Vilbert sells her a love potion, and Little Father Time symbolically anticipates the withering of the roses. In his original Preface, Hardy called Jude's experience 'the tragedy of unfulfilled aims', which is manifested in the series of human betrayals and self-betrayals. Sue's final capitulation to convention is brought about by the horrific deaths of her children at the hands of Little Father Time, who acts out her deepest feeling. Her dread of divine authority reasserts itself in her penitence for her 'insolence of action' (*JO*, 6: 3) in living with Jude. Ignorant of the destructive power of her neurotic nature, she punishes herself by returning to Phillotson. Hardy's allusions to tragic Greek drama (*Antigone* and *Agamemnon* are quoted by Jude), culminate in a tragic conclusion intensified by the extraordinary suffering of Jude and Sue, and by the overwhelming sense of waste. Jude's tragic death, lamenting in the words of Job, 'Let the day perish wherein I was born', is profoundly ironic and absurdist. Betrayed finally by Arabella, who goes off with Vilbert, the dead Jude lies alone in his room surrounded by the cheers of the celebrating crowd applauding the conferment of degrees on the aristocracy. However, society's implication in the tragedy of Jude is qualified by Hardy's emphasis on psychological determinism in his allusions to the Fawley curse of proneness to insanity and suicide. The neuroses of Jude and Sue reinforce each other in a way that intensifies the novel's tragic experience.

In the 1912 Postscript to the original Preface, Hardy said he thought that the cruelty of marriage to one of the parties rendered it 'essentially and morally no marriage', and that this 'secured a good foundation for a tragedy'. *Jude the Obscure* is an angry novel in which marriage is treated bitterly as a tragic farce **[39, 79]**. Jude is married twice to Arabella, Sue is married twice to Phillotson. Arabella the lawless sensualist and irresponsible mother subverts the stereotype of the fallen woman who traditionally suffers shame and social exclusion, by committing bigamy with Cartlett, marrying Cartlett, and at the end of the novel is pursuing Vilbert with a further marriage in view. The polarised treatment of these marriages is represented by Arabella and Phillotson. Governed by earthy realism, Arabella regards a husband as a convenient provider of sexual and material comfort, while Phillotson becomes, with his cynical friend Gillingham, the spokesman for the supremacy of social convention. Marriage is revealed as a meaningless contract institutionalising sexual inequality.

These patterns of futility, in which action is negated by the way individuals end where they began, draws attention to what Hardy admitted is an almost geometric narrative structure. It is evident in the way Jude and Sue change intellectual positions, but more significantly it offers a pattern of repetition that gives emotional intensity to the novel's tragic design. Each part of *Jude the Obscure* begins optimistically but records a process of disillusion and defeat. Jude's sense of high purpose at the beginning of Part First is thwarted by his marriage to Arabella, and the part ends with his attempted suicide. At the beginning of Part Second, Jude enters Christminster with a sense of renewed mission, but this ends in his despairing self-judgement by the well at Marygreen. The third part sees the flowering of an alternative dream of love with Sue, only to find it dashed by her marriage to Phillotson. Part Fourth promises a new relationship with Sue, but ends with a frustratingly spiritual bond. The fifth part begins with Sue's divorce from Phillotson, but ends in destitution; while the final part opens with the gaiety of the Christminster Remembrance Day crowds and Jude's hope of finding some work, but ends with his death.

This inexorable but intermittent decline towards tragedy underpins the fatalistic structure of a novel which Hardy himself described in the 1912 Postscript as containing 'certain cathartic Aristotelian qualities'. Jude, the sensitive, idealistic tragic hero, in striving to overcome the social obstacles to his vision and his need for love, brings upon

himself his own nemesis, but through suffering he gains a tragic understanding of his identity, and also of the forces that have shaped his
experience.

Further reading

Howe (1968) is one of the succession of critics to draw attention to
this novel's modern climate of intellectual crisis, doubt, and anxiety,
and to its presentation of an intellectual woman. D. H. Lawrence (1936)
points out that Sue Bridehead wishes to subdue the body and contain
it within the mind. Feminist critics on the whole admit Sue's sexual
timidity, but argue for her struggle for independence and selfhood.
Boumelha (1982), who regards this novel as 'unique in its siting of
Jude and Sue at the conjunction of class and sexual oppression'
(Boumelha 1982: 137), suggests that as a New Woman Sue's sexual
reserve 'is a necessary stand against being reduced to the "womanly" '
(Boumelha 1982: 143), and in any case Sue is read through the distortions of Jude's consciousness. For Morgan (1988), on the other hand,
Hardy consciously allies himself with the voice of Sue. Morgan defends
her lack of sexuality as being culturally determined, and reinforced by
Jude's tragic denial of her true sexuality. Jacobus (1975), also focussing
on Sue's consciousness, explores her process of self-discovery and her
modern and complex relation to Jude, but concludes that she is broken
by her 'femaleness' after the loss of her unborn child. Langland's essay
on gender (Higonnet 1993), concentrates on Jude's ambivalent response
to the feminine and to the discourse of masculinity, as he strives to
define his inner self. Sumner (1981) regards Sue as being sexually repressed in a classically Freudian way; Wright (1989) explores her inability
to evade in her New Woman role the status of erotic object; Meisel
(1972) concentrates on Jude, who combines the differing needs of Tess
and Angel Clare and 'whose consciousness of [his ego's] own anchorlessness defines the meaning of *modern*' (Meisel 1972: 139). Goode's
essay (Jacobus 1979) examines the New Woman question from a
Marxist perspective. De Laura (1967) argues in a cultural analysis that
Jude is torn between Victorian ethical idealism and the modern
experience of paralysis of will. Kramer (1975) sees the 'self-validation
of tragic consciousness' (Kramer 1975: 161) as being weakened by the
novel's lack of absolutes and its relativisim of judgement, so that Jude's
tragic confrontation with ultimate issues occurs 'in a context that
permits no answers' (Kramer 1975: 161). The humanist, Gregor (1974)
points to the modern nature of this text in its abandonment of plot to
focus on the consciousnesses of its central figures and on Jude's

'wandering ego' (Gregor 1974: 139); while in a structuralist analysis, Miller (1970) argues that like Hardy's other major characters, driven by the death of God to achieve an integral self, Jude seeks the annihilation of consciousnesss. In a provocative essay, Kincaid (Higonnet 1993) adopts a psychoanalytic approach to investigate the reader's implication in the gratification derived from child-beating, voyeurism and sadomasochism. Taylor (1998) finds individual legal and social codes inadequate as individual targets of Hardy's anger, because his sense of pain was general. Suffering and mercy, which lie outside the letter of the law, suggests Taylor, are 'Hardy's two great principles, and they stand as his great late Victorian alternatives to the Letters that Kill' (Taylor 1998: xxxiii).

(b) LESSER NOVELS

Desperate Remedies

George Meredith's advice, on reading *The Poor Man and the Lady*, that Hardy should concentrate on producing a stronger plot produced his first published novel, *Desperate Remedies* **[19]**. Its heroine, Cytherea Graye, left impecunious by her father's sudden accidental death, is taken up by Miss Aldclyffe, an older wealthy woman and a former beauty, who coerces her into marriage with her steward, Aeneas Manston, a man who fascinates her, but whom she finds sinister. Her instinctual fears prove well founded when it is revealed not only that Manston is Miss Aldclyffe's illegitimate son, but that he murdered his first wife. This offers Cytherea an escape, and marriage to her earlier suitor, Edward Springrove, an architect. On Miss Aldclyffe's death, as Manston's widow, Cytherea inherits her estate and lives in Knapwater House.

Although skilfully constructed, *Desperate Remedies*, written at the end of a decade that saw the rising popularity of sensation fiction in the novels of Wilkie Collins and Mrs Braddon, is overburdened by its plot (Hardy placed it among his 'Novels of Ingenuity'). It draws not only on the genre of the sensation novel, but also on those of Gothic romance and the detective story. There are a murder, a suicide, a fire, a ruin, a powerful waterfall, and an unearthly storm that accompanies Manston's playing of the organ. There are also impersonations, plotting and counterplotting, while one of several striking coincidences is the fact that the picture in a locket shown Cytherea by Miss Aldclyffe is that of her own father. The influence of contemporary stage melodrama is evident in the stereotyped figures of the innocent female victim and her villainous sexual oppressor. Hardy fails to integrate these different fictional modes, and this tentativeness may also be seen in his excessively pedantic use of literary and biblical allusions at inappropriate points in the narrative. The fragmentation of the novel's form is a focus of debate among recent critics **[181, 185, 203]**.

The strength of *Desperate Remedies* lies in its portrayal of Cytherea Graye and her companion Miss Aldclyffe. The docile Cytherea is beautiful, flirtatious, and intensely aware of her sexuality. Her brother Owen, who suffers from a mysterious illness and for whom she feels responsible, persuades Cytherea to marry Manston out of duty, but although she enjoys her attractiveness to Manston, she finds him sexually threatening. And she is jealous of Springrove's fiancée, Adelaide Hamilton. Cytherea's beauty also attracts Miss Aldclyffe, a possessive woman, who seems to regard her young companion almost as a lover. In a remarkably powerful episode, in which long-suppressed sexuality is released, she makes an approach to Cytherea in bed. If not an explicitly lesbian passion, her intense physical expression of love for Cytherea is at least highly ambivalent sexually. As a mother, Miss Aldclyffe is given some psychological depth, and a degree of moral self-judgement is evident in her recognition of the consequences of following Manston's request to undeceive Springrove about Cytherea's love.

Some of Hardy's concerns that were to be developed more fully in later novels may be detected in *Desperate Remedies*: conflict between social obligation and individual happiness, the divisive social class system, and the oppressive marriage contract. Elements of Hardy's later powers are here; his capacity for description (for instance of the Three Tranters Inn and the cider-making), his control of visual perspective, when Cytherea looks through a window at her father plunging from the scaffolding to his death, and his psychological treatment of sexual relations and social constraints.

Further reading

Bayley (1978) is unusual in having a high regard for this neglected novel, finding its strength in its disunity. More typical is Howe (1968), who sees it as powerful, but possessing a raw art. The view of this text as containing warring elements stems from its debts to the sensation novel, which are explored by Rutland (1938) and Pinion (1977). Millgate (1971) suggests that these constituents reveal Hardy's aim to write a sensation novel which has as its centre a psychological interest. Morrell (1965) argues that Hardy employs the form of sensation fiction in order to subvert its providential emphasis. While Hardy's excessive use of allusion is defended by Springer (1983), the process of naming and allusion is seen by Fisher (1992) as an aspect of Hardy's subversion of his traded text, regarding this novel as a 'Trojan Horse' (Fisher 1992: 21), which mocks the genre it imitates. Fisher's materialist approach coincides with Ingham's feminist reading (1989), which views the plot as undermining rather than enforcing patriarchy, and as challenging accepted views of women. Sumner (1981) points to Hardy's tentative exploration of lesbianism in the bedroom scene between Miss Aldclyffe and Cytherea. But Ebbatson (1993), from a Marxist materialist standpoint, regards this encounter as an exploration of the issue of power in sexuality, gender and class. He also examines the relation between the detective element of the novel and Hardy's narrative strategy.

A Pair of Blue Eyes

Hardy classified *A Pair of Blue Eyes* [20–1] among 'Romances and Fantasies'. A favourite of Tennyson, its melancholy treatment of youth, love and death is expressive of late nineteenth-century susceptibilities. Not unnaturally in an early novel, Hardy draws freely on his own life [18–21]. Like Emma Gifford, Elfride Swancourt, the possessor of the blue eyes, is girlish, impulsive, flirtatious and naïve. In the face of her father's snobbish refusal to contemplate Stephen Smith as a suitor because of his lower class status, she agrees to elope, but vacillates and then retreats in cowardice from the venture, absurdly blaming her horse for her indecision about keeping her marriage appointment. She regards her returning by night train from London to Plymouth with Stephen as a wicked escapade. Her nervous temperament anticipates those of Eustacia Vye and Sue Bridehead. Elfride and Stephen Smith are too immature to make a successful marriage; she is vacillatory and he lacks the forcefulness to secure her commitment to him. Smith is somewhat boyish and feminine in character, and an autodidact (anticipating Jude Fawley), who taught himself chess and Latin by correspondence. He disappears from the text for much of its length.

Stephen's rival in love for Elfride, Henry Knight, his somewhat older mentor, a man of intellect and a book reviewer, is drawn from Hardy's close friend Horace Moule [11–13, 23]. Hardy succeeds in presenting a fine psychological study of an arrogant idealist, whose emotional coolness and moral rigidity looks forward to Angel Clare. His neurosis takes the form of having to be the first man to have been the focus of his woman's affections, and while he is unable to forgive Elfride her previous trivial defiance of convention, he is shaken by the eruption of his repressed sexual life. A man strangely and tragically out of touch with the world, even failing to purchase earrings successfully, he is also the focus of a remarkable scene as he hangs perilously from a cliff, reviewing past geological ages recorded in the cliff face, before being rescued by Elfride, who makes a rope from her underclothes.

Elfride's inconstancy is evident only nine months after Smith's departure for Bombay, when she finds herself attracted to the handsome Lord Luxellian whom she encounters in Hyde Park. Then her attention is drawn to Henry Knight. Her greatest weakness, however, is her passivity and cowardice in concealing from Henry Knight her relationship with her first suitor Felix Jethway, who died. She is out of her depth with the older, sophisticated man and cannot measure up in the end to Knight's expectations. This leads to the collapse of their relationship, her marriage to the ultra-worldly and uncomplicated Lord Luxellian, who desires her in a direct way, and to her death in childbirth (in later editions). From a potential tragic heroine, she declines into a figure of pathos, and there is a mordant irony in the railway porter's description of the carriage containing her body on its last journey to Endelstow, as 'Light as vanity; full o'nothing' (*PBE*, 39).

One of the novel's main concerns is social class. Hardy's indignation at the denigration of the stonemason's trade by Elfride's father has its source in bitter personal experience with Emma's father. The barrier of social class is the obstacle to Smith's happiness, a factor too in the ebbing of Elfride's passion for him, and also in her eventual marriage into the aristocracy. The scenes in Hyde Park are a broader satirical treatment of social pretension. But Hardy's anger is most engaged against Parson Swancourt, a hypocrite as well as a snob, who rejects Smith's suit but will marry Charlotte Troyton for her money.

The immaturity of *A Pair of Blue Eyes* may be seen in Hardy's use of material from his unpublished novel, *The Poor Man and the Lady*, and his debts to characters from *Desperate Remedies*. As in the latter novel, his style is inflated by allusions to literature and art. He also uses the occasion of the publication of Elfride's romance to intercalate his comments on fiction and parody reviews of his earlier novels. Structurally, Hardy attempts to unify the narrative by tight parallelism. Elfride's confessions of former sweethearts to Smith and Knight echo each other, as do the scenes at the grave vault for the deaths of Lady Luxellian and later Elfride herself. Hardy also uses the sexual symbolism of the game of chess to reveal the shifting balance of power between the rivals for Elfride's hand. Elfride condescends to the self-taught Smith, while Knight who has the upper hand in his game, patronisingly lets her escape defeat.

This over-tight control of the narrative is balanced by slackness else-where. The serious action is compressed into the later stages of the novel, while Elfride is allowed to fade as a potentially tragic figure because in the final chapters she ceases to be the main focus of the narrative. Information about her experiences from the time of her rejection by Knight up to her death is given by her maid, Unity. The conclusion is abrupt, and there is also a serious failure of tone at the end when after the comic encounter between Smith and Knight, which clears up doubts about Elfride's sexual purity, the two rivals renew their pursuit of her on the very train that is bearing her corpse to Endelstow. This irony does not get beyond the grimly farcical.

Further reading

A starting-point is Taylor (1982), who offers an extensive and sensitive reading. Millgate (1971) is also an alert interpreter, who sees Henry Knight as a Hamlet figure. However, both of these critics regard this novel as irretrievably minor, a view challenged by Lucas (1977), who offers a sympathetic account of Elfride's endeavour to achieve selfhood. Morgan (1988) develops a feminist case, endorsing Elfride's attempts to evade her lovers' prescribed roles for her, and interpreting the narra-tor's censorious commentary on her behaviour as Hardy's strategy 'to placate the Grundyists' (Morgan 1988: 12). Ingham's study of narrative syntax (1989) finds in this text a number of discourses that register Hardy's anxiety about female stereotyping. Rimmer's essay (Rimmer 1993) argues that these anxieties are foisted onto an 'obviously fallible' narrator (Rimmer 1993: 214). Ingham and Rimmer also explore the subtle interrelation of class and gender, while Goode (1988) finds Hardy strategically playing a 'scientific game' with the conventional expec-tations of his readers and his 'real thoughts', like the game of chess in the novel, 'by which with practice you can learn to give pieces away in order to secure victory' (Goode 1988: 10–11). Sumner's interest (1981) is in the psychological problems of Henry Knight as representative of modern man; while the concern of Jacobus (1982) is with Knight's experience on the cliff, and she develops a sophisticated discussion of Hardy's view of the imagination as a destructive force.

The Hand of Ethelberta

Hardy described *The Hand of Ethelberta* **[25]**, which followed *Far from the Madding Crowd*, and was later classified among 'Novels of Ingenuity', as a 'plunge in a new and untried direction' (*LW*, 105).

Ethelberta Petherwin, a beautiful young widow and the daughter of a large family in Wessex, supports them through her career as a professional story-teller in London. Eventually she marries an old *roué*, Lord Mountclere, in order to secure her family's welfare, though her father and brothers in particular are upset at her desertion of her social origins. Ethelberta's social mobility, and her having a father in service, allow Hardy, as he said in the 1895 Preface, to offer a view of the upper class 'from the point of view of the servants' hall'.

Hardy draws on his experience of London in the 1860s in portraying Ethelberta's career, which parallels his own in Ethelberta's family origins, and in her desire to write an epic poem (Hardy's idea for *The Dynasts* came to him while he was writing this novel). Hardy's anxiety about social class is projected onto Ethelberta as a means of detached exploration of his own situation among the mobile middle class. Ethelberta is corrupted by the sophisticated ways of the urban world, while her brothers Sol and Dan are content with their work as craftsmen in Sandbourne. The point of reference for Hardy's satire remains Wessex, the benchmark for human relationships.

Ethelberta's social mobility as a widow, a woman of beauty and intelligence, and a professional story teller, enables Hardy to use her as a means of bringing the upper and lower classes into satirical conjunction. The cynicism of the aristocracy is revealed in Lord Mountclere's admission to Ethelberta that his rank permits him to overlook her humble origins with impunity, while the absurdity of the class system is pointed up by the farcical pursuit of Ethelberta by her carpenter brother Sol and Mountclere's brother, the Honourable Edgar Mountclere, united in class antagonism and fear of the appalling marriage in prospect. The oppressiveness of the social structure is presented graphically by the way that Mrs Doncastle's servants emerge from below ground at the bidding of their masters like a sub-human species. Its hypocrisy is symbolised by the dignified opulence of Lord Mountclere's house, Enckworth Court, achieved by cosmetic use of paint and plaster to suggest marble, and by facing the brickwork with stone. The aristocracy's veneer of superiority is destroyed by the revelation that Alfred Neigh's social position is supported by horse-knackering, satirically captured in the horrific, surrealistic picture of the dying horses at Harefield. The world of the aristocracy is encapsulated at the beginning of the novel in a proleptic Darwinian image of a hawk pursuing a duck, which Ethelberta watches with intense sympathy for the intended victim. But although she is born into the class on which upper class men like Lord Mountclere habitually prey, she outmanoeuvres her pursuer, conquering him in the end.

Extremely self-conscious in its craft, in many ways *The Hand of Ethelberta* is an exploration of fiction as illusion, which involves parody of the conventions it employs; romance, melodrama and farce, and a rejection of realism for absurdist and surrealistic effects. The 'hand' of Ethelberta is an obvious, ironic allusion to courtship, and the sub-title, 'A Comedy in Chapters', suggests the novel's affinity with the conventions of Restoration and eighteenth-century comedy of manners. There is the quick-witted heroine who is pursued by various suitors with quasi-allegorical names, such as Ladywell and Neigh, her triumphant battle of wills with an elderly suitor, Lord Mountclere, and a number of situations drawn from farce. This self-reflexive novel alludes explicitly with satiric force to its own subversion of literary genres, when a society lady, Mrs Doncastle, remarks on the strangeness of the times, when the traditional comic parent attempting to prevent his daughter's marriage is a servant, and the suitor is a member of the peerage.

Ethelberta's motives for such a perverse choice as Lord Mountclere remain ambiguous. Initially, her desire to provide an income for herself and her family simply involved the construction of a *persona*, Mrs Petherwin, an English lady of refinement, who tells romances of which she is the heroine. However, Ethelberta's whole life becomes the performance of a fiction. She can speak warmly of her family, yet refers to her brothers condescendingly as mere workmen. Driven by her powerful will and social ambition, she becomes a divided personality, alienated from her family by her acceptance of the absurdity of the class system that requires them to live parallel lives. By the end of the novel, Ethelberta has repressed her emotional life and her sexuality, rejected alternative suitors, and has subdued her husband. Her life now revolves around overseeing the efficient operation of his estate and the writing of an epic poem. There is a sense in which she has become the victim of her own mutually reinforcing obsessions with social class and fiction-making, and has surrendered the simpler values of her humble family from Wessex for an uneasy place in a new world. Potentially *The Hand of Ethelberta* is a psychological tragedy, but Hardy avoids this by leaving Ethelberta's feelings unrecorded, so that she remains an enigma. Not surprisingly, this novel has given rise to recent critical debate among both materialist and feminist critics **[181, 185, 189]**.

Further reading

Two critics who offer extensive commentaries on this neglected novel are Millgate (1971) and Richard Taylor (1982). Millgate pinpoints a major theme as the relation between appearance and reality, which involves comedy and which also conceals the true character of Ethelberta. Taylor, on the other hand, finds the social triumph of Ethelberta a moral tragedy. Materialist critics have found this novel rewarding. Widdowson (1989) sees Hardy's foregrounding of the artifice of realist fiction as a way of exposing for scrutiny the issues of class and gender; while Fisher (1992) views Ethelberta's rewriting of her class, and her use of her sexuality to gain control of the male social structure as overthrowing 'at least fictionally, a crucial erotic paradigm' (Fisher 1992: 75). Ingham (1989) offers a feminist approach. She regards this novel as reversing the male hegemony implied in the title; while Sarah Davies (1993) argues that the feminine character offered by the realist novel is revealed to be a mythical male construct. Dolin (1997) regards this novel as employing elaborate literary pastiche that masks Hardy's treatment of his negotiation of the literary marketplace. As a subversive countertext, the novel satirises the style and conventions of the *Cornhill*, in which it was first serialised, and challenges its editor's standards of sincerity, morality and realism in fiction. Far from being a unified subject, Ethelberta is simply the creation of her audiences, and is a vehicle for exposing lies: 'The codes and conventions, social, moral, or cultural, which are mobilized to explicate individual experience in various instances of language' (Dolin, 1997: xxxviii).

The Trumpet-Major

The Trumpet-Major **[27–8]** is a historical novel set in the era of Napoleon, the bogey man who exercised a lifelong fascination over Hardy. It is based on Hardy's extensive research in the British Museum, but his personal involvement is also evident in the use of his grandmother's anecdotes about local preparations against the threat of invasion, and in the introduction of his ancestor, Captain Hardy (later Vice-Admiral), who was present at Trafalgar **[7, 28, 115, 136]**. As Hardy's research suggests, he was determined to achieve historical accuracy as well as the period flavour suggested by the reference in its opening sentence to those 'days of high-waisted and muslin-gowned women' (*TM*, 1). *The Trumpet-Major* is the fictionalised history of ordinary folk, encompassed by the larger movement of history which suddenly intrudes into their lives. The little world of Overcombe in Wessex is presented as an idyllic pastoral spot, sheltered by downland, its timeless quality represented by the mill at its heart, where have lived generations of 'corn-grinders whose history is lost in the mists of antiquity' (*TM*, 2). Hardy tactfully establishes the community's values; work, stability, mutuality, respect for tradition, and tranquility. However, as Anne Garland looks at this timeless landscape, it is invaded by soldiers scattering the sheep and pitching their camp, representing the disruptive force of national history.

In the foreground of Hardy's subtle interplay between the machinations of war and personal histories is a domestic tale that itself has a timeless quality. It is an ironic comedy of courtship that hinges on the social and sexual weakness of Anne Garland, the daughter of a landscape painter living with her widowed mother next to the mill, who has the problem of choosing a husband from between the miller's two sons, the harum-scarum merchant seaman Bob Loveday, her first childhood sweetheart, and his stolid, worthy brother John, the trumpet-major, who lacks sexual assertiveness. At the centre of Anne's vacillation between the two brothers is social class and sexual attraction. Hardy makes much of Anne's insistence on her genteel sense of superiority to miller Loveday and his sons. But she rejects the squire's son, Festus Derriman, through sexual aversion and fear, while Bob's cause is aided by his promotion to lieutenant, probably the result of Anne's brief conversation with King George. Her scruples are finally overcome by the reappearance of her fickle scapegrace, safe from war, in his dashing uniform. By a mordant irony, the couple's elevated social status is confirmed when Anne inherits Oxwell Hall from Squire Derriman, which bestows on them the position in society that Anne had craved.

In *The Trumpet-Major* there are several sources of disturbance to the even-paced tenor of life in Overcombe. Most grandly, the King comes to review the troops on the downs. Matilda Johnson, the actress whom Bob Loveday brings home from Portsmouth, represents the intrusion of the debased culture of the town. The war symbolically penetrates the ancient walls of the mill itself, when Bob Loveday is pursued there by the naval press-gang. And when he goes back to sea to fight at Trafalgar, and his brother John is called to service in Spain, the Garlands and the Lovedays are truly caught up in the war. The scene most symbolic of this turning upside down of ordinary lives caught up in historical process is that in which Anne encounters King George.

The figure of the ogre, Napoleon, casts a long shadow over the narrative. However, at one level the threat of invasion is presented positively. Hardy uses the stereotype of the gallant soldiers in their scarlet uniforms as a symbol of national pride. There is the pleasure of viewing their ranks formed on the green downland. For the women there is the sexual interest, and for the community a feeling of excitement in being involved in events of significance in the world. Nevertheless, Hardy's concern with historical context cannot evade the irony of the soldiers' temporary welcome. At the homely miller's party, Sergeant Stanner's mockery of 'Boney' is placed in perspective by narrative information about his ignominious death under a horse's hoofs at Albuera, and Hardy recounts in a dispassionate tone their ironic ignorance of the hazard of chance that will produce for some glory and for others death. This bleak moral view encompasses the Lovedays and the Garlands. While the foolish, shallow and inconstant are rewarded, the worthy John Loveday is destined to die in the service of his country. The larger narrative viewpoint, which includes the bitterly laconic allusion to his death in the novel's final paragraph, intensifies the poignancy of his parting from his father, his face and uniform framed by the candlelight, and deepens the callousness of Bob's brusque farewell with the news that he will stoop to claim Anne Garland after all.

This historical perspective also undermines Hardy's hopes for the continuity of an older England. The mill, symbolising traditional communal values, is at the centre of the novel. It is given a significant presence at the beginning, and later when the soldiers are entertained there, and also at the end, where it is the scene of Loveday's parting from one son and his presiding at the marriage of the other. One son dies and the son who remains is feckless, has no leaning to the trade, is marrying a snob, and has come into property. The mill thus serves to locate Hardy's despair for the future of an ancient culture.

Hardy's ultimate context, of course, as its personification in the text suggests, is not history but time. While the mill represents family and communal history, this sense of human significance is quietly undermined by the water of the mill-stream, which 'with its flowing leaves and spots of froth, was stealing away, like Time, under the dark arch' (*TM*, 1). Hardy's comment on the permanence of the downs places all human history in an ironic perspective that redoubles the irony of Napoleon's frustrated threat to England and derisory end on Elba. Indeed all human folly is examined and placed in a compassionate frame. Squire Derriman, so fearful of both Napoleon and his own blustering nephew Festus, a parody of Napoleon, dies. Festus, who has coveted his uncle's property, does not inherit. Failing to win Anne Garland, he succeeds instead with the theatrical Matilda Johnson. The traditional comic closure afforded by the wedding of Anne Garland and Bob Loveday also receives an ironic treatment. Having discovered their weaknesses, each settles for second best. And John Loveday is dead.

However, Hardy's idea of the permanence of human nature is endorsed by the stagey sub-plot, involving Festus and his uncle Benjy, who form part of a collection of stereotypes. To the traditional comic miser and his cowardly braggart nephew, a clown figure, are added the genteel widow and her eligible daughter, the two brothers, sailor and soldier, who are rivals for her hand, and their father the robust miller. Human nature, with all its weaknesses and follies, Hardy suggests, will endure long after individual histories, and even the histories of nations, are forgotten. *The Trumpet-Major* is a sombre, ironic and complex novel, which has recently received greater critical attention **[181]**.

Further reading

Recent interpreters have found this novel more interesting and significant than earlier critics. A central concern has been the problem of its relation to history, since most of its characters are ordinary, humble people who stand outside the historical record. Thomson (1962), noting the movement of the narrative back into the past in several sections of the novel, argues that this enforces a sense of life that is 'quickly lost in the vast reaches of unrecorded history' (Thomson 1962: 54). Indeed the materialist critic, Goode (1988) suggests that history itself may have been regarded by Hardy as an absurd concept, and that his fascination with Napoleon the *arriviste* may have had to do with Hardy's own conquering 'by writing the culture which did not know him' (Goode 1988: 65). Another materialist, Wotton (1985) takes the view that Hardy deliberately ignored the recorded history of powerful property owners to reveal 'the *real* but unwritten history of the Lovedays and the class they represent' (Wotton 1985: 47). In a similar vein, Ebbatson (1993) comments on the instability of the past, which itself is a complex social and economic process. Interestingly, Ebbatson also pays attention to the neglected heroine, Anne Garland, invoking Lacanian theory to reveal her transformation from observer to the status of fetishistic object. He also suggests that the violence of the war and of the emperor is mirrored in the male aggression of Festus Derriman and the Loveday brothers. Taylor (1982) finds in the prim and passive Anne Garland a source of moral irony, in that her perversity receives its appropriate reward in marriage to the callous Bob Loveday. Shires (1997) argues that Hardy employs the genres of history, romance and comedy to offer an essentially modern perception of the illogicality of experience. History is exposed as a juxtaposition of various time-scales, the story is 'largely anti-romantic' (Shires 1997: xxix), and the traditional patterns of comedy are overturned.

A Laodicean

This novel **[28–9]**, which deals with the love between a young architect, George Somerset, and Paula Power, the wealthy daughter of a railway engineer, is a variation on the subject of the poor man and the lady. Hardy implied that this intellectually ambitious novel contained a lot of his own ideas. The sub-title, 'A Story of To-day', announces Hardy's interest in the later-Victorian transition from the lingering influence of the medieval world to the modern. Its conflicts of ideology centre on the mind of Paula Power, who has inherited a medieval castle, and who is the Laodicean of the title. However, she regards her lukewarmness in religion and social thinking as a provisional necessity.

Critics are divided about the degree of success achieved by *A Laodicean*, classified by Hardy among his 'Novels of Ingenuity'. It begins with great assurance as ironic social comedy, but Hardy's illness and limited imaginative energy during the writing **[29]** may account for his reliance on travelogue, when Paula takes an extended holiday in Europe, which draws on his own recent tour. It may also help to explain the movement into crude melodrama. This area of the novel produces concealed identities, blackmail and arson, which do not develop its main concerns, nor sit comfortably with its dominant genre. This tension may be deliberate, for Hardy also combines the medieval form of the morality play with modern social realism. William Dare, Captain De Stancy's illegitimate son, is a diabolic figure; while George Somerset undergoes knightly ordeals in order to rescue Paula from De Stancy. Hardy's ironic playing with this theme is apparent when Somerset, rather than the maiden, is trapped in the turret of Stancy Castle and has to be rescued. Hardy also makes some ironic inter-textual use of Shakespeare's *Love's Labours Lost*, in which De Stancy plays the King of Navarre, who also has renounced the company of women, to Paula's Princess of France.

Paula is a somewhat alienated woman. Divorced from the sustaining life of the community by her status as an orphan, her wealth and her castle, she has to create her own values. Her Laodiceanism, her luke-warmness, is essentially a modern condition, part of the restlessness that leads her to renovate the castle and to travel abroad. Like Hardy, a humanist sceptic, uneasy with orthodoxy and dogma, Paula eventually commits herself to Somerset and to the modern. Her vacillation expresses all areas of her personality, as it does in Sue Bridehead in *Jude the Obscure*. Like Sue, she is a New Woman, feeling her way towards a self-conscious identity and political awareness. Her divided personality includes pagan inclinations, sexual reticence, the enjoyment of power over Somerset, and an ambiguous relationship with Charlotte De Stancy. Her attitude to medievalism is equally complex. Like Hardy, Paula regards it as outmoded, but is susceptible to some aspects of its romantic appeal. And her attitude to it remains equivocal at the end. When her castle is burnt down, she elects to build a new house next to the ruin, 'and show the modern spirit for evermore' but she also says to George Somerset, 'I wish my castle wasn't burnt; and I wish you were a De Stancy!' (LA, 6: 5).

The influence of Matthew Arnold **[28, 85, 89, 121]** is strongly evident in Hardy's presentation of Paula's character. She rejects the Hebraism of the Baptist faith of her late puritan father and views the modern world in the light of Hellenism. Quoting from Arnold's essay on 'Pagan and Medieval Religious Sentiment', in which he advances the beauty and value of pagan life, she enquires whether George Somerset wishes to be a perfect 'representative of "the modern spirit" ', standing for 'what a finished writer calls "the imaginative reason" ' (AL, 6: 5). This underlines Paula's plan to restore her Gothic castle by introducing into it, with disastrous eclecticism, a Greek court. The castle itself is an ambiguous symbol for Hardy, who was attracted by its romance. Paula's living there is, as he says in his 1896 Preface, characteristic of the period that witnessed the 'changing of the old order in country manors and mansions', and the ancient and modern are juxtaposed when George discovers that the newfangled telegraph that Paula uses enters the castle through an arrow slit.

Essentially the medieval world of the De Stancys is dead, and the end of the novel registers the virtual extinction of their family, together with the ruin of their ancestral home. Captain De Stancy, who symbolises the predatory instinct of the aristocracy, is a complex character, an honourable man riven by warring elements, and suffering the penitence of the liaison that produced his malevolent son. Losing Paula, he remains isolated and disgraced. Old Sir William has withdrawn from society into a self-contained, self-serving individualism. Charlotte, ambiguously in love with both Paula and Somerset, after preventing her brother's wedding, withdraws into the religious life. While the satanic William Dare may have died in the fire he started at the castle.

Whereas Paula's lukewarmness represents her inability to commit herself to fixed ideologies, and allows her to evade prescribed social roles, George Somerset's lukewarmness is expressed by the quiet preservation of flexibility of mind. He rescues Paula from her immersion in medievalism, but he also enjoys the company of the aristocratic Charlotte De Stancy, and he is willing to accommodate the past, by altering his plans when he discovers the ancient foundation of Stancy Castle. George's profession permits Hardy to explore social attitudes, for as Taylor (1982) points out, like John Ruskin he believed that architectural styles express a society's culture and values. The beauty of Gothic architecture has been supplanted by a utilitarianism, seen in the functional design of the new Baptist chapel. Hardy's pragmatic and sceptical attitude to modernity, like his attitude to conservation, is reflected in George Somerset. His own house, Max Gate was functional, designed for maximum convenience. Somerset learns from a process of disillusionment that the ideal has never been achieved. He retains a commonsense attitude that allows him to study with real enthusiasm the English Gothic, while building a modern house next to the ruins of a medieval castle. Paula Power and George Somerset remain undogmatic and flexible, in a world of increased social and geographical mobility, new ideas and beliefs. Symbolically, the castle is destroyed very publicly. Equally symbolically, their wedding takes place off-stage in Europe.

Further reading

Millgate (1971) offers an interesting account of Hardy's Laodiceanism, while Taylor (1982), acknowledging the inadequacy of the novel's melodramatic episodes, pays sustained and detailed attention to Hardy's analysis of the modern temperament in Paula Power and George Somerset. He also examines the intellectual problems occasioned by living in the transitional culture of late-Victorian England. Bayley (1978) also finds merit in this novel, suggesting that its negative form allows Paula and Somerset to 'remain suitably unrealized and negative figures' (Bayley 1978: 155). The interest of Sumner (1981) lies in Hardy's exploration of Paula Power's efforts to cope with her strongly implied bisexuality. From a very different point of view, Cunningham (1975) examines the Baptist elements in the novel; while Wing (1976), focussing on the relation between genre and Hardy's social interests, sees the melodramatic villains as outcasts from middle-class English society.

Two on a Tower

In his *Life*, Hardy recorded his 'infinite trying to reconcile a scientific view of life with the emotional and spiritual, so that they may not be interdestructive' (*LW*, 153). In *Two on a Tower* **[29–30]**, which he placed among his 'Romances and Fantasies', this attempt at reconciliation is focused on astronomy. The young astronomer, Swithin St Cleeve, represents scientific rationalism, while an older woman, Lady Viviette Constantine, with whom he forms a relationship, stands for sexual passion and loving-kindness. The science was important, since Hardy's aim, as he made clear in a letter to Edmund Gosse, was 'to make science, not the mere padding of a romance, but the actual vehicle of romance' (L, I, 110). The tower of the title, which is situated in a remote spot on Viviette's estate, is for Swithin a retreat from a society in which, as the son of a curate and a farmer's daughter, he is ambiguously placed. It is where he and Viviette meet, where their relationship develops, and where she dies. The tower also has a centrally symbolic importance. As Hardy said in the 1895 Preface, he intended to 'set the emotional history of two infinitesimal lives against the stupendous background of the stellar universe' in order to show the true importance of human scale. St Cleeve's introduction of Viviette to the immensity of the universe makes her feel that 'it is not worthwhile to live' and that 'nothing is made for man' (TT, 1: 4). The tower thus offers a perspective of an annihilating nullity.

In a novel structured around contrasts, the main opposition is between Swithin St Cleeve and Lady Viviette Constantine, who are presented as binary figures in a series of ways: aristocratic and lower class, youthful and mature, single and married, fair and dark, religious and agnostic. But the central opposition is between the scientific rationalism of Swithin and Viviette's generous humanity. Hardy shows how Swithin's research becomes increasingly obsessive, to the point where he considers suicide when he finds that a discovery he has made has been anticipated. Gazing into the heavens, he becomes increasingly cut off from the human. The Comtean influence [14, 23, 68, 121] in Hardy's rejection of the tyranny of scientific reason, may be seen even more strongly in his portrayal of Viviette, whose love countervails the terror of an empty universe and redeems the emotionally immature Swithin through passion.

Viviette Constantine is successfully realised as a complex character. Her motivation is realistically conceived. She is twenty-nine, temperamentally 'either lover or dévote' (TT, 2: 7), and has been abandoned by her boorish husband, Sir Blount, who is hunting game in Africa, to social isolation at Welland House. Her encouragement of the handsome young astronomer leads naturally to love, and to the anxieties of their clandestine marriage after her husband's death. Impulsive and generous, she is also deeply conventional, absurdly wishing to conceal their marriage until Swithin has achieved social status through his scientific work, which gives rise to uncontrolled ironies and tragic-comic misunderstandings. Hardy points the irony of Lady Constantine's encouragement of Anthony Green to marry the pregnant Gloriana to satisfy convention. With Swithin banished because of the illegality of their marriage (due to an error over the date of her husband's death) when Lady Constantine finds herself pregnant she marries the Bishop of Melchester to conceal her plight.

While at the Cape studying the southern skies and the Transit of Venus, his true, scientific goddess, Swithin learns of Viviette's marriage, the birth of a child and the early death of the bishop. Viviette is now free to enter into a legal marriage with Swithin, but he delays his return from Africa, and when he does come back after three years' immersion in astronomy, his response when they meet on the tower in the company of her little son is emotionally sterile. Tragedy, bitter irony and melodrama interact in the conclusion, when as Viviette's despair turns to joy on hearing that he will fulfil his promise of marriage, she dies from an excess of emotion. The narrative does not anticipate so melodramatic an ending, but the conclusion is realistically ambivalent, as the genre of romance is turned on its head. The appearance at the moment of Viviette's death of a village girl, Tabitha Lark, close to Swithin's age and now a London musician, has been prefigured by Swithin's earlier attention to her in the church, and by more recent conversations between them. However, it is left unclear whether her power of sexual attraction will succeed in drawing him away from science, while it is equally uncertain whether the child, symbolically the offspring of both reason and emotion, offers hope for the future.

Hardy's deliberate incorporation of the Transit of Venus (December 1882) into the novel signals his intention to emphasise its modernity. In addition to the issues of science and female sexuality, it addresses contemporary cultural preoccupations with social class, marriage and religion, within the realistic social landscape bounded by Welland House, the village, Swithin's cottage, and the tower. In the 1895 Preface, Hardy defended the morality of the novel, but he amended the text to make it clear that Viviette's child is conceived on her final night with Swithin, after the illegality of their marriage is known to them. And the absurdity of the concept of a marriage contract is satirised further by Viviete's desperate conventional marriage with a man she does not love to save the reputation of the child of the man she does love.

The novel's schematic design, its remorselessly ironic drive, and its counterpoint of intellectual ideas makes it seem a rather abstract and detached production; while Hardy's attack on the marriage contract, and his satire on the arrogance of the Church is unsuccessful. The Bishop is too obvious and easy a subject for Hardy's irony, and there is a complete failure of tone in the novel's final sentences: 'Viviette was dead. The Bishop was avenged.' Two redeeming elements of realism stand out, however; the character of Viviette, and Hardy's treatment of the villagers, when they meet at Swithin's cottage for choir practice, and when they gather at the foot of the tower in response to his invitation to look at the comet, speculating about the relationship between Viviette and Swithin, who will be ruled by the 'plannards' (*TT*, 1: 13). However, Hardy's general uncertainty of treatment leaves this novel uncomfortably stranded between tragedy, comedy, fable, melodrama, romance and social satire, each element of which predominates at some stage of the narrative, but which resists integration into a unified form.

Further reading

In a suggestive chapter, Millgate (1971) follows Hardy in directing attention to the novel's status as a romance, but finds its examination of the issues it raises somewhat limited. Miller (1970), as part of his structuralist study, discusses the novel's philosophical and scientific contexts, arguing that the lack of inner depth of Hardy's characters leads to their roles as spectators of life. In this text, the human mind gazing at the stars symbolises the essentially modern experience of 'nullity reflecting nullity' (Miller 1970: 19). Taylor (1982), while acknowledging the tension between the human and the universal, feels that this gets lost in the complications of the love plot. He regards the heroine's sudden death as symptomatic of Hardy's failure to cope with tragi-comedy, with resultant lapses in tone. Bayley (1982) makes a case for regarding Hardy's portrayal of a love relationship as highly successful, though he concedes that its scientific concerns remain uneasily connected to the love interest. Sumner (1981) sees this novel as 'containing some of Hardy's most original and adventurous experiments', and draws attention to the heroic character of Viviette, suggesting that 'Hardy has an almost Lawrentian delight in Viviette's sensuality' (Sumner 1981: 78–9). Pursing the idea of the erotic, Wright (1989) argues that much of the pleasure of the text is voyeuristic and resides in the secrecy of the encounters between Viviette and Swithin St Cleeve. For Shuttleworth (1999), this novel 'describes an arc across the horizon of late nineteenth-century social and cultural concerns: sexuality, class, history, science and religion' (Shuttleworth 1999: xvi).

The Well-Beloved

Hardy subtitled *The Well-Beloved* **[37–8]** 'A Sketch of a Temperament'. Generically, it is a *Künstleroman*, a novel about an artist, which is developed around three stages in the life of the successful London sculptor Jocelyn Pierston, who pursues ideal feminine beauty, both in life and as inspiration for his art, at the ages of twenty, forty and sixty. The novel's epigraph, 'One shape of many names', comes from Shelley's *The Revolt of Islam*, and the doctrine of Platonic love that informs Jocelyn's pursuit is expressed in Shelley's 'Epipsychidion' **[91, 121, 192]**. While as his friend Somers implies, this obsession is an expression of normal male sexuality, for Jocelyn it is also an aesthetic quest which he channels into his work, giving sculpted form to the elusive vision. Unlike Somers, who marries the socialite Nichola Pine-Avon, Jocelyn is an uncompromising idealist, who in spite of fame and wealth, resists the vagaries of fashion in his art, and in his life successively falls in love with Avice Caro, her daughter and her granddaughter, as each in turn becomes the repository for his vision of the well-beloved.

The Well-Beloved reveals that Hardy's capacity for experiment remained undiminished. Its anti-realist thrust is implied in his description of it as a 'fantastic tale of a subjective idea' (*LW*, 303), though he qualifies this: 'There is, of course, underlying the fantasy followed by the visionary artist the truth that all men are pursuing a shadow, the Unattainable' (*LW*, 304). In *The Well-Beloved* Hardy reviews his own pursuit of elusive women who became material for his art **[10, 38, 45, 52, 118, 127]**; he asserts his own retention of emotional and creative vigour, as his poem 'I Look into My Glass', written at approximately the same time, reveals; and he defends his own artistic ideals against the sniping of critics and the constraints of censorship.

This novel possesses a somewhat abstract pattern because, as Hardy said in his 1912 Preface, 'the interest aimed at is of an ideal or subjective nature, and frankly imaginative, verisimilitude in the sequence of events has been subordinated to the said aim'. At the same time, this schematic fable contains a strong element of psychological realism in the way Hardy traces the compulsive rhythmic patterns of obsession and reveals its underlying insecurities. There is a deep fear of personal commitment behind Jocelyn's passivity as a lover and his discovery that his hauntings are always fleeting. A generous and humane man, he embarks on a spiritual quest that is accompanied by perpetual frustration and genuine suffering. His urge to return to the place of his birth, the Isle of Slingers (Portland), is symptomatic of a search for a deeper sense of identity. The symbolic solidity and changelessness of the Isle of Slingers is a point of reference for charting Jocelyn's increasing sense of the transience of life, as Hardy tactfully shifts the focus of the narrative from the migration of ideal beauty from woman to woman to the preoccupation with lost love, and the bitter recognition of the ineluctable truths of age.

The Isle of Slingers contributes to the novel's strangely symbolic power. Avice Caro, Jocelyn's first love, is representative of the fierce independence and primitive nature of the Isle of Slingers. His perception that the vision of the well-beloved has left her to reside in Marcia Bencomb is his tragic error. After learning of Avice's death, he thinks he has found it in her daughter, a washerwoman on the island, and then in her daughter, the third Avice. Tragic irony governs Jocelyn's discovery that the original Avice Caro was his only true love, that the ideal and the real were identical, releasing profound feelings precisely at the moment when the well-beloved becomes ultimately inaccessible. Avice the second and third are simply shadows of that reality. Hardy's poem 'The Well-Beloved' reveals the tragic implications of a mismatch between the idealised construction and the human object, between the vision of the beloved and the woman herself. But Hardy also described the novel as a 'tragic-comedy' (*LW*, 304), and there is a univeral tragic-comic irony in the experience of growing old while remaining emotionally youthful. The return of Marcia Bencomb, also at one time an inhabitant of the Isle of Slingers, underlines the remorseless march of time. She has lost her beauty and Jocelyn can offer her only friendship. His Platonic vision of the well-beloved is unable to sustain itself in contest with the depredations of age.

Another aspect of the design of *The Well-Beloved* is the oscillation of its action between the remote Isle of Slingers and London, where Jocelyn works and mainly lives. Like Hardy for a period of his life, he is a *déraciné* figure, a symbol of rootless modernity. Hardy's satire of the superficiality and dullness of the artistic and social circles of London, drawn from his own experience, is somewhat muted because his principal aim is to establish a schematic counterpoint between them and those direct and intimate relationships on the Isle of Slingers. Massive and primitive, with its origins in pre-history, and alive with superstition, it is a powerful presence in the novel. Jocelyn is drawn back to his roots repeatedly, and at the end of his life he abandons London for the sense of permanence offered by home. He settles on the Isle of Slingers with Marcia in a conventional marriage, becoming prominent in the community. Fascinatingly, while Hardy was able to make art out of his experience, Jocelyn Pierston is artistically destroyed by his. When the energising vision has left him, disillusionment sets in and he finds 'his sense of beauty and art and nature absolutely extinct' (*WB*, 3: 8). Ironically, he succumbs to the opposing claim of modern materialism and replaces damp Elizabethan cottages with new well-ventilated houses.

The Well-Beloved is classified among 'Romances and Fantasies'. Its subject and style are fabular, but because it is based on Hardy's own artistic experience, it has a realistic depth and subtlety of characterisation. The symbolic use of landscape is convincingly handled, but the London scenes are awkward and overdone, while the schematic nature of the story sometimes obtrudes, as for instance in the chapter with the reading-direction 'Juxtapositions', when Somers and Nichola Pine-Avon are incongruously found on the Isle of Slingers. The novel's chief interest perhaps lies in Hardy's use of the fable to review his writing life to date.

Hardy's boldness may be judged in the light of the extensive revisions that he made to the serial version, which he regarded as experimental, when it came to be published in volume form. Jocelyn's early marriage to Marcia and his later marriage to Avice the third were removed, as was the opening chapter; the sexual nature of Jocelyn's infatuation was made more explicit, while the original ending was replaced by his loss of the capacity for any aesthetic enjoyment. Hardy's rewriting not only made the novel tauter, but also considerably more daring, and more profoundly ironic.

Further reading

The problem of genre in this novel has baffled readers' expectations. Miller (1970) was the first to rescue it from critical neglect, stressing its 'antirealistic' texture (Miller 1970: 169), and linking it to his 'Poems of 1912–13', particularly to 'The Well-Beloved'. The major work on this novel has been done by Miller, in his Introduction to the New Wessex edition (1975) and in his essay in his book, *Fiction and Repetition: Seven English Novels* (1982). Miller argues that this text is 'one of a group of important nineteenth-century novels about art' (Miller 1982: 148). He focuses on its 'interlocking repetitions' which 'make it impossible to solve or resolve the story once and for all' (Miller 1982: 174), and suggests how, in anticipation of modern fiction, 'the problem of endings is thematised in the story' (Miller 1982: 156). Millgate (1971) draws attention to the element of romance and relates its 'carefully wrought fable' (Millgate 1971: 307) to Hardy's own experience. Taylor (1982) develops this idea, arguing for the similarity of artistic temperament between Jocelyn Pierston and Hardy, and seeing the novel as Hardy's detached scrutiny of his career as a novelist. From a psychoanalytic perspective, Wright's interest (1989) is in Hardy's exploration of the relation between the erotic and artistic creativity; while Sumner (1981) finds parallels between Jocelyn's behaviour and Jung's theory of the anima, and regards this novel as 'very largely a vehicle for theory' (Sumner 1981: 32). It is also examined in the context of the Aesthetic Movement of the 1890s, in Ryan's essay (1979), which reads Hardy's treatment of Jocelyn's clinging to youth as an ironic riposte to Oscar Wilde's *The Picture of Dorian Gray* (1890). Textual variations are discussed by Hetherington (1986). Ingham (1997) argues that the major differences in plot between the serial and the volume versions make them alternative texts, constituting a double form in which a male plot is counterpointed against a female plot, so that 'Actuality itself becomes provisional' (Ingham 1997: xxxii).

(c) SHORT STORIES

Hardy produced nearly fifty short stories between 1860 and 1900. Thirty-seven of them were collected in four volumes, *Wessex Tales* (1888), *A Group of Noble Dames* (1891), *Life's Little Ironies* (1894), and *A Changed Man and other Tales* (1913). Hardy's stories frequently appeared in American periodicals, because while British readers preferred the three-volume novel, the American market favoured the short story. And since his stories did not attract much attention in Britain, Hardy felt freer to experiment.

Wessex Tales **[34]**, categorised by Hardy among 'Novels of Character and Environment', captures the variety of cultural and economic life in Dorset, which functions as a microcosm of Wessex. Set in the past from Napoleonic times up to the mid-nineteenth century, they are an act of fictional memory. The stories are told as though each emerges from an oral tradition, and they draw on parish records and newspapers. *A Group of Noble Dames* **[34]**, classified with 'Romances and Fantasies', is a cycle of stories about aristocratic ladies, told to each other by middle-class members of the Wessex Field and Antiquarian Club, who have been driven indoors by bad weather. These tales are collected from historical Wessex, and are set mainly in the seventeenth and eighteenth centuries. Although they are fiction, their source is mainly John Hutchins's *History and Antiquities of the County of Dorset* (1774). The various narrators' minute scrutiny of the unconventional social lives of these titled women reveals Hardy's concern with sexual relationships that transgress class boundaries. Hardy's next volume, *Life's Little Ironies* **[38]**, explores contemporary issues. It deals predominantly with the domestic life of the middle class, which he criticises for its philistinism and stultifying conventionality, and which he increasingly came to see (possibly influenced by Ibsen's plays which he attended) as tragic.

Hardy refuses to offer a sense of resolution to the dilemmas he raises. The final collection, *A Changed Man and Other Tales* [47], is an eclectic grouping of miscellaneous stories. It holds less interest as a volume, and apart from the remarkable, 'The Romantic Adventures of a Milkmaid', the stories are undistinguished.

Hardy took his short stories very seriously, revising them carefully for publication, and although there are overlaps, he aimed for a coherent grouping of stories in each volume. In order to achieve this, occasionally he transferred tales from one volume to another; for instance in 1912 'A Tradition of Eighteen Hundred and Four' was reallocated to *Wessex Tales*, while 'An Imaginative Woman' was moved from *Wessex Tales* to *Life's Little Ironies*. However, each volume is varied in subject matter, narrative strategies and style. Hardy experimented with varieties of style, and also with different narrative voices, mixing genres and exploring, with unusual daring, issues of class and sexuality. With these features in mind, the following discussion will concentrate on a representative selection of the best stories in order to illustrate their range.

Set in the 1820s, 'The Three Strangers' [30, 34] records the dramatic encounter one night, in a remote shepherd's cottage, between two refugees from a storm, an escaped convict and the public hangman, who is due to execute him next morning at Casterbridge. An additional ironic depth is given to this black comedy by the appearance of the convict's brother, who finds the two men helping to celebrate a christening with the shepherd's fast diminishing stock of mead. The central contrast, which is achieved with elemental symbolism, is between the simple generosity of rural society, represented by Shepherd Fennel's humble cottage, and the oppressive urban world brought uncomfortably close by the hangman's callous condescension. The sheep-stealer, Timothy Summers, whose crime was dictated by absolute need, achieves minor heroic status by escaping from the hangman, as natural justice triumphs over law. The social, moral and economic conditions of rural life create a human solidarity with the hunted outcast and contempt for the power of law, which Hardy comically deconstructs in the farcical figure of the constable.

'A Tradition of Eighteen Hundred and Four' [38] moves further back in time. Its unusual narrative structure points to Hardy's interest in the relation between oral tradition, history and the imperative of fiction [7, 28, 101, 136]. It is a framed narrative, the first person narrator recounting the words of Solomon Selby as he told the story around the inn fireside a decade before. However, Solomon is identified as an unreliable narrator. His claim to have witnessed as a boy the night-time reconnaissance of the Dorset coast by none other than Napoleon himself is undermined, not only by the romantic tales of battle he has been fed by his uncle Job, but also by Hardy's intercalation into the narrative of alternative interpretations, such as the presence in the area of the King's German Legion, or smugglers. The convincing details of the story have to be weighed against the unreliability of its teller. Nevertheless, this story of threatened invasion has been kept alive by being incorporated within local tradition.

The narrator of 'The Melancholy Hussar of the German Legion' **[38]** is very different. He is a thoughtful middle-aged man, who is concerned to link the historical context of the story to the present of the reader. In this tale, the connection between the narrative voice and Hardy is particularly close, because as Hardy makes clear in the 1896 Preface to *Life's Little Ironies*, he had heard the story from the original of Phyllis, one of its central characters. The narrator feels compelled to defend her reputation, explaining her sheltered life with her eccentric father, and establishing her as a vulnerable figure. Her choice is between social elevation with prosperous Humphry Gould and sexual passion with glamorous Corporal Matthäus Tina in the King's German Legion camped at Budmouth, who is lonely and homesick. These two alienated characters Phyllis and Tina, idealise each other, but are ironically destroyed by social convention and martial law. Ironically, while Phyllis is waiting to elope with her German lover, Gould reveals to her that he has married another woman. Tina and his friend Christoph are shot for desertion, an execution that Phyllis witnesses from a distance. In telling her story, the narrator establishes Phyllis as part of the local history of Wessex and its oral traditions, just as the soldiers' graves have become part of the landscape.

Oral tradition occupies 'The Withered Arm' **[34]** in a different way entirely. It is a tale of superstition of the kind that Hardy heard from his mother and grandmother. It depends on a faith in a macabre folk remedy, the 'turning of blood' by touching the fresh corpse of a convicted man, of which Hardy had personal knowledge. The story is located in the folklore tradition by Hardy's memory of tales of over-looking (causing evil to another), and by his establishment of the familiar contrast between the ladylike Gertrude and the dairy worker Rhoda. However, Hardy's use of a third person narrator secures a distance from events that seem incredible. Abandoned by a wealthy local farmer, who marries a young wife Gertrude, Rhoda brings up the child of the relationship. At the very moment that Rhoda, in the throes of a nightmare, violently repels the evil spirit oppressing her, Gertude experiences a sharp pain in her arm, which over time withers into paralysis, affecting her looks and her place in her husband's affections.

The story is carefully based in realism, by the concrete descriptions of Rhoda's cottage and the dairy where she works, by Gertrude's journey over Egdon Heath to Conjuror Trendle, and by Trendle's ordinary job as a trader in products of the heath. But it has a psychological truth as well. Its core of superstition enforces more compellingly the power of the mind which the withered arm symbolises, as Rhoda comes to dominate her rival. Ironically, as the women form a friendship, Gertrude's plight comes to absorb Rhoda's thoughts. Their antagonism flares again at the hanging at Casterbridge, for the corpse that is to cure Gertrude is that of Rhoda's son, the victim of parental neglect. Folktale, modified in this way by human feeling, and by the exploration of the psychology of revenge, develops into tragedy.

The supernatural is approached with greater sophistication in 'The Fiddler of the Reels' [38], a story in which form and content are artistically unified, permitting ampler thematic development. At one level, the story works symbolically in the ballad mode. Mop Ollamoor, the horse doctor, uses the hypnotic power of his fiddle-playing to seduce women, in this instance the impressionable Car'line, whom he makes pregnant. Foreign-looking and of unknown origins, he plays only secular tunes, has never entered a church, and his music is associated with the demonic. His playing symbolises his sexuality. As such he is regarded as a threat to women, to marriage, and to the social fabric.

The story's symbolism is supported by realism. Car'line's second encounter with Mop, when she is again compelled to dance to exhaustion at the behest of the fiddle, is at the Quiet Woman inn, where she has had too much to drink. Mop is also the father of Carry, whom he claims. His rival for Car'line's affections, Edward whom she marries, is an unimaginative mechanic with little sexual presence. The larger realistic context is given by the modern world of the Great Exhibition, railways and America. Mop's presence at the Crystal Palace and later in America, where he performs with the middle-aged Carry, suggests that in spite of its denial by scientific rationalism instinct, in this case the primitive relationship between sexuality and music, has a hold over individual lives that is neither understood nor controlled.

The contemporary world occupies the foreground in 'On the Western Circuit' [38]. A young country girl, Anna, is seduced by a youthful London barrister Charles Raye, whom she encounters at the fairground during his visit to Melchester. He romanticises her rural origins, and in turn her letters lure him into marriage. When he discovers that these were written on behalf of the illiterate girl by her mistress, a lonely, passionate woman in an unfulfilling marriage with a well-to-do wine merchant, he feels trapped and socially ruined. Her sterile marriage is replicated by his. It is a wonderfully economical and deeply ironic plot, in which the triangular relationship, the sexual dimension of which is treated boldly, develops a logic and momentum of its own.

Particularly powerful is the psychological exploration of the sexual fantasist, the childless wife, Edith Harnham, who increasingly lives vicariously through her maid, finally usurping her identity as Charles Raye's mistress and the mother of his child. This narrative focus is elaborated by the moral pattern: Charles has seduced Anna, Anna has concealed from him her illiteracy, and Edith has deceived both Anna and Charles Raye by conducting an emotional affair. When Charles and Anna marry, Edith's loss of Charles is intensified by their futile recognition of the bond between them, symbolised by their kiss. However, the narrative enacts a rhetoric of sympathy and irony in which no moral judgement is made.

Another exploration of modern marriage is developed into a subtle examination of contemporary middle-class provincial life in 'An Imaginative Woman' [38]. This story challenges the constraints of realism. Edith Marchmill, the imaginative woman of the title (probably based on Florence Henniker [10, 38, 45, 52, 111, 127]), who is married to a gunmaker, revolts from his vulgar materialism and her empty marriage, by seeking relief in poetry and in private fantasy. Her inner life progressively takes over from reality, as desire becomes associated with poetry and she develops a powerful sexual attraction for the poet Robert Trewe (based on Dante Gabriel Rossetti). The futility of this compensatory imaginative relationship with the poet is revealed when she becomes pregnant by her husband, and she implies that the child is Trewe's. Hardy's bleak and daring conclusion is symbolically appropriate, ironic and tragic. Edith dies in childbirth, while Marchmill disowns the child because he believes it resembles the poet.

Hardy's experimentation with mixing different genres may be seen in 'The Romantic Adventures of a Milkmaid' [30]. Set in the 1840s, this narrative begins by providing the context of ordinary rural life, with a realistic portrayal of the dairy in which Margery Tucker works. But then it moves rapidly into fairytale. An exotic stranger, Baron Xante, who has overtones of the demonic lover, is fascinated by Margery as a symbol of innocent Nature, while for her he represents the allure of the mysterious. Hardy uses their misinterpretation and romanticisation of each other to engage in a comparison of the rural and urban worlds, as the Baron introduces Margery into society. She is overwhelmed by its wealth and sophistication, particularly at the ball where his power over her is most keenly felt. On the point of fleeing together, they recognise the enormity of the proposed deed, and instead she returns to her husband and to domestic reality. This melodramatic tale, which is perhaps too long for its subject matter, also rehearses common Hardyan themes: the lure of sexual excitement and the power of romance as destructive forces, the tedium of marriage, the insuperable barriers of social class, and the disruptive intrusion of the outsider into Wessex.

There are other fine stories that extend Hardy's range still further. Four of these concern marriage. 'The First Countess of Wessex' records the intensity of social expectations encountered by aristocratic young women in seeking to make an appropriate match. 'The Distracted Preacher' **[34]** is a humorous study of the dilemma facing a young Methodist minister in love with a beautiful widow, when he discovers her to be a smuggler. There is a study of a liberated woman, who rejects marriage on any terms other than romantic and remains defiantly single, in 'Interlopers at the Knap' **[34]**; while a sombre contrast of marriages is explored in 'Fellow-Townsmen' **[34]**, a story which focuses on the human propensity to blame fate for individual failures of nerve and will.

Further reading

Hardy's stories have received relatively little critical attention. The major critic is Brady (1982), who offers an excellent close reading of Hardy's narrative effects, which she regards as being more intense and experimental in his stories than in his novels. The theoretical approach of Ebbatson (1993) examines the children's story 'Our Exploits at West Poley' through Kristevan linguistics, a critical approach that synthesises materialist and psychological theories in order to understand language in relation to the self. Ebbatson also offers a historicised reading of social class in 'An Indiscretion in the Life of an Heiress'. More recently, Ray (1997) has produced a thorough textual study of the short stories.

(d) POETRY

Hardy's career as a poet, from the 1860s, when he commenced writing, through to the 1920s, spanned a period that included not only great social upheavals, but also considerable changes in poetic style. During this time Hardy composed over a thousand poems, but while *The*

Collected Poems follows the order in which they were published, this obscures the sequence of composition, because of Hardy's habit of publishing new poems together with those he had written years before. Moreover, the task of discovering a clear line of development in Hardy's poetry is made even more difficult by the fact that in many cases the date of composition cannot be identified.

In his early poems Hardy experimented with poetic forms, notably sonnets and ballads. There was a broadening of range during the years of his career as a novelist and the 1890s, when he resumed poetry full time. This output included poems arising from his pilgrimage to places associated with Keats, Shelley and Byron, poems about the universe, war poems, love lyrics, as well as narrative poems and ballads. His poetry had achieved considerable technical assurance, was more reflective, with a greater development of metrical form. From the turn of the century until Emma's death in 1912, although Hardy continued to produce significant verse, his poetic energy seems mainly to have gone into the writing of his monumental epic-drama *The Dynasts*.

The period following 1912 saw the publication of two volumes, *Satires of Circumstance* (1914) and *Moments of Vision* (1917). The first of these includes the famous sequence of poems about his dead wife ('Poems of 1912–13'). Together these volumes, which represent some of Hardy's finest verse, contain a wide range of poems: love poems, philosophical poems, nature poems, elegies, war poems, poems on public events, and a tribute to his revered Swinburne. Hardy's later poetry, which he continued to write up to his death in 1928, reveals a degree of anxiety, an inclination towards the surreal, and a sense of increasing detachment, expressed through a variety of subjects and poetic forms. Hardy's status as a poet, his influence on other poets, and the 'canon', the core of his poetic achievement, have all been the subject of critical debate **[190–1, 193]**.

Hardy's relationships with both his Romantic predecessors and his Victorian contemporaries are linked inextricably to his response to the age in which he lived. Although his earliest poem 'Domicilium' is written in Wordsworthian blank verse, and expresses Hardy's sense of the relationship between the natural landscape in which he lived and its beneficent effect on the growth of his personality, he soon rejected this Wordsworthian view of the natural world:

Nature's defects must be looked in the face and transcribed ... I think the art lies in making these defects the basis of a hitherto unperceived beauty, by irradiating them with 'the light that never was' on their surface, but is seen to be latent in them by the spiritual eye.

(*LW,* 118)

For Hardy, 'The "simply natural" is interesting no longer' (*LW*, 192). In *Tess of the d'Urbervilles* Hardy refers bitterly to Wordsworth's ode, 'Intimations of Immortality' as a 'ghastly satire'. In this post-Darwinian world, the mode of vision available to the Romantics was no longer possible; the poet was simply an observer of an empty, seemingly chaotic universe. Hardy's poem 'Shelley's Skylark' extols Shelley's capacity for prophetic thought and high poetic art **[91, 111, 192]**, but it insists on the mortality of the bird, and its status as the object of the poet's mind. 'Shut out that Moon', with its reliance on the idiom of romance, also turns its back on Romantic gestures: 'Close up the casement, draw the blind, / Shut out that stealing moon' (*CP*, 201). Its rich language is undercut by the reductive imagery and bleak diction of the final stanza, which replaces the ideal by reality: 'Within the common lamp-lit room / Prison my eyes and thought' (*CP*, 201). Hardy's recognition of the impossibility of the Romantic mode of vision in an industrial and increasingly urban society, and in an age that the poet Matthew Arnold described as 'deeply unpoetical' **[28, 85, 89, 106]**, is evident in his poem 'We are Getting to the End', which opens with the lines: 'We are getting to the end of visioning / The impossible within this universe' (*CP*, 886). Written in response to the First World War, this poem also alludes to the loss of the ideal of human progress – 'We are getting to the end of dreams!' (*CP*, 887).

The death of God, confirmed for many by Darwin's theory of evolution, is recorded in Hardy's poem 'God's Funeral' **[12, 77, 81, 201]**. He denied that the poem was atheistic, and strictly speaking it maintains an agnostic stance, but it regards the concept of a powerful and loving creator as the construct of the human imagination. The decline and death of this faith leaves Hardy 'dazed and puzzled, 'twixt the gleam and gloom' (*CP*, 309). Hardy substituted the Immanent Will **[27, 43, 126, 138]** for God, and following thinkers such as Auguste Comte **[14, 23, 68, 108]** and John Stuart Mill **[14, 85]** he replaced Christianity with social meliorism. This is explained in his lengthy Apology to *Late Lyrics and Earlier*: 'pain to all upon [this globe], tongued or dumb, shall be kept down to a minimum by loving-kindness, operating through scientific knowledge, and actuated by the modicum of free will conjecturally possessed by organic life when the mighty necessitating forces – unconscious or other – that have "the balancings

121

of the clouds", happen to be in equilibrium, which may or may not be often'.

Hardy's doubts about the Christian faith are hinted at in such poems as 'The Impercipient', and 'The Oxen', but they are registered in tones of obvious regret. Traditional perception of the divinity of Christ had been challenged by historical scholarship, such as David Friedrich Strauss's influential *Der Leben Jesu* (*The Life of Jesus*, 1836), translated into English by George Eliot in 1845, which emphasised the humanity of the historical Jesus. Although Hardy keeps to the Biblical narrative in his poem about Peter's denial of Christ, 'In the Servants' Quarters', he introduces details that give the episode a historical authenticity; Peter's interrogation by a maiden who has noticed his shudder at the clink of Christ's chains, and the laughter of the constables at the dialect speech Peter shares with his master.

However, for Hardy the possibility of poetry's traditional function of transcendence remains, but in a more limited form. In Hardy's work the poet transcends himself towards humanity, affirming the central values of loving-kindness and fellowship. In 'At the Railway Station, Upway', a convict, a constable and a young boy occupy a timeless limbo between trains. The boy's act of playing his violin to cheer the convict, the convict's ironical singing of freedom, and the complacent constable's involuntary smile, create the grounds for the convict's transcendence of his state and their achievement of human solidarity.

Strength is derived from the perception of the continuity of human life in a personal poem such as 'Heredity', or in a more universal poem about war, for instance 'In Time of "The Breaking of Nations"'. A visionary poem that achieves this sense of continuity is 'Old Furniture', which depends on the exercise of poetic will. Hardy's imagining the hands of previous generations with wraithlike movements at work on the pieces of furniture, like a series of fading images of a candle-flame seen in a mirror, is a celebration of simple acts of human assertion. It is also a resurrection that offers a means of spiritual renewal; while in the 'turn' that Hardy employs at the beginning of the final stanza, he wryly defines his own sense of alienation from the modern world, with its devotion to purpose, action and progress: 'Well, well. It is best to be up and doing, / The world has no use for one to-day / Who eyes things thus – no aim pursuing!' (*CP*, 456).

Hardy's magnificent poem, 'During Wind and Rain' is another poem of humanistic strength. It draws on memories of Emma's family home, and is divided into four discrete moments of vision that embrace human fellowship and harmony as positive joys. Each is undercut by a remorseless, ballad-like refrain, 'Ah, no; the years O!', and 'Ah, no; the years, the years' (*CP*, 465–6), that reminds the reader both of the ineluctable passing of time and of mortality. However, this simple structural irony is modified by the incorporation of a sense of transience and dissolution within the vivid, positive imagery: in the autumn the candles 'mooning' the faces of the singers are burning down, the creeping moss threatens the family's creation of a garden in the spring, the sea is a symbol of mutability, and the furniture on the lawn in the summer suggests vulnerability. The awareness of a terrifying nullity at the heart of things, shared by the inhabitants of the poem, and endorsed by the refrain, is nevertheless transcended by their will to pursue actions that celebrate the human values of love, fellowship, adventure and gaiety.

The equally famous poem, 'The Darkling Thrush' (which owes debts to Keats's 'Ode to a Nightingale' and Shelley's 'To a Skylark') is a poem about solidarity with nature. However, unlike their unseen, ecstatic, blithe birds, Hardy's is visible and ordinary. His description – 'An aged thrush, frail, gaunt, and small, / In blast-beruffled plume' (*CP*, 137) – avoids the Romantic imagery of Keats and Shelley. Apparently a modern lament for the death of God and of nature (the sky is both the landscape's and the century's crypt), the poem records the end of place and time. Set at the turning-point between the old century and the new, the awful nullity developed in the image patterns of the first two stanzas is mirrored in the consciousness of the poet himself. The century's outleant corpse makes a parallel with the poet who 'leant upon a coppice gate' (*CP*, 137); the 'weakening eye of day' (*CP*, 137) creates a metaphor for the poet's darkened vision, while the tangled bine-stems scoring the sky 'Like strings of broken lyres' (*CP*, 137) is a further image of poetic sterility. There is a sudden change from perception to sound. The muteness of the poet, for whom the universe is dead, gives way to the thrush, which expresses hope and joy. Like Hardy himself (aged, frail, gaunt and small) the thrush is the governing symbol for continual creative activity. Like the poet, who is both observer and agent, the thrush creates his essential self by an act of will. He has 'chosen thus to fling his soul / Upon the growing gloom' (*CP*, 137) – a defiant act of affirmation. It is also an unwitting act of loving-kindness that forges a contact between itself and the poet, creating a sense of solidarity with all living things. This is given a particular existential force by the poem's terrible context of non-being.

Much depends on humanity's capacity to perceive and act in such moments. In 'The Self-Unseeing' **[42]** Hardy records an occasion in his boyhood when he danced in the parlour, intoxicated by the music of his father's violin, while his mother gazed entranced into the fire; a moment of joy apparently annihilating the tyranny of time. But the opportunity for transcendence was lost because their actions were involuntary, passive and self-regarding. Hardy's use of heraldic imagery and clichés of emotion in the final stanza suggest that their pleasure was won at the cost of a moment of more profound relationship:

Childlike, I danced in a dream;
Blessings emblazoned that day;
Everything glowed with a gleam;
Yet we were looking away!

(*CP*, 152)

The double vision recorded here is an example of Hardy's fidelity to what he called 'impressions'. Insisting that his writing did not offer a philosophy of life, Hardy claims that each poem was an 'impression', intensely subjective and evanescent. In his Introductory Note to *Winter Words*, his last volume, he says that 'no harmonious philosophy is attempted in these pages – or in any bygone pages of mine, for that matter'. Hardy's impressions of life were not wholly bleak. There is the wry humour of 'The Ruined Maid', which manages the simultaneous deconstruction of two myths, the pastoral and the fallen woman, as a poor Dorset peasant girl encounters a former friend who has escaped to a life of prostitution in London; there is the acerbic wit of 'An Ancient to Ancients', in which Hardy addresses the coming generation of poets; and there is the comic debunking of sentimentality about animals in 'Ah, are you Digging on my Grave?' (in which the dog's fidelity is not to his buried mistress, but to his buried bone). However, Hardy's main preoccupations are loss, the inevitability of decay, the passing of time, and regret. Alongside his humorous verse, we must set that early lyric, the major imagist poem 'Neutral Tones', which numbly recalls the loss of love in a baffling universe. 'A Wish for Unconsciousness' expresses directly a desire for oblivion. There is also that great lyric of despair, 'In Tenebris I', each self-contained stanza of which records a dialectic between nature, characterised by winter, decay, death, storm and blackness, and the poet's own even more profound darkness of soul.

Sometimes Hardy's examination of tragic experience is located in the past, fictionalised and given an appropriate generic form, such as the ballad. 'A Trampwoman's Tragedy', set in the 1820s, records with a degree of detachment gained by the stereotypical narrator, a familiar pattern of love, jealousy, murder and execution, which takes place in a rural environment. Hardy considered it his most successful poem. A more modern use of the ballad, though it retains archaic language and

traditional stanza form, occurs in 'A Sunday Morning Tragedy', a poem
about a growing social problem. It tells the story of a girl's attempt to
procure an abortion and her subsequent death. However, because of
its uncomfortable social realism, it was rejected by magazine editors,
eventually appearing in the *English Review*.

Generally, however, poetry gave Hardy greater freedom of expression
than did fiction to flout conventional opinion. As he put it in the *Life*:
'To cry out in a passionate poem that (for instance) the Supreme Mover
or Movers, the Prime Force or Forces, must be either limited in power,
unknowing, or cruel ... will cause [readers] merely a shake of the head.
... If Galileo had said in verse that the world moved, the Inquisition
might have let him alone' (*LW*, 302). 'Nature's Questioning' is typical
of Hardy's use of personal reverie as the source of controversial
philosophical speculations, here occasioned by the reciprocal gaze of
the poet as teacher and representative elements of Nature 'Like
chastened children sitting silent in a school' (*CP*, 58). But nature's
questioning of the purpose of existence and pain – the possible product
of some conscious 'Vast Imbecility' (*CP*, 59), or some unconscious
'Automaton' (*CP*, 59), or some incomprehensible 'high Plan' (*CP*, 59) –
is unanswerable:

> Thus things around. No answerer I. ...
> Meanwhile the winds, and rains,
> And Earth's old glooms and pains
> Are still the same, and Life and Death are neighbours nigh.
>
> (*CP*, 59)

Hardy's poetry displays an extraordinary range of variations on
major themes – nature, time and memory, death, and love. The well-
known poem 'Afterwards' is particularly revealing about Hardy's
perception of nature, but also about his art and his attitude towards
himself as a poet. Enormous care went into the crafting of the poems,
which meant considerable revisions. The seemingly inevitable opening
line of 'Afterwards': 'When the Present has latched its postern behind
my tremulous stay' (*CP*, 521) was refined from 'When night has closed
its shutters on my dismantled day'. The poem's focus is the animals and
birds that are memorably imaged, and Hardy's observation is especially
intense, for instance, of the almost imperceptible alighting of the hawk
'like an eyelid's soundless blink' (*CP*, 521). Hardy celebrates the life he
will be leaving, but his marginal impact on the world will, he implies,
not be as a poet, but as an ordinary observant countryman, alive in his
neighbours' memories as one who 'used to notice such things' (*CP*, 521).

Time is used very precisely by the countryman. The time of 'After-wards' is May. In 'Overlooking the River Stour', when Hardy is watching swallows catching insects above the river in wheeling figures of eight, it is June. 'An August Midnight' finds the coming together in Hardy's study, as he is writing, of the humble longlegs, a moth, a dumbledore (bumblebee) and a fly, bringing the number of creatures in the room to five. But he is the only one of them barred from 'Earth-secrets' (*CP*, 134). These superbly understated observations and evoca-tions of the rhythms of life in the countryside are often allied, as in 'At Middle-Field Gate in February', in which Hardy recalls the amorous summers of girls now dead, to his profound understanding of transience, and of the destructive power of time.

Poems mentioned earlier suggest how Hardy's observation of nature may prompt philosophical speculation about the relationship between the natural and the human worlds. 'The Convergence of the Twain', on the loss of the *Titanic*, records a symbolic confrontation between man and nature. Here modern technology (also embraced in other poems that deal with railways, cars or the telegraph) represents 'human vanity', and the 'Pride of Life' (*CP*, 288). In particular, Hardy points to the self-indulgence of the wealthy, to their opulence and sensuality, which receive satiric comment from the undersea creatures, who perceive the incongruity of the presence of that 'vaingloriousness' (*CP*, 289) in the depths of the ocean. Nature, in the shape of an iceberg, is the agent of the 'Immanent Will' (*CP*, 289) **[27, 43, 121, 138]**, and the whole poem leads up to the metaphysical as well as physical shock of nature's violent negation of the ideological equation of technology with human progress.

The passing of time and personal loss give rise to some fine elegiac poems that can be identified with Hardy's family. In addition to those already glanced at are 'Thoughts of Phena, at News of her Death', about his cousin Tryphena Sparks, his 'lost prize' (*CP*, 55), 'A Church Romance', recording the courtship of his parents, and 'One We Knew', an affectionate memory of his grandmother. These poems, which arise from memories of the homely and familiar, have an extraordinarily artless intimacy. The description in 'The Oxen', for instance: 'We pictured the meek mild creatures where / They dwelt in their strawy pen' (*CP*, 439), immediately involves the reader in the yearning for the faith of childhood, and belief in the myth of the cattle kneeling on Christmas Eve.

The love lyric, 'A Broken Appointment', with its rhythmic, clock-like refrain 'You did not come', 'You love not me' (*CP*, 124), is an expres-sion of Hardy's recognition of the failure of his one-sided romantic involvement with Florence Henniker **[10, 38, 45, 52, 111, 118]**. The speaker presents himself as a 'time-torn man', and the broken appointment enacts the failure of time to fulfil its promise to soothe and heal. Time, as much as the woman who lacks 'lovingkindness', is the betrayer. As so often, Hardy's skill is evident in his indebtedness to traditional poetic forms, in this case his adoption of the Petrarchan sonnet sestet. Hardy's treatment of love is also dominated by a powerful feeling of loss. 'To Lizbie Browne' whimsically laments another 'lost prize', a girl who grew up and married before Hardy could declare his love. With teasing self-mockery, he dwells on her ripening sexuality, which intensifies his mortification, and this is capped by his recognition that while she inhabits his memory he is lost to hers.

Aging is confronted fearlessly in 'I Look into My Glass', a poem that engages with the paradox of emotional vitality coupled with physical decline. In 'Nobody Comes', by contrast, Hardy places the aging poet in a surreal technological landscape, where the telegraph wire 'Intones to travellers like a spectral lyre' (*CP*, 704), and where the headlights of a passing car signal the arrival of the mechanistic and the utilitarian, leaving Hardy, self-divided in the darkness of an existential world in which nobody comes: 'And mute by the gate I stand again alone, / And nobody pulls up there' (*CP*, 705).

The passing of time is altogether a more complex matter in that impressive poem 'Wessex Heights', written at a point of crisis in Hardy's life, during the 1890s when he felt his marriage to have been a great mistake. Tryphena Sparks had died, he found novel-writing unrewarding, *Jude the Obscure* was being attacked, and he feared to venture out in case he were accosted and insulted. His social life was also uncongenial. A deeply reflective poem, 'Wessex Heights' is a confessional review of Hardy's misery, developed steadily with a disciplined syntax. Topographically, for Hardy the heights symbolise freedom, while the lowlands represent his fear of ghostly detectives tracking him in the towns. This paranoia is amplified by the ghosts of six women (only one of whom, 'one rare fair woman' (*CP*, 301), Florence Henniker, can be identified with any certainty), who inhabit different areas of the landscape, and whom he seeks to exorcise.

Hardy's poems of loss naturally include the experience of bereavement, thoughts of death, and memories of the dead. 'In Death Divided' is a whimsical, self-pitying poem lamenting his ultimate separation from Florence Henniker, buried in some distant spot, her stately headstone registering even in death her social superiority to his 'simply-cut memorial' (*CP*, 302). In 'Something Tapped' Hardy is haunted by his beloved's face at the window; while there is the memory of his sister in 'Logs on the Hearth', as he remembers climbing with her the very apple tree he is in the act of burning. And he anticipates his own death in 'Who's in the Next Room?'.

Hardy's seeking to shape his own attitude to death may be seen not only in those poems of loss in which he celebrates loved ones, but also in those extraordinary poems of affirmation in which he resurrects friends from his community. 'Friends Beyond' imagines the voices of the dead in Mellstock churchyard, from the squire down to William Dewy and Tranter Reuben (characters who appear in *Under the Greenwood Tree*), whom he imagines whispering to him in triumph at having achieved oblivion. He finds consolation in their philosophical approach to death. However, this elegy also engages with life, and it turns on the irony that, although the local dead ritually renounce, each according to his or her social status, all material concerns, all care for reputation and all family ties, the poem celebrates the material and emotional wealth of their lives. A further irony lies in the fact that though they may have dismissed the poet from their minds, Hardy has not forgotten them, and their continued existence is assured, both in his memory and in his verse.

Death was also viewed by Hardy as a return to nature. In the surreal poem, 'Voices from Things Growing in a Churchyard', he insists on the reality underlying the abstract concept of our eventual assimilation into the natural world. The voices he imagines are not those of the long-dead inhabitants of the churchyard, but of plants that they have become, each ironically appropriate to the individual's character and status in life. The poem opens, 'These flowers are I, poor Fanny Hurd' (*CP*, 590), and continues, 'Once I flit-fluttered like a bird / Above the grass, as now I wave / In daisy shapes above my grave' (*CP*, 590). The humour, the jingling refrain, the insouciance of the voices, and the beauty of the plants and trees emphasise the unthreatening naturalness of the process of dissolution, while again bringing the dead to life in Hardy's imagination.

During Hardy's lifetime there were two major wars which engaged him emotionally, the Boer War in South Africa, and the Great War **[41, 48–9]**. They prompted the writing of some distinguished war poems. Hardy eschewed patriotic jingoism. The poem, 'Drummer Hodge', in which a young Wessex countryman (the derogatory term for rural workfolk was 'Hodge') is swept up by imperial conflict, is superbly achieved. Ignorant of the country in which he had come to fight, he is killed almost on arrival in South Africa, and lies uncoffined in a strange land. The incongruity of his situation is captured bitterly in the title, signifying both the soldier and the rustic. Hardy avoids sentimentality and diminishes war by placing the dead drummer in a universal perspective of cosmic alienation:

> Yet portion of that unknown plain
>   Will Hodge for ever be;
> His homely Northern breast and brain
>   Grow to some Southern tree,
> And strange-eyed constellations reign
>   His stars eternally.
>
>   (*CP*, 83)

The same war occasioned 'The Souls of the Slain', a brooding reflection on the illusory nature of the fame and glory achieved in combat. This is discovered too late by the ghosts of dead soldiers returning home from the southern hemisphere. The speaker's meditation is prompted by the setting, the edge of the ocean on a still, intensely dark night. The poem closes with the return from the ghosts' conversation to the poet's brooding mind and the 'Sea mutterings' (*CP*, 87).

'The Man he Killed' operates very differently. Hardy's humanistic debunking of the heroics of war here takes the form of setting human realities against the clichés that justify slaughter, as a soldier reflects on the curious fact of killing a man who, away from the field of conflict, he would have treated to a drink:

> 'I shot him dead because –
> Because he was my foe,
> Just so: my foe of course he was;
> That's clear enough ...'
>   (*CP*, 269)

In his concentration on the pity of war, Hardy anticipates the poet of the Great War, Wilfred Owen. But he also manages a savagely satirical attack on war in 'Channel Firing'. The dead are awakened by the sound of gunnery practice at sea and sit up thinking that it is Judgement Day, until advised by God that it is merely the same old human madness. The speaker is one of the skeletons, who in the opening line addresses the reader in inclusive blame: 'That night your great guns, unawares, / Shook all our coffins as we lay' (*CP*, 287). The closing conversations of the disturbed dead register their despair of human progress and the futility of preaching the Christian gospel. The poem's surreal, comic gothic is grounded in the real through the physical detail of the church, around which lie the dead.

Hardy's treatment of war was varied and he was extremely versatile in discovering appropriate poetic forms for the expression of his views. Among his finest is 'In Time of "The Breaking of Nations" ', a comment not only on the Great War, but on all war. It is a complex poem, but it is organised around artfully simple pastoral images embodying profound feelings, which are understated with the utmost economy. The image of the man harrowing, the burning of the couch-grass, and the young lovers who enter the rural landscape are brought together in the third and final stanza:

> Yonder a maid and her wight
>> Come whispering by:
> War's annals will cloud into night
>> Ere their story die.
>> (CP, 511)

The militarism of European dynasties is dismissed as ephemeral compared with the endurance of nature and human love.

Many of Hardy's poems have women as their subject. Hardy writes about women from different social classes, in various situations and dilemmas, with sympathy, psychological insight, amusement, wit, anger and admiration. Some of these poems have already been mentioned. The girl in 'The Ruined Maid' defends her exploitation of her sexuality in a society that treats women as cheap labour, either in the cornfields of Dorset or more frankly on the streets of London. 'A Trampwoman's Tragedy' voices, but cannot explain, the mystery of sexual instinct that leads a pregnant woman to tease her lover to distraction and murder. The psychology of sexual passion is explored in 'The Coquette, and After'. The perverse desire for sexual domination is ironically inverted, as farce turns to tragedy and the speaker voices her recognition of the social penalty she must pay: 'Of sinners two / At last *one* pays the penalty – / The woman – women always do!' (CP, 127). By contrast, 'Former Beauties', given from the point of view of a middle-aged man, looks back nostalgically on a past in which women he knows were courted on country summer evenings. Hardy explores the relation between sexuality and musicality in an extraordinary, dramatic poem, 'The Chapel-Organist'. A young female organist is driven to suicide by the spiritual and financial meanness of the chapel elders, who fear her disturbing sexuality and who learn that in order to pursue her passion for music she has prostituted herself.

A more personal poem, in which a woman's voice is given full scope is 'In a Eweleaze near Weatherbury'. Almost certainly, from its dating and from its reference to her 'term as teacher', the voice is that of Hardy's cousin Tryphena Sparks, recalling the passing of the years since she danced on the sheep-meadow 'With one who kindled gaily / Love's fitful ecstasies!' (*CP*, 62). It is a poem of self-assertion and of a realistic accommodation to life. Despite the insidiously debilitating physical ravages of time, she remains emotionally the same, and continues to value sexual beauty above the spiritual: 'Still, I'd go the world with Beauty, / I would laugh with her and sing' (*CP*, 63). Yet she bravely accepts its inevitable fading, and the futility of resuming its worship. The poem's dance-like rhythms, its cheerful recollection of amorous triumphs, and its clear-sighted understanding of self, combine to produce a positive statement of female sexuality.

The woman who dominates some of Hardy's finest poetry, however, is Emma. 'Poems of 1912–13' is an outpouring of lyric verse after her death. These poems encompass the full expression of grief. They proceed from remorse, from an attempt to cancel the intervening years, and an endeavour to resurrect the young Emma. Though plangent, they are crafted with extraordinary care, and arranged in a sequence that offers contrasts of mood, point of view, and form. Hardy marks the difference Emma's death has made to his life in various ways. In 'The Walk' he communes with her in a quietly relaxed way, reflecting that his walking alone to the 'hill-top tree' (*CP*, 320) was not unusual, since latterly her lameness had prevented her accompanying him. The difference when he returns to the house is registered with wonderful emotional precision, understatement, and economy of language: 'Only that underlying sense / Of the look of a room on returning thence' (*CP*, 320).

'The Voice', in which Hardy hears Emma calling to him, has a naked honesty; in his admission that she is 'much missed' (*CP*, 325), in his remembering her first appearance to him in an 'air-blue gown' (*CP*, 326), in his appeal to her to let him view her, and in his bleak acknowledgement that in truth he hears only the wind. The conclusion, with its stuttering syntax and rhythm, offers a striking image of the aging, haunted lover:

> Thus I; faltering forward,
> Leaves around me falling,
> Wind oozing thin through the thorn from norward,
> And the woman calling.
>
> (*CP*, 326)

Some of the poems devoted to Emma are visionary. In 'At Castle Boterel' Hardy's primitive sense of place permits the continued

existence of Emma as a phantom who remains on the slopes long after
they have both gone, for the primeval rocks that have noted the
transience of life, have recorded 'that we two passed' (*CP*, 331). The
image of the past is shrinking as he looks back at it for the very last
time, feeling keenly his own mortality and the realisation that 'I shall
traverse old love's domain / Never again' (*CP*, 331). However, by an act
of poetic will place may be seen as containing time and so preserving
the significance of human actions. The revelation, in 'After a Journey',
of Emma's presence by the waterfall, ignored by the preening birds
and lazy seals, allows Hardy to address her in intimate, loving tones,
and to assert his selfhood in the final stanza:

> Trust me, I mind not, though Life lours,
>> The bringing me here; nay, bring me here again!
>>> I am just the same as when
> Our days were a joy, and our paths through flowers.
>>>>> (*CP*, 329)

A particularly complex poem is 'The Phantom Horsewoman'. In it
Hardy employs a highly formal structure to confront reality and to
embody vision. In the first three stanzas he describes himself from the
detached perspective of an observer who sees only a man in 'a careworn
craze' (*CP*, 332), and imagines he is fantasising obsessively about 'A
phantom of his own figuring' (*CP*, 333). This tone of pity reinforces
the dominant image of the desolate shore on which the poet stands
staring at the empty waves. However, the final stanzas hold in tension
the horror of a desolate universe, imaged by the vacant sands and the
bewildering sea mist, and the poet's vision itself. The achieved meaning
of being there is symbolised in the final stanza:

> A ghost-girl-rider. And though, toil-tried,
>> He withers daily,
>> Time touches her not,
>> But she still rides gaily
>> In his rapt thought
>> On that shagged and shaly
>> Atlantic spot,
>> And as when first eyed
> Draws rein and sings to the swing of the tide.
>>>>> (*CP*, 333)

Life and death are held in careful balance in Hardy's description of
Emma as a 'ghost-girl-rider' (*CP*, 333). He creates Emma, in defiance of

the terrible void of her absence, as the source of continued meaning in his life.

Hardy's poetry is pre-eminently about ways of seeing. This is evident in the numerous angles of vision he employs in so many poems. Sometimes it involves creating a picture, as in 'Snow in the Suburbs', which allows the eye to follow the cascading snow set off by a sparrow alighting on a tree; or it employs the camera effect, as in 'On the Departure Platform', which tracks the gradually diminishing form and disappearance of a muslin-gowned girl among those boarding the train. However, Hardy is also a poet of social observation. His humanistic sympathies emerge in a variety of poems drawing upon his experience of both Dorset and London. 'We Field-Women' records the hardships of female rural labour, 'The Old Workman' ambivalently notes a mason's pride in his work on a mansion, his lack of complaint at the permanent injury he received in the process, and his deferential attitude to his employers. Hardy also gives a voice to the socially marginalised. In 'No Buyers' the dispirited travellers selling brushes and baskets are precisely observed. 'Dream of the City Shopwoman' explores the life of a girl, 'Oppressed by city people's snap and sneer' (*CP*, 576), who lives in a garret and fantasises about an idealised rural world. It is a cry of despair:

> O God, that creatures framed to feel
> A yearning nature's strong appeal
> Should writhe on this eternal wheel
>   In rayless grime ...
>   (*CP*, 577)

A similar sense of entrapment is conveyed in 'Coming up Oxford Street; Evening', in which Hardy describes, with cumulative harsh imagery, the glaring sun from the west reflecting from the windows the *bric-à-brac* of the commercial world, dazzling a city clerk 'Who sees no escape to the very verge of his days / From the rut of Oxford Street into open ways' (*CP*, 680). The narrowness of city lives is developed in 'An East-End Curate', which reveals poignantly the pinched life of a young religious zealot among uncomprehending neighbours in 'A small blind street off East Commercial Road' (*CP*, 676).

Much used to be made of alleged obstacles to the comprehension of Hardy's poetry created by his choice of language. One Wordsworthian influence Hardy did not outgrow was his moral and aesthetic choice of what Wordsworth called in his Preface to *Lyrical Ballads* 'the real language of men'. Hardy's language serves the artistic demands of each individual poem. It involves among other features, coinages, archaisms, dialect words, pedantic usages, hyphenated words, grammatical misusages and wordplay. Virtually every poem throws up an example. His tactic of opening up the language of poetry to encompass various linguistic areas serves his fundamental aim of jolting the reader into accepting his angle of vision.

Hardy's diction and syntax are partly defined by his setting his face against the late-Romantic ideology of the hugely popular poets, Tennyson and Swinburne. The attraction of these poets for Hardy is evident in his ability to write a pastiche of Tennyson in 'Shut out that Moon', and in his memorialising of Swinburne in 'A Singer Asleep'. However, with self-conscious deliberation, he rejected their sonorous, cadenced diction and self-indulgent syntax, as 'An Ancient to Ancients' reveals:

> The bower we shrined to Tennyson,
>   Gentlemen,
> Is roof-wrecked; damps there drip upon
> Sagged seats, the creeper-nails are rust,
> The spider is sole denizen ...
>
> (*CP*, 659)

Hardy's tougher, bleaker view of life leads to his description of himself at the end of 'In Tenebris I' as 'One who, past doubtings all, / Waits in unhope' (*CP*, 153), where his coinage 'unhope' is precisely and successfully chosen. Syntactically, the conclusion to 'Midnight on the Great Western' is appropriately awkward, as Hardy endeavours to develop his observation of a child travelling alone, with a label of identification, into a significant metaphor:

> Knows your soul a sphere, O journeying boy,
>   Our rude realms far above,
> Whence with spacious vision you mark and mete
> This region of sin that you find you in,
>   But are not of?
>
> (*CP*, 483)

Hardy's astonishing technical versatility has won the admiration of major poets from Ezra Pound and Cecil Day Lewis to Philip Larkin. Among other genres he employs the lyric, narrative, ballads, and the sonnet. He also moves easily between the amplitude of dramatic monologue and the compression of imagism. He experiments continually with an ingenious variety of stanza forms and rhyme schemes, rejecting the fluidity of contemporary poetry for his own idiosyncratic style, based on a real understanding of the variety of speech rhythms and registers. Each individual poem is designed to express in its language and form, and with utter honesty, Hardy's impressions of life. Therein lies their authority, expressed so profoundly in the conclusion of his final poem, 'He Resolves to Say No More':

> And if my vision range beyond
> The blinkered sight of souls in bond,
>   – By truth made free –
>   I'll let all be,
> And show to no man what I see.
>
>   (*CP*, 887)

Further reading

Among critics interested in poetic influences on Hardy, Hands (1995) argues convincingly for Hardy's turning away from the Romantics and their legacy among Victorian poets, and Taylor (1988) shows how Hardy developed from imitation 'through modified convention to original forms' (Taylor 1988: 78). Taylor has also written a comprehensive survey of Hardy's poetic career (1981), in which he argues for a pattern of development in his work, based on his main achievement, the 'meditative lyric'. Taylor's book also includes an extensive analysis of Hardy's war poetry. Hynes (1961) was the first critic to engage fulllength with Hardy's poetry, and to tackle the thorny issues of his philosophy and his style. Marsden (1969) offers a sound introduction, and writes perceptively about Hardy's language. The authority on Hardy's language, however, is Taylor (1993), who explores the relationship between Hardy's literary language and Victorian philology. He discusses the self-conscious heterogeneity of Hardy's language, which challenges contemporary language from within, and is also involved in his scrutiny of class. Richardson (1977) is interested in Hardy's ideas, especially about necessity and possibility, and he considers Hardy's affinities with Browning. Buckler (1983) relates Hardy's *Life* to his poetry, arguing for his transformation of the confessional into the dramatic, and attending perceptively to the individual voices in his poems. Larkin (1966) acknowledges Hardy's influence on him, which led him to reject Yeats as his model. Davie (1973) in an important book argues that, compared with the modernists, Hardy's is a quietist poetry of withdrawal, and has been a pernicious influence on succeeding generations of poets. Davie also pays attention to Hardy's craftsman-ship. Ward (1991) is also interested in influences, tracing Hardy's place in an English line from Wordsworth and Clare through to the Movement poets, particularly Larkin. From a socialist perspective, Lucas (1986) extols Hardy as a poet of community and human solidarity, while the materialist Widdowson (1996), tackling the vexed question of the establishment of Hardy's poetic 'canon', convincingly suggests that looking carefully at poems outside it reveals a more interesting and complex poet. Zietlow (1974) offers a comprehensive examination of the poetry, divided according to type of poem, arguing for the human-ising influence of Hardy's idealism. Paulin (1975), in arguably the best study, examines in depth Hardy's aesthetic perception, taking account of his positivism and scepticism, and produces a number of detailed readings; while Harvey (1995), explores the relation between Hardy's imagination and his existential humanism, and argues for his occasional visionary liberation.

(e) *THE DYNASTS*

Hardy's interest in the Napoleonic period originated in his boyhood **[7, 28, 101, 151]** and his first tentative thoughts about a work with a vast European setting appeared in a note in 1874. Subsequently, he researched the period diligently. Hardy's conception of *The Dynasts* **[42–3]**, a hugely ambitious attempt to chronicle the Napoleonic Wars, gradually evolved from a narrative composed of ballads that concen-trated on Napoleon's early career. The form that Hardy's idea finally took was that of an epic verse-drama encompassing Napoleon's rise and fall and its catastrophic consequences.

One of Hardy's triumphs is his deliberately ambivalent portrayal of Napoleon as a charismatic, courageous leader, who is also a megalo-maniac seeking to subdue Europe. Unaffected by the widespread terror and suffering he has unleashed, he is nevertheless subject to nightmares about the officers he has been obliged to sacrifice. As Hardy records Napoleon's reduction, especially after the Battle of Borodino, from an imperial figure to one of simply human scale, he takes on a tragic dimension. Through a vision of the appalling carnage he has caused, and the protesting gaze of his dead officers, he comes to recognise the ironic gulf between his view of his destiny and that preordained for him by history. He gains some understanding of the operation of the Will: 'Why hold me my own master, if I be / Ruled by the pitiless Planet of Destiny?' (*D*, 3.6.3).

The major characters in Hardy's great drama are historical. With conscious patriotism, he introduces heroes such as Nelson, Sir Arthur Wellesley (later Duke of Wellington) and Sir John Moore, as well as Marshall Ney and General Kutuzov, representing the French and the Russians. There is also a host of figures – royal, military and political, as well as ordinary folk – all caught up in the cataclysm. Hardy was concerned both with the mysterious forces of history that energised whole nations, and with the question of what the historical process achieved. Examining these issues involves a double perspective. There is his dramatisation of the war with Napoleon, and at the same time his presentation of the observation of that action by an Overworld peopled by Spirits, who represent Hardy's epic machinery. This visualising frame is the source of cosmic irony, especially the objective commentary of the Spirit of the Years and the sympathetic commentary of the Spirit of the Pities, one seeing history as a web being spun without direction, and the other regarding it as a meliorist process. These act as a powerful counterpoint to the tragic human drama as it unfolds.

Hardy's compassion is engaged both for the slaughtered fighting men and for the civilians whose lives are blighted by Napoleon's devastation of whole regions of Europe from the battlefields of western Spain to Borodino and Moscow. Hardy's horror at the waste of war extends to a poignant consideration, by the Chorus of the Years, of the destruction not only of men, but also of animals, insects and flowers on the battlefield of Waterloo. In order to encompass not only Waterloo, but also Moscow, London and rural Dorset, corresponding to Hardy's concept of humanity as a great panoramic web, he experiments with narrative point of view, describing scenes from the perspective of enormous height; an artistic venture which, in its scope, flexibility and objectivity, anticipates cinema:

> Europe is disclosed as a prone and emaciated figure, the Alps shaping like a backbone, and the branching mountain-chains like ribs, the peninsular plateau of Spain forming a head ... The point of view then sinks downwards through space, and draws near to the surface of the perturbed countries, where the peoples, distressed by events which they did not cause, are seen writhing, crawling, heaving, and vibrating in their various cities and nationalities.
>
> (D, 3: Fore Scene)

The Dynasts is governed by a structure of philosophy not dissimilar to that of Edward von Hartmann in his Philosophy of the Unconscious (English translation 1884) and Arthur Schopenhauer in The World as

Will and Idea (English translation 1890), who emphasised the human will as a means to understanding. The Immanent Will **[27, 43, 121, 126]** of *The Dynasts* is a force that is essentially the sum of all wills, which works obscurely and imperceptibly, without either emotional or moral sense. The hundreds of thousands caught up in the war, even Napoleon, whatever their own apparent intentions, are in fact acting out the unconscious Will. The Immanent Will is immune to the universal human suffering that is the result of its tragic operation. However, Hardy believed that in the distant future it *may* evolve some degree of consciousness, some awareness of the human tragedy, and work to ameliorate it. The final word is given to the Chorus of the Pities:

> But – a stirring thrills the air
> Like to sounds of joyance there,
>   That the rages
>   Of the ages
> Shall be cancelled, and deliverance offered from the darts that
>   were,
> Consciousness the Will informing, till It fashion all things
>   fair!
>
> (*D*, 3: After Scene)

In 1914 Hardy commented to his wife that had he foreseen the Great War, he would not have ended *The Dynasts* on a note of melioristic optimism.

Although *The Dynasts* was produced in Hardy's own lifetime, he insisted that it was for 'mental performance', and the reader's visual imagination is heavily involved in cooperating with Hardy's dramatisation of history. *The Dynasts* involves many modes of writing, including dialogue, stage directions, dumb shows and songs, in addition to panoramic shots of historical events. While some of the dramatic scenes are compelling, the extensive counterpointing of the historical narrative by the Overworld reduces its effectiveness, and so too does the extensive prosaic narrative. However, the commentaries of the Spirits, which express some of Hardy's own ideas, occasionally make a powerful emotional impact.

Further reading

Hardy's major poetic work has attracted limited critical interest. It has been regarded as a quarry for his most important ideas. Southerington

(1971) examines the thinking that informs it as both drama and philosphical poem. Dean (1977) has a convincing study of Hardy's use of various planes of vision, using the analogy of the Victorian diorama, in order to include a double show of the war and its celestial spectators. Orel (1963) is concerned with its divergence from classical epics in its invention of celestial machinery, its debased hero, and its anti-war stance. Wright (1967) examines exhaustively Hardy's use of his extensively researched source material. Morrell (1965) an existential humanist, sees even in this text a positive margin for the exercise of human will, while Miller (1970), in his structuralist phase, regards it as evidence of Hardy's strategy of using detached and objective narrators as a way of exploring reality through fictive indirection. There is a brief dissident analysis in Armstrong (1993), who argues that attending to the grotesque characteristics of *The Dynasts* reveals it to be an unheroic study of power. Orel (1979) also has an interesting essay on what this work meant to Hardy.

(f) *THE LIFE AND WORK OF THOMAS HARDY*

The first biography of Hardy, written by his wife Florence, and known since its publication in a single volume in 1933 as *The Life of Thomas Hardy* [49–50], was in fact an elaborate deception, for it was ghosted by Hardy himself. It is really a third person autobiography, which carefully creates the illusion of a disinterested record, presenting itself as a conventional official biography.

An intensely private person, Hardy resented the intrusions of journalists, hated speculation about the relationship between his life and his writings, and as he became increasingly famous he fended off enquirers in pursuit of material for biographies. Eventually, however, he succumbed to the coaxing of Florence and his friend Sydney Cockerell and decide to pre-empt the possible appearance of somewhat critical biographies after his death, by publishing an authoritative work of his own.

Hardy and Florence divided responsibility for the research; he looked through his notebooks, while she made notes based on conversations with him. Hardy drafted the manuscript, which Florence typed and then destroyed. Hardy's passion for secrecy was such that his extensive revisions for the printer were made in the handwriting he had used as a practising architect. All but the final four chapters were written by

Hardy. Two of these were completed by his wife from preliminary work, while the concluding two chapters, based mainly on his memoranda book, were hers alone.

Hardy's *Life* is designed to present a portrait of a successful author at the height of his fame. Written from that perspective, it is circumspect and sometimes includes a measure of deception. Hardy is very much concerned to be remembered as a major poet (and the author of his masterwork *The Dynasts*), so it is not surprising to find him assiduously creating that image for himself. It is strange, however, in the light of the care that he took in revising his novels, to read his assessment of his fiction as popular work, which was written merely for an income.

Not only does Hardy show little interest in the novels, but he disavows the existence of any autobiographical elements in them. He goes to great lengths, for instance, to conceal any connection between himself and Emma Gifford and the characters Stephen Smith and Elfride Swancourt, in the early novel, *A Pair of Blue Eyes*; just as at the end of his writing career he strenuously denied any autobiographical content in *Jude the Obscure*. At other points in the *Life*, the typescript revisions reveal that Hardy reined in any impulse to give away too much of his private self, for instance deleting a romantic thought about Julia Augusta Martin, who was close to him as a child, and whom he later encountered as a young man in London.

Florence took advantage of Hardy's permission to intervene in the text. She omitted a number of Hardy's intemperate outbursts against critics under whose attacks he had smarted. She also reduced the diary entries that recorded notable figures whom he had met in London society. However, at the last minute she also included information sent her by Sir James Barrie, on whom she was relying for advice, which offer glimpses of Hardy's intense emotional life; his silent worship of the wealthy farmer's daughter Louisa Harding, about whom he wrote three poems in later life, and his overwhelming sense of despair when he read the negative criticism of his first published novel *Desperate Remedies* in the *Spectator*.

It is now possible to get closer to Hardy's original autobiographical intentions, since Michael Millgate reconstructed the text from surviving typescripts and published it in 1984 as *The Life and Work of Thomas Hardy*, over Hardy's own name. Hardy's projection of himself as an important public figure derives its authority in part from the accumulation of facts, attested to by many quotations (not all of them accurate), principally from diaries, letters, and notebooks. Prominent among them are lists of the important people he encountered in London society, including aristocrats, politicians and famous literary figures.

However, by contrast a private matter such as his honeymoon with Emma is dismissed as a 'short visit to the Continent' (*LW*, 104), and the growing problems of his first marriage are ignored. Also omitted is his significant relationship with Florence Henniker.

Hardy's extreme sensitivity to his humble social origins resulted in an extraordinarily brief coverage of the influential early years at Higher Bockhampton and at Dorchester. He mentions only the immediate members of his family, and makes much of his distant noble ancestry, presenting the Hardys as an important local family in decline; while he perverts the truth in claiming that the Giffords favoured Emma's marriage with him, for in fact it was opposed on the grounds of his lower class status. The *Life* is essentially a work of fiction, created out of the materials of Hardy's life, in order to preserve for posterity the image of the great man of letters. It is ironic that because Hardy destroyed the documents used in the construction of the *Life*, while it is an important biographical resource, it is also an unreliable narrative.

Further reading

Buckler (1980) offers an illuminating essay on Hardy's construction of a textual self-image in the *Life*. Gregor and Irwin (1984), consider Hardy's *Life* as both the story of a writer's life and an account of his life. Rosemarie Morgan (1988) argues that in spite of Hardy's creation of a public persona, inscribed in his text are clues to his private self. The major work is Millgate (1984), which includes a comprehensive Introduction. Millgate has restored what Hardy originally wrote, removing his wife's additions, which appear as an appendix.

PART III

CRITICISM

This section of the book offers accounts of the major critical approaches to Hardy's writing, giving weight to significant topics and issues. In the long period from the close of Hardy's career as a novelist up to Albert J. Guerard's pivotal book (1949) that pointed out Hardy's anti-realism, critical studies endorsed the view of Hardy as a realist, a tragic writer and the creator of Wessex. The Modernists' response was divided between enthusiasm (Virginia Woolf, 1932 and D.H. Lawrence, 1936) and puzzled disdain (F.R. Leavis, 1932 and 1948). However, the 1940s were ushered in by the Hardy Centenary issue of the *Southern Review* (1940), which included laudatory essays. Especially important were those by W. H. Auden on the poetry, and by Morton Dauwen Zabel on the aesthetic of the fiction.

The 1950s saw new directions in Hardy criticism, stimulated by the continuing rise of English studies in the universities, and by John Crowe Ransom's book, *The New Criticism* (1941), which by the 1950s had launched a movement bearing its name. Its methodology, based on the close reading of poetry, excluded other disciplines, such as history or philosophy. Its liberal humanist slant, with its emphasis on individualism and on moral values, was in conflict with the countervailing ideology of Marxist criticism, oriented towards sociology and history. Marxist criticism had existed before, but it gathered momentum in the 1950s and continued to be developed and refined during the rest of the century. Under the stimulus of the New Criticism, the 1960s and 1970s saw the rise of humanist formalism, which was drawn to the values of individualism and the integrity of the organic society in Hardy's work, although the picture is many-stranded. The 1970s also saw the development of structuralism, a theory that was applied to Hardy in an endeavour to identify the hidden structure within individual works which permits a comprehensive understanding of his *oeuvre*.

The 1980s witnessed radical advances in the theorisation of the study of literature in the universities. It had begun in France in the 1960s and it made a large impact on the higher education establishments of Britain and America. New life was breathed into psychoanalytic and Marxist theory, while structuralism gave way to post-structuralism. The stability of the text as a focus of study was challenged by deconstruction, a theory developed by the French philosopher, Jacques Derrida, which represented a complete fracture with the old liberal-formalist mode of reading. Coherence and unity were seen as illusory and readers were liberated to aim at their own meanings. Hardy's texts were at the centre of these theoretical movements, including one that came to prominence in the 1980s, feminism. Feminism had gradually gathered momentum as a cultural and political force in the preceding two decades, but its academic base now lay in newly established women's studies courses in universities. Some of its methodologies derive from Marxist cultural criticism, while others draw their energy from broader post-structuralist theory.

In the 1980s, Marxist criticism received renewed impetus and further developed the reaction against the traditional humanist construction of Hardy as the creator of a timeless Wessex. Marxism is a methodology that finds embedded in realist texts the representation of a whole society, and studies its internal contradictions for the reflection of the history of class struggle. The radical diversity of Hardy criticism in the 1980s co-existed, however, with sophisticated examples of more traditional studies.

By the conclusion of the 1980s, as the process of splintering into various political and theoretical groupings continued, the dominant tradition of liberal humanist criticism had been dislodged from its position of cultural supremacy. In the 1990s new approaches to Hardy drew widely upon, among others, psychoanalytic theorists, such as Jacques Lacan, and Marxist theorists, such as Fredric Jameson and Louis Althusser; while feminist theory remained strongly influential.

(a) TRAGEDY

Like other nineteenth-century writers, Hardy inherited a tradition of Classical and Renaissance tragedy, which belonged to the theatre, and which drew in different ways on a framework of religious belief. The intellectual climate of the period in which Hardy lived did not offer the Christian cosmos of the Renaissance, nor since the universe was empty, the gods of Aeschylus and Sophocles. Modern tragedy was seen increasingly as having its origins in contemporary society, suffering having now a merely human scale, and embodied within it were elements of realism, satire and comedy.

Hardy's remarks on tragedy in the *Life* reflect his preoccupation with the different facets of human experience that he was exploring in various novels. The picture that emerges is of a restless experimenter. A comment of April 1878, when he had completed *The Return of the Native* **[66–71]**, summarises the thrust of its tragic action:

A Plot, or Tragedy, should arise from the gradual closing in of a situation that comes of ordinary human passions, prejudices, and ambitions, by reason of the characters taking no trouble to ward off the disastrous events produced by the said passions, prejudices, and ambitions.

(LW, 123)

Thinking about the patterns of fate and the relation between fate and character in *The Mayor of Casterbridge* **[71–6]**, Hardy notes that: 'a tragedy exhibits a state of things in the life of an individual which unavoidably causes some natural aim or desire of his to end in a catastrophe when carried out' (*LW*, 182). Hardy's interest in *The Woodlanders* **[77–82]** and *Tess of the d'Urbervilles* **[82–8]** in the social shaping of tragic outcomes is reflected in a bald comment of 1892: 'That which, socially, is a great tragedy, may be in Nature no alarming circumstance' (*LW*, 228). His preoccupation with the weight of social oppression in *Jude the Obscure* **[88–94]** led to this response to some of the reviews: 'Tragedy may be created by an opposing environment either of things inherent in the universe, or human institutions. If the former be the means exhibited and deplored, the writer is regarded as impious; if the latter, as subversive and dangerous' (*LW*, 290).

The first full-length book on Hardy, which appeared before *Jude the Obscure*, was that of Lionel Johnson (1894). Its discerning comments on Hardy's tragic practice laid a foundation for later critical commentary. Johnson's point of reference is Greek tragedy and the theory of Aristotle, and he draws attention to the tragic inexorability of Hardy's logic in *The Return of the Native*. But it is in *The Mayor of Casterbridge* that he finds Hardy's plot fulfilling 'the great demands of Aristotle' (Johnson 1894: 188) in its 'exact and relentless retribution' (Johnson 1894: 188).

However, Johnson is aware that Hardy has added 'the concerns of modern thought' (Johnson 1894: 52), which enhance the impressiveness of the novels, as his 'tragic, passionate figures' (Johnson 1894: 52) are troubled by modern anxieties. For the most part, Hardy integrates classical tragedy and modern subtlety of thought successfully, but in *Tess of the d'Urbervilles*, which Johnson examines closely, he finds a bitterness absent from Aeschylus, who has faith in divine justice. Johnson objects to Hardy's scientific rationalism, and also to his emphasis on determinism as the mainspring of the tragedy:

> But, winning and appealing as she seems, there remains in the background that haunting and disenchanting thought, that upon the determinist principle, she could not help herself: she fulfilled a mechanical destiny. There is nothing tragic in that, except by an illusion: like any other machine, she 'did her work', and that is all

147

... The tragedy of Tess does indeed rouse in us 'pity and fear': it does indeed purge us of 'pity and fear': but with what a parody of Aristotle!

(Johnson 1894: 244–5)

Another notable landmark in Hardy criticism, D.H. Lawrence's essay (1936) tackles Hardy's tragic vision from the point of view of his own preoccupations as a writer. Lawrence's penetrating psychological interpretation of human sexuality argues that Hardy's characters are striving blindly for some form of self-definition against the oppressive forces of society. One element of Hardy's tragic power resides in his understanding of the consequences of social rebellion:

This is the tragedy of Hardy, always the same: the tragedy of those who, more or less pioneers, have died in the wilderness whither they had escaped for free action, after having left the walled security, and the comparative imprisonment, of the established convention.

(Lawrence 1936 in Draper 1975: 65)

A second source of Hardy's tragic profundity, for Lawrence, is his comprehension of nature. Lawrence identifies Egdon Heath as the 'great, tragic power' (Lawrence 1936 in Draper 1975: 65) of *The Return of the Native*. It is the source of instinctual life, from which humanity separates itself at its peril. In his ability to locate the modern social dilemmas of his characters in the context of the mythic dimensions of the natural universe, 'this setting behind the small action of his protagonists the terrific action of unfathomed nature' (Lawrence 1936 in Draper 1975: 71), as he does in *The Return of the Native, Tess of the d'Urbervilles* and *Jude the Obscure,* Hardy stands among the great tragic writers, Shakespeare, Sophocles and Tolstoy. However, his tragic authority is muted by the submission of his characters to social regulation:

... Anna, Eustacia, Tess or Sue – what was there in their position that was necessarily tragic? Necessarily painful it was, but they were not at war with God, only with Society. Yet they were all cowed by the mere judgment of man upon them, and all the while by their own souls they were right. And the judgment of men killed them, not the judgment of their own souls or the judgment of Eternal God.

(Lawrence 1936 in Draper 1975: 72)

A counterweight to Lawrence's persuasive rhetoric is a subtle study by Jean R. Brooks (1971), embracing the range of Hardy's writing. A formalist work in the liberal humanist tradition, it defines Hardy's uniquely multiple-faceted vision of experience as 'poetic', and its theoretical discussion is supported by extensive textual analysis that offers a modern, existential humanist account of Hardy's tragic vision.

Brooks argues that Hardy's writing, as in the comic scene in *The Mayor of Casterbridge*, when the furmity woman confronts Henchard in the courtroom, is close to the Absurdist form of tragi-comedy, or comi-tragedy.

> The dissonance of the multiple vision dramatically enacts Hardy's metaphysic of man's predicament as a striving, sensitive, imperfect individual in a rigid, non-sentient, absurd cosmos, which rewards him only with eternal death.
>
> (Brooks 1971: 14)

The tragic greatness of Hardy's heroes is life-enhancing, yet flawed by a vulnerability that renders them tragically unsuited to their situation, such as Jude's sexual impulses and self-degradation. For all their individuality, Brooks suggests, Hardy's characters with their tragic strength are types interacting ritually with fate. But while 'Hardy's poetic pattern stresses the action of fate, it does so to stress too the human responsibility to deflect fate from its path before it is too late' (Brooks 1971: 18–19).

The core of Brooks's account of Hardy's tragic vision is her perception of his existential humanism:

> Hardeian man, sustained only by his own qualities as a human being, defies the chaotic void as Hellenic and Shakespearean man, placed in reference to cosmic myth, defied powers which were, if cruel and unknowable, at least *there* to be defied.
>
> (Brooks 1971: 16)

This, says Brooks, makes Hardy's authentic tragic voice important to the modern world. Whether it be Giles Winterborne's selfless love, or Eustacia Vye's self-assertion:

> ... the sense of tragic waste is tempered by tragic joy because in the tragic confrontation with futility and absurdity Hardy affirms some of the highest values men and women can achieve. ... These

values remain unchanged when the people who embodied them are destroyed, and whether the gods are alive or dead.

(Brooks 1971: 15)

Jeannette King's starting-point (1978) is different. Her book involves the exploration of the effect of theories of tragedy on the fiction of George Eliot, Thomas Hardy and Henry James. She investigates how these writers attempt to accommodate the novel form to the creation of realistic tragedy, and how in different ways they seek to bring classical models and concepts into artistic relationship with modern tragic experience.

Her study of Hardy begins with his knowledge of the *Agamemnon* and *Oedipus*, his Aristotelian conviction that *peripeteia,* or reversal, is the basis of tragedy, producing a cyclical pattern in which the hero has to confront his past. King also bases her discussion on Aristotle's belief in the central importance of plot in creating tragedies of situation, a view that Hardy shared. Referring to Hardy's reference to Sophocles in *The Woodlanders,* and to his quotation from Aeschylus at the end of *Tess of the d'Urbervilles,* King concludes that in Hardy's fiction 'Heredity and environment, character and society, are each conceived as modern Fates' (King 1978: 26), but that he also extends the novel and re-focuses tragedy by evoking pity and fear for humble characters suffering class oppression.

Each of Hardy's novels, argues King, may be seen as an experiment with tragic form. *The Return of the Native* accommodates heroic tragedy (Eustacia Vye) and modern tragedy (Clym Yeobright); *The Mayor of Casterbridge* reveals the unified form of Greek tragedy; *Tess of the d'Urbervilles,* a 'typically female tragedy' (King 1978: 120), offers an Aristotelian tragedy of situation, informed by an Aeschylean belief in education through suffering. However, *Jude the Obscure* requires a new concept of tragedy because: 'the novel deliberately questions the traditional classical concepts of law and character in a way that points towards twentieth-century ideas of "modern tragedy" ' (King 1978: 121).

The view represented by King's study is opposed to that of Dale Kramer (1975):

… though *The Mayor of Casterbridge* is modelled to a large degree on Aristotle and though Hardy attempted to employ the unities of time and place in *The Return of the Native,* he does not adhere consistently to Aristotle's ideas on tragedy or to those of any clearly defined school.

(Kramer 1975: 14)

In Kramer's view, the application of Aristotelian criteria to Hardy's fiction has given impetus to the post-New Critical emphasis on the rhetoric and unity of the novel, shifting the search for the core of the novel's tragic experience to the substance of the text. Kramer employs a sophisticated formalist argument, which seeks to show how: 'Hardy in each novel uses a dominant aesthetic feature, or organising principle, that informs the entire work and creates the peculiar quality of tragedy that distinguishes it' (Kramer 1975: 21).

Kramer finds Hardy's first effort at tragedy, *The Return of the Native*, his least successful; 'a student's idea of tragedy, with Hardy borrowing features from and alluding to classical stories' (Kramer 1975: 69). However, it is unique because it has two protagonists, Eustacia Vye and Clym Yeobright, who 'inhabit different psychic worlds and evoke from us different tragic reactions' (Kramer 1975: 50). In the Aristotelian scheme of *The Mayor of Casterbridge*, Dale Kramer discerns two structures: the individual struggle that is an aspect of the cycle of change within society, and the tragedy of Michael Henchard. Henchard's second violation of the natural order reaches beyond the cyclical structure of his rise and fall and produces Hardy's sole example of universal tragedy.

For Kramer, *The Woodlanders*, which begins the process of Hardy's 'democratization of tragedy' (Kramer 1975: 136), is the most pessimistic of the Wessex novels. Hardy's reference to Sophocles suggests that the humble surroundings of Little Hintock have the potential for universal tragedy, and Hardy's complex employment of the narrative point of view ensures that no one character occupies the central tragic role. Society is identified as the tragic cause, thwarting the happiness of a diverse group of characters unable to reconcile their desires with its demands. Tragic experience in *Tess of the d'Urbervilles* is different, for in this novel, Kramer argues, Hardy is concerned with defending the integrity and absolute moral value of the individual consciousness against judgements based on social conventions. The unique quality of its tragedy is that 'within the pages of the novel Tess is tragic only to herself. To others, she is a puzzling daughter, a temptingly lovely girl and woman, an image of purity, a fallen woman' (Kramer 1975: 117).

The form of Hardy's final tragic novel, *Jude the Obscure*, Kramer suggests, reflects his concern with the relativism of judgement which weakens 'the self-validation of tragic consciousness' (Kramer 1975: 136). Paradoxically, this seemingly doctrinaire novel achieves the objectivity and balance of tragedy through authorial distance, because the 'relative validity of the several viewpoints of the characters and the narrator is supported by the lack of absolutes in the story' (Kramer 1975: 156). This tragedy presents profound issues: 'Jude confronts basic and ultimate matters – the relation between the individual and a universe that seems to offer him no genuine freedom or opportunity for happiness – and he confronts those issues in a context that permits no answers' (Kramer 1975: 161).

(b) WESSEX

The fictional county of Wessex was created in *Far from the Madding Crowd* **[61–6]**. It was subsequently developed into the setting for the majority of Hardy's novels, short stories and poems. He mapped his personal psyche onto the landscape of his 'partly real, partly dream-country', as he calls it in the Preface to the 1895 edition of *Far from the Madding Crowd*, where he also describes how it originated:

> The series of novels I projected being mainly of the kind called local, they seemed to require a territorial definition of some sort to lend unity to their scene. Finding that the area of a single county did not afford a canvas large enough for this purpose, and that there were objections to an invented name, I disinterred the old one.
>
> (quoted in Ian Gregor 1974: 145)

The old Wessex was the Saxon kingdom situated, after the Roman occupation, in the south of England. Hardy's Wessex is centred in his native county of Dorset (South Wessex), with the county town of Casterbridge (Dorchester) at its social hub. Topographically and socially it is a varied region, with a range of agriculture, occupations and distinctive local cultures. It includes the university city of Christminster, the barrack city of Melchester, as well as the seaside resorts of Sandbourne and Budmouth. Hardy also draws on the deep and varied cultural history of his chosen region, but as he made clear in his Preface to *Far from the Madding Crowd*, his county was also 'a modern Wessex of railways, the penny post, mowing and reaping machines, union workhouses, lucifer matches, labourers who could read and write, and National School children'.

His creation of Wessex is based on realistic social observation. He records unsentimentally the economic basis of rural life, the functioning of the rural economy, the subsistence level of the labourer, and the socio-economic relations between these workers and their landlords. He also records the process of change in the advent of more efficient mechanised farming. As a countryman he could see, as he remarked in his essay 'The Dorsetshire Labourer', that it would not be in the interest of farm workers to 'remain stagnant and old-fashioned'.

Hardy quickly recognised the commercial opportunity that his fictional county afforded. He advertised 'Wessex' when new editions of his novels were published, and when he was choosing titles for volumes of short stories and poems. He even provided readers of his novels with a Wessex map. It is this Wessex that is the subject of an entire chapter in Lionel Johnson (1894). Hardy's fidelity to life receives high praise. The 'exact truth' (Johnson 1894: 114) of the landscape, the ordinary world of rural work, and the coherence of his Wessex, are perceived as the basis for the tragic power of *The Return of the Native* [66–71] and *Tess of the d'Urbervilles* [82–8], novels that depend on a clash between rural and urban cultures. These emphases were to characterise critical discussions of Wessex until relatively recently. Lord David Cecil (1943) finds in Hardy's Wessex an idyllic world of tradition and stability, so attractive in the period of social upheaval and anxiety in which Cecil was writing:

> Rural Wessex was still feudal, pre-industrial Wessex, with its villages clustered round the great houses and church, with its long-established families and time-hallowed customs, its whole habit of mind moulded by the traditions of the past.
>
> (Cecil 1943: 148)

Of course, this is a carefully edited version of Hardy's Wessex, but one essentially followed later by Irving Howe (1968), a mainstream liberal humanist critic, who finds a Wordsworthian presence in the natural world of a Wessex that represents 'the seemliness of an ordered existence, of all that is natural, rooted and tried' (Howe 1968: 17), where 'there survives the memory of a life in which nature and society are at peace' (Howe 1968: 17), an English countryside of which 'the Wessex novel forms a prolonged celebration' (Howe 1968: 19).

Douglas Brown, in an influential work (1954), sought to redress the balance by studying Hardy's presentation of Wessex as a historical rural society. Brown uses documentary evidence of the depression of British agriculture through the various impact of free trade, poor harvests and cheap imports [8, 178]. He also uses close textual analysis to support his historical readings. However, his conclusion that *The Return of the Native* concerns the rejection of urban life, *The Mayor of Casterbridge* [71–6] records agricultural decay, and *Tess of the d'Urbervilles* signals the defeat of a community, depends on his thesis that Hardy is dismayed by the invasion of Wessex by an alien culture:

His protagonists are strong-natured countrymen, disciplined by the necessities of agricultural life. He brings into relation with them men and women from outside the rural world, better educated, superior in status, yet inferior in human worth. The contact occasions a sense of invasion, of disturbance ... and the theme of urban invasion declares itself more clearly as the country, its labour, its people and its past consolidate their presence ... This pattern records Hardy's dismay at the predicament of the agricultural community in the south of England during the last part of the nineteenth century and at the precarious hold of the agricultural way of life.

(Brown 1954: 30)

Douglas Brown's view is developed further by George Wing (1980). For Wing, the processes of change and invasion eventually affect people and places throughout the whole of Wessex. Also following Brown in drawing on historical evidence, and in reinforcing the view of Wessex as accurately representing the severe economic conditions in agriculture, is William J. Hyde (1958), though he cautions against seeing Hardy in terms of straightforward realism. This caution is heeded by Maire A. Quinn (1976), for whom Hardy's presentation of Wessex is permeated by literary effects that proceed from his anxiety not to be designated as merely a provincial novelist. Hence his incorporation of erudite references, his overt displays of craftsmanship, his cosmopolitanism, and his attempt to give universal significance to the local.

Raymond Williams (1973), in a penetrating essay, draws attention to the issue of regionalism in Hardy. He sees Hardy's preoccupation with the social forces of education and mobility implicit in the Wessex communities as part of his awareness of the wider impact of the non-regional: 'It is this centrality of change, and of the complications of change, that we miss when we see him as a regional novelist: the incomparable chronicler of his Wessex, the last voice of an old rural civilization' (Williams 1973: 239–40). Following Hardy, Williams stresses the modernity of Wessex, the inadequacy of the term 'peasant' to describe the complex structure of rural society, and the internal market forces and educational processes that were changing it. Hardy's affection for the old ways is of course part of the structure of his feeling for Wessex, but his understanding of change is sociological and psychological:

The profound disturbances that Hardy records cannot then be seen in the sentimental terms of neo-pastoral. The exposed and separated individuals, whom Hardy puts at the centre of his fiction, are only the most developed cases of a general exposure and separation. Yet they are never merely illustrations of this change in a way of life. Each has a dominant personal history, which in psychological terms bears a direct relation to the social character of change.

(Williams 1973: 254)

While Williams clearly regards Hardy's writing as separated from traditional regionalism, W.J. Keith (1988), in a lucid exploration of Hardy's regionalism, disagrees:

Against Williams, however, I would argue that this development does not make Hardy's novels any the less regional. By according the relation between regional and universal so important a place in his fiction, he was drawing attention to one of the most significant trends of the age ... he was bringing the regional dilemma to the forefront of the contemporary consciousness.

(Keith 1988: 88)

Hardy is placed within the historical development of the genre of the regional novel. His major contribution to it is seen as his creation of a series of novels, all of which centre on a particular geographical area, which offer a variety, but also allow scope for broader fictional possibilities.

Keith finds Hardy's claim to be the historian of Wessex substantiated less in the novels than in the short stories, the best of which are characterised by a narrator with a historical curiosity, a story linked to a particular place, or a narrative demonstrating communal memory. Like other critics, Keith finds Hardy preoccupied by change:

When we come to examine the regional elements in Hardy's novels, we find that a development is discernible in his presentation of the increasing tensions between country and town, between local traditions and national objectives, between dialect speech and 'standard English', between regional culture and a rootless cosmopolitanism. ... His Wessex is not a closed, immutable society; on the contrary, it is buffeted on all sides by the forces of change.

(Keith 1988: 100–1)

Keith's theme then is in a line of criticism that charts the decline of Wessex life. The migration of rural labour, in *Tess of the d'Urbervilles* and the destruction of Marygreen in *Jude the Obscure* **[88–94]**, signal both the end of the village regional community and the acceleration of a process of cultural dispossession:

> I believe we miss much of the significance of Hardy's work if we fail to recognize the multi-faceted ironies implicit in his presentation of increasingly anti-regional elements within a developing regional series.
>
> (Keith 1988: 102)

However, this historical emphasis, shared by critics such as Merryn Williams (1972), is concerned to avoid a schematic and reductive reading of the novels. She seeks to overturn earlier nostalgic views of rural society and uncover the social complexity of Wessex. Grounded in historical evidence, and contextualised by the work of rural writers such as Richard Jefferies, her study reveals Hardy's understanding of the complexity of the rural economy. However, her argument for Hardy's realism is based on a simple reflectionist assumption of the historical 'reality' of Wessex.

R.P. Draper (1985) suggests that Hardy succeeds in producing a regionalism that avoids idealisation and sentimentality; while Michael Millgate (1987) has usefully compared Hardy's Wessex with Faulkner's Yoknapatawpha, arguing that Hardy's Wessex gave authority to the value of regionalism by his creation of an autonomous and believable system of characters, language and social relationships. However, these humanist views are challenged by a materialist, Peter Widdowson (1989). Widdowson argues that Hardy's description of Wessex as a 'partly dream-country' suggests that it is really a landscape of the mind. He goes on to show how this landscape and the concept of English cultural identity have been hijacked for ideological purposes by liberal-humanist critics, a process accelerated by times of national crisis: 'His fiction thus comes to represent a mode of what we might call "humanist-realist-pastoral" ' (Widdowson 1989: 61). In a refreshing discussion, Widdowson argues that liberal-humanist critics' opposition to industrialisation and urbanisation has produced Wessex as a location of nostalgic pastoralism and essential Englishness. It is a process that began with early criticism, and may be seen differently inflected in Lord David Cecil's presentation of Hardy as occupying a place in the heritage of English literature stretching back to Shakespeare; in Douglas Brown's perception of Hardy's dismay at the decline of the rural community; in Irving Howe's sense of Wordsworthian harmony of nature and society; and even in Merryn Williams's unproblematic acceptance of the 'reality' of Hardy's historical Wessex. Widdowson asks rhetorically:

> ... to what, then, does Hardy's 'Wessex' allude? Was he writing about the 'universal' themes of Man, Fate, and Nature set in a mythic and elemental rural environment? Was he elegizing the loss of a 'peasant community' beset by Victorian capitalism and industrialism? Or was he, from his own contradictory *déclassé* and *déraciné* position of meritocratic, metropolitan, professional man of letters, refracting the historically determinate process of the transformation of the rural community of which he both was, and was not, a part?
>
> (Widdowson 1989: 199–200)

Widdowson argues strenuously for Hardy's understanding of this historical process at work in rural Wessex; poverty, exploitation, the dispossession of people from their homes, rural depopulation, and urban slums, all registered in precise sociological detail. Widdowson goes on to use Hardy's accurate eye for historical process as the basis for an examination of social class in his novels:

> Whatever else Hardy may have had in mind, their basic structural and textual crux was not so much 'Wessex' and the agricultural community, but the problematic relations of a class society in rapid change.
>
> (Widdowson 1989: 205)

As Widdowson's rhetorical question, quoted earlier, implies, his discussion places firmly, at the centre of Hardy's construction of Wessex, his preoccupation with his contradictory class position.

Simon Gatrell (1999) tackles the issue of the evolution in Hardy's *oeuvre* of a Wessex, which 'did not exist in the novelist's imagination when he first began to write' (Gatrell 1999: 19) and which only appeared in the form modern readers recognise with the production of his last novels. Working with the first editions of Hardy's texts, Gatrell reveals how, with the increasingly complex development of Wessex, the early novels were subsequently revised to fit in with what had grown into a much larger scheme.

The essential Wessex, Gatrell argues, is to be found in *Under the Greenwood Tree*, which concerns the threat to the traditional rural community. A reference to Casterbridge tenuously links the Cornish setting of *A Pair of Blue Eyes* to Wessex, while Wessex seems to represent

Dorset in *The Hand of Ethelberta*. The name 'Wessex' is first used in *Far from the Madding Crowd*, though its geographical extent remains unclear. In this novel a measure of continuity is introduced by the reappearance of Keeper Day from *Under the Greenwood Tree* and geographical realism is enhanced by the fact that Weatherbury is based on Puddletown.

Aspects of Wessex are delineated in subsequent novels; its society and social rituals in *The Return of the Native*, where the heath is 'quintessential Wessex' (Gatrell 1999: 23) and its unofficial history in *The Trumpet-Major*. Although *A Laodicean* and *Two on a Tower*, did not significantly develop Wessex, Hardy's short stories, such as 'The Distracted Preacher' and 'The Three Strangers' show his deepening sense of the profound bonds uniting a rural community.

After *The Mayor of Casterbridge* established Wessex as a social, and historical entity, it remained a point of reference, so that although the setting of *The Woodlanders* is remote, Hardy is careful to make clear that it is part of Wessex; and the idea of Wessex was confirmed publicly by the appearance of *Wessex Tales* in 1888. Gatrell points out that Wessex was first significantly extended beyond Dorset in *Tess of the d'Urbervilles*: 'So we can say with some confidence that in September or October of 1890 Hardy first formulated for himself the idea of Wessex as twentieth-century readers have been accustomed to experience it' (Gatrell 1999: 27), while the boundaries of the new Wessex are also established by the 'heights' in the poem 'Wessex Heights'.

With the publication of *The Wessex Novels of Thomas Hardy*, argues Gatrell, Hardy saw himself as the historian of a culturally cohesive Wessex. The early novels were revised to confirm to this comprehensive idea. Gatrell concludes that Hardy 'chose Wessex as a homogeneous historical object over Wessex as subjective process, and undertook the work of bringing *The Return of the Native*, *The Trumpet-Major*, *A Laodicean* – to mention three of the more recalcitrant texts – into the nineties pattern of Wessex' (Gatrell 1999: 31).

(c) HUMANIST FORMALISM

The ideology of liberal humanism found expression in the earliest reviews of Hardy's writing and remained a dominant force until the explosion of literary theory in the 1980s. It is a broad and still influential category. It endorses the moral value of the individual, and the strength of the human spirit. It prefers the integrity of an organic rural society to the anonymity and materialism of an urbanised and technological world. Applied to fiction, this ideology involves the naturalisation of the novel's world and its values, and the recognition of fictional character as presenting a unified subject.

An important strand in liberal humanist writing on Hardy has been influenced by New Criticism. A reaction against the impressionism of earlier criticism, and also opposed to contemporary historicism, Marxism and psychoanalytic criticism, among other competing methodologies, it is a programme based on the close reading of individual texts. It stresses the autonomy of the individual work, its creation of meaning internally through language and structure, and its organic unity. An early example of New Critical humanist criticism is John Holloway (1953), who discusses Hardy alongside other Victorian prophetic writers; Thomas Carlyle, John Henry Newman, Benjamin Disraeli, George Eliot and Matthew Arnold. Their humanist aim, partly philosophical and partly moral, was to 'express notions about the world, man's situation in it, and how he should live' (Holloway 1953: 1). In the case of Hardy, whose values remain unobtrusive, Holloway suggests that wisdom is acquired, not through logical thought, but through the structure of feelings in the novels which awakens understanding 'by the whole weave of a book' (Holloway 1953: 11).

Hardy regards Nature, in Holloway's view, as an organic unity, of which human life and society are microcosms, wholly subject to its governance. Thus his novels reveal a 'determined system of things which ultimately controls human affairs without regard for human wishes' (Holloway 1953: 281). Hardy's sense of this great web is evident in *The Woodlanders* **[77–82]**, the limiting effects of environment on human lives in *The Return of the Native* **[66–71]**, and the organic relation between a society and its surrounding landscape in *The Mayor of Casterbridge* **[71–6]**. A larger view emerges in *Tess of the d'Urbervilles* **[82–8]**, where South Wessex 'from the standpoint of human society [is] a single organism' (Holloway 1953: 275). *Jude the Obscure* **[88–94]** stands outside the view offered by these novels, argues Holloway, because of its limited treatment of Nature. The novels which most fully articulate Hardy's philosophy are *Far from the Madding Crowd* **[61–6]**, *The Return of the Native*, *The Woodlanders* and *Tess of the d'Urbervilles*. However, Hardy's moral position emerges in novel after novel. Right conduct involves living naturally, that is 'in continuity with one's whole biological and geographical environment' (Holloway 1953: 281), as do Gabriel Oak, Clym Yeobright, Diggory Venn and Giles Winterborne. His 'bad' characters are those who like Henry Knight in *A Pair of Blue Eyes* **[96–8]**, 'pursue some private self-generated dream instead' (Holloway 1953: 283). It follows that for Hardy the greatest disaster is for an individual to be rootless.

Holloway's critical method involves a Jamesian assumption about Hardy's artistic removal of the author's voice, allowing his view to emerge imperceptibly from the conflicting voices of his characters. But more importantly, it proceeds from a close reading of passages from the novels in which attention is paid to Hardy's figurative language – metaphor, symbolism and imagery – his dominant effect that carries the structure of feeling. Holloway finds the unifying relation between form and meaning in language, which enables him to incorporate Hardy's use of improbable incident, embarrassing in a 'thinker and a realist' (Holloway 1953: 247) into a symbolic pattern supporting Hardy's system of necessity. The socio-economic conditions of Hardy's plots are subordinated to proleptic imagery that foreshadows the course of events.

In Dorothy Van Ghent's pioneering study (1953), which covers a range of major novels from the eighteenth to the twentieth centuries, John Holloway's approach through language converges with the analysis of structure. Her idea of the relation between a novel's form and its function is:

> ... one complex pattern, or *Gestalt* ['form'], made up of component ones. In it inhere such a vast number of traits, all organised in subordinate systems that function under the governance of a single meaningful structure, that the nearest similitude for a novel is a 'world'.
>
> (Van Ghent 1953: 17)

The overall unity of the novel's form, its 'integral structure' (Van Ghent 1953: 17) is an indication of its quality, but for Van Ghent, unlike Holloway, symbolism does not take precedence over incidents: they are in a co-operative relationship as elements of pattern.

Like a number of other leading humanist formalists, Dorothy Van Ghent finds *Tess of the d'Urbervilles* a challenging text on which to deploy her methodology. And like them Van Ghent is concerned with realism, with Wessex, and with tragedy. Her reading of Tess's tragic heroism in terms of a mythology that links the 'spectacular destiny of the hero with the unspectacular common destiny' (Van Ghent 1953: 238) rests on her analysis of the novel's symbolism, which is found to have an organic relation to its larger structure. A telling instance is the accident with the mail cart that links together the whole sequence of events in Tess's tragedy. Van Ghent frees herself to focus on Hardy's symbolism by ignoring the intrusive narrative voice that offends against her aesthetic criteria, dismissing its pronouncements as 'bits of philosophic adhesive tape' (Van Ghent 1953: 238).

Dorothy Van Ghent insists simultaneously on the power of Hardy's realism and his symbolism, but the critical centre of her essay is her perception of an organic relation between his symbolism, his realistic presentation of the earth, and the mythical construction in which it is dramatised as an antagonist that obstructs human purposes. She also manages to link Hardy's realism and coincidentalism with the fatalism and belief in magic of the country folk, as a bridge between the mysterious, omnipresent earth and Tess's moral dilemma. Hardy's use of symbolism is identified as a magical strategy that allows the accommodation of the supernatural within his view of life.

Tony Tanner (1968) is also concerned with the relation between the form of the novel and the meaning of its tragic experience. Tanner's perception of the novel's Sophoclean profundity, focussed in the experience of Tess, is of humanity's place in a universe fundamentally in conflict with itself. For him, the ultimate mystery of experience is visualised symbolically, and in presenting it Hardy's detached observation achieves a necessary impersonality. This mystery is manifested in the novel's form through the extensive pattern of imagery of colour and movement which Tanner's subtle close reading reveals. Colour imagery has individualising and proleptic functions, which Tanner traces in Hardy's use of the colour red. Tanner's study of movement in the novel relates to a second aspect of its form, Hardy's use of the architectonic: 'the overall architecture of the novel is blocked out with massive simplicity in a series of balancing phases – The Maiden, Maiden No More, the Rally, the Consequence; and so on' (Tanner 1968: 220). By this means the story achieves the anonymity of the folk tale or the ballad. Hardy's lack of interest in the causative in his narrative, suggests Tanner, 'enhances the visibility of the most basic lineaments of the tale' (Tanner 1968: 220). Each phase of the novel, he notes, commences with a figure moving, beginning with Jack Durbeyfield and then focussing on Tess, thus underlining the schematic, reductive quality of Hardy's visualisation, which implies her place in a larger tragic world. Tess of the d'Urbervilles is also examined from a formalist perspective by David Lodge (1966). Lodge regards the novel as demanding the close reading the critic would give to poetry. He links his rigorous and lucid linguistic analysis of selected passages, notably the famous scene in the garden at Talbothays, to his formal interest in narrative patterns, and also to the problem of Hardy's two narrative voices, those of the creator and the pedant.

The humanist who sought to challenge these New Critical approaches was Roy Morrell (1965). His thesis is that a careful critical reading of Hardy's fiction, and of *The Dynasts* **[136–9]**, reveals that far from holding a fatalistic belief in a deterministic universe, Hardy had faith in the human capacity for choice, in the exertion of individual will, and that individuals who failed to assert their humanity were culpable. This provocative study runs counter to the established critical view of Hardy's pessimistic fatalism, established by William R. Rutland (1938), and developed by Harvey Curtis Webster (1947). Morrell argues convincingly for the dogged sagacity and realism of Gabriel Oak in *Far from the Madding Crowd*, who 'neither evades [reality] nor resigns himself to it; he makes something out of it' (Morrell 1965: 63). Even in *The Dynasts*, in spite of the operation of the Immanent Will, there remains a significant margin for independent human assertion, as exemplified in Wellington's tactics against Napoleon: 'Hardy's *Dynasts* certainly does not present us with a world in which human endeavour counts for nothing. The value of discipline, co-operation, and carefully timed effort is recognized clearly' (Morrell 1965: 84).

Morrell lays the blame for misreadings of Hardy partly at the door of the New Critics, exemplified primarily for Morrell by John Holloway, whom he castigates for distorting the novels through his focus on language, in particular through his focus on proleptic imagery, which is not in fact proleptic at all, and which in any case is the product of a limited methodology:

> The New Critics will have nothing but bored contempt for my simplicity in supposing that mere incidents can weigh in an argument against *images* – the latter being regarded as in some way more essentially part of the book, part of its 'weave'.
>
> (Morrell 1965: 18–19)

From the point of view of analysing character in action – incident or plot – *Tess of the d'Urbervilles* may be seen as the tragedy of Tess's failure to act, in 'choosing not to choose' (Morrell 1965: 91). Morrell argues that she continually postpones, lacking the moral courage to translate potential alternatives into actualities. Her quasi-mystical experience in the garden at Talbothays serves to reveal how much she has lost touch with reality. Roy Morrell offers an existential view of experience, in which fate and society play only a contributory part, where the tragedy arises from human weakness, and success, however modest, depends on the exercise of human will.

The most significant humanist formalist study of Hardy is that of
Ian Gregor (1974). His book is the culmination of earlier essays on
Hardy's work, and an extended development of the theme of an article
(1966). Gregor's approach is concerned with exploring the central
importance to his fiction of his perception of humanity as one great
network:

> When we come to reflect on the relationship that exists between
> the kind of fiction Hardy writes and the substance of that fiction,
> we find an interesting correspondence. On 4 March 1885 we find
> Hardy making an entry in his journal: 'The human race to be shown
> as one great network or tissue which quivers in every part when
> one point is shaken, like a spider's web if touched'. I would suggest
> that in that image we have a ruling idea in Hardy's development
> as a novelist, an idea which at once determines the shape of the
> fiction and its substance.
>
> (Gregor 1974: 33)

Gregor's subtle formalist examination of the major novels
approaches a poetic reading rather along the lines of Jean R. Brooks,
though with greater attention to the narrator and to the response of
the reader. Gregor proposes a flexible conception of fictional form in
Hardy, based on the story conceived of as an 'unfolding process' (Gregor
1974: 26) experienced by the reader both as a movement through the
novel and as a mode of revelation. For Gregor, the plot is 'mimetic of
Hardy's metaphysic ... an analogue both for the plots men make for
themselves, and for the plots over which they seem to have no control'
(Gregor 1974: 27). But the importance of the story is shared with that
of the narrator. A 'dialectic of feeling ... is operative between the
narrator and his narrative' (Gregor 1974: 29), into which the reader is
inserted, with the understanding that the 'narrator's reading [is] only
as sharp and as fitful as our own' (Gregor 1974: 32).

The coherence and unity of Hardy's major fiction, Gregor argues,
should not be sought in the novels' various strands of interest – ballad,
social history, contemporary science and philosophy – for Hardy's
description of his novels as a 'series of seemings' suggests a

> seeking for a truth whose form is always provisional, whose
> dynamic is the tension between the story-teller and the sage, the
> author and the reader, a tension which, for Hardy, was the essential
> condition for the imaginative vitality of the quest.
>
> (Gregor 1974: 33)

For Hardy, fiction, like a web, is a 'provisional design flung across the vacancy of miscellaneous experience' (Gregor 1974: 41). A corollary of Gregor's approach is his recognition that characters, ideas and the presence of a narrator, cannot be separated for the purposes of criticism, and he proceeds by close, sensitive readings that attend to the narrative voice.

Gregor explores the complex genesis of Wessex in *Far from the Madding Crowd* as a dialectic between a dream-country, as Hardy described it, and a utilitarian region. In *The Return of the Native*, Gregor argues, Hardy discovers the parameters of his imagined world, concerned with the evolution of consciousness and self-estrangement. In *The Mayor of Casterbridge* there is a movement towards the consideration of human relatedness in the connection between Henchard's private history and the history of Casterbridge and Wessex. From *The Woodlanders*, a novel without a dominating figure onwards, Gregor suggests, using Hardy's own reference in that novel to the 'great web of human doings' (Gregor 1974: 3) as his starting-point, Hardy examined human relatedness as part of a process that includes both sexual and economic possession. The distinctive rhythm of *Tess of the d'Urbervilles* is identified as the continuous oscillation between the world and the consciousness of an individual character, as Tess develops from subjectivism to an understanding of the social and economic forces of which she is the tragic victim. *Jude the Obscure*, Hardy's finest novel, Gregor argues, 'marks [Hardy's] furthest advance in fiction on two fronts: in its structure and style, and in the nature of its subject' (Gregor 1974: 136). In revealing how the endeavour of Jude and Sue to achieve personal freedom is thwarted by social forces, Hardy focuses on the portrayal of consciousness, and the formal implications of this involve the abandonment of plot: '*Jude the Obscure* is the only novel in which plot, the essence of Hardy's fiction in the past, is superseded by what the artist himself calls "a series of seemings" ' (Gregor 1974: 138), anticipating too in its focus on Jude's 'wandering ego' (Gregor 1974: 139), the procedures and concerns of modern fiction.

(d) STRUCTURALISM AND DECONSTRUCTION

The major structuralist study of Hardy is J. Hillis Miller (1970), which seeks to identify the underlying structure common to all his writing. Ranging over Hardy's works, Miller pursues the single pattern that unites them: 'distance and desire – distance as the source of desire and

desire as the energy behind attempts to turn distance into closeness'
(Miller 1970: xii). This dualistic pattern is a response to the death of
God, and to the 'definition of man as pure consciousness' (Miller 1970:
19). Hardy's characters are driven by an emotional emptiness to replace
separation and an inner void by presence, by the possession of another
person and the achievement of an integral self. Involved in a dance of
desire that dies with contact and sexual consummation, they are led
to a moment of illumination of the cause of their sufferings, but come
to an essentially modern 'suicidal passivity, a self-destructive will not
to will' (Miller 1970: 219); to the annihilation of consciousness sought
by Henchard, by Jude in his dying curse, and by Tess in the poem,
'Tess's Lament'.

Miller's strategy is to insert himself into the text through the
language he shares with the text, entering its texture of words, its
'threads and filaments' (Miller 1970: viii). He is of course aware of the
subjectivity of his readings. An essential aspect of his argument is that
Hardy exists only in the language of the voices he employs. In this
radical approach, Hardy is seen as exploring the real, which would
otherwise remain invisible, through fictive indirectness, distancing his
narrators from their stories and placing them in the role of detached
and objective, though also in an obvious sense present and sympathetic,
spectators of events. This strategy is even more in evidence in *The
Dynasts* **[136–9]**, where the detachment is achieved by the chorus of
spirits.

Miller's sophisticated thematic approach to Hardy, with its attention
to patterns of recurrence, is particularly illuminating as it is applied to
The Well-Beloved **[110–14]**, which is 'the fullest exploration of that
law of mediated desire in Hardy's work which dictates that love will
be inflamed by whatever separates the lover from his goal while at the
same time providing him indirect access to her' (Miller 1970: 175). In a
brilliant essay, Miller (1968) has also produced a structuralist analysis
of the major poem, 'Wessex Heights' **[127]**, pursuing in its language
the insistent pattern of repetition that characterises Hardy's work.
Through language the poet's mind 'becomes aware of itself and of its
texture' (Miller 1968: 340), as it endeavours to enact an escape from
the structure of space and time; the characteristic withdrawal of the
mind from life in Hardy's work. Miller finds in the language of the
fourth stanza, with its image of the chrysalis, a complex description of
the relation between past and present self: 'Human temporality is
characterized by a paradoxical combination of presence and absence,
continuity and discontinuity, similarity and difference' (Miller 1968:
351). The betrayals and self-betrayal associated with the lowlands in

the poem, a Hardyan obsession, are compounded by the suffering caused by the withdrawal of the love of the 'one rare fair woman', who has authenticated his existence. Miller draws together the strands of his argument by suggesting that the poem 'concludes with a choice of disengagement from life which is characteristic of Hardy's protagonists near the end of their lives' (Miller 1968: 355), symbolised by the heights. Yet the lowlands also form 'an inescapable part of his mind' (Miller 1968: 357). Miller concludes that the poem shows the speaker moving towards a future which offers, as its closing words suggest, 'some liberty', if only in his recurrent attempts to free himself completely from his imaginative re-enactment of past events:

> This perpetual present of repetition is one version of authentic human temporality, which, as long as a man is alive, is an endless movement towards a future which will be, but never yet is, the perfected assumption of the past.

> (Miller 1968: 359)

The suffering speaker of the poem 'remains both out of time and within it' (Miller 1968: 359).

Miller's work assumes a subject-centred discourse and the possibility of a unified text. However, in a later, distinguished study Miller (1982), influenced by the French philosopher, Jacques Derrida, embraces poststructuralism. Derrida's radically sceptical theory of deconstruction undermines the structuralist principle of binary opposition, based on the relationship between linguistic signs and what they represent. Boundaries that support ideology are eroded by the arbitrariness of the sign, and by what Derrida identifies as the continual play of difference (*différance* – difference and deferral). An endless play of deferred meanings produced by the text challenges the conception of it as a stable structure. Derrida's strategy of reading in the margins of the text became an influential method of analysis. Repeated key words, identified in the margins of the text, produce doubleness and contradiction, undermining the text's intelligibility. Readers are free to produce their own meanings because coherence and unity are illusory goals. The basic concepts of deconstruction; difference, repetition and marginality, inform Miller's sceptical reading of *Tess of the d'Urbervilles* **[82–8]**. Scrutinising the passage describing Alec d'Urberville's violation of Tess, Miller points out how the text insistently raises the issue of Tess's suffering as a question to be answered, but denies the reader an answer. Identifying the marginal element in the passage as the metaphor of the tracing of a pattern on Tess, Miller suggests its multiple significance: 'It assimilates the real event to the act of writing about it. It defines both the novel and the events it represents as repetitions, as the outlining again of a pattern which already somewhere exists' (Miller 1982: 120). This is Miller's central statement of his deconstructionist strategy:

> It is possible to distinguish chains of connection which are material elements in the text, like the red things; or metaphors, like the figures of grafting or of writing; or covert, often etymological associations, like the connection of grafting with writing or cutting; or thematic elements like sexuality or murder; or conceptual elements, like the question of cause or the theory of history; or quasi-mythological elements, like the association of Tess with the harvest or the personification of the sun as a benign god. None of these chains has priority over the others as the true explanation of the meaning of the novel. ... Taken together, the elements form a system of mutually defining motifs, each of which exists as its relation to the others. The reader must execute a lateral dance of interpretation to explicate any given passage, without ever reaching, in this sideways movement, a passage which is chief, original, or originating; a sovereign principle of explanation. The meaning, rather, is suspended within the interaction among the elements. It is immanent rather than transcendent. ... This does not exempt the reader from seeking answers to the question of why Tess is compelled to repeat herself and others and then suffer through those repetitions. The answers, rather, must lie in the sequence itself.
>
> (Miller 1982: 126–7)

The reader, Miller concludes, is drawn into the pursuit of an explanation for Tess's tragic experience by Hardy's insistent questioning of the reason for her suffering, only to retreat baffled by the plethora of mutually contradictory explanations available in a text that is over-determined.

(e) PSYCHOANALYTIC APPROACHES

A strong thread of psychoanalytic criticism runs through Hardy studies from the 1970s to the present, based mainly on the early theory of Sigmund Freud and the more recent work of the French psychologist and theorist Jacques Lacan. Its underlying assumption is that, by analysing Hardy's characters, it is possible to uncover his essential psychological preoccupations. Perry Meisel (1972) focuses on the psychological conflict within Hardy between his profound emotional allegiances to the Christian faith and his own rural community, and the influence of the conceptual tendency of nineteenth-century scientific rationalism represented by Darwin. Meisel traces the impact of this conflict on the developing form of Hardy's fiction, arguing that as the bonds of community evident in the early novels are gradually weakened, the isolated individual self increasingly becomes the focus of examination. Meisel identifies *The Mayor of Casterbridge* **[71–6]** as the novel in which the isolated ego becomes the object of study, as Hardy recognises that 'the unconscious is the true psychic reality' (Meisel 1972: 92).

The culmination of this process, suggests Meisel, may be seen in *Tess of the d'Urbervilles* **[82–8]** and *Jude the Obscure* **[88–94]**, which explore the psychological conflict between humanity's 'natural and social components' (Meisel 1972: 118). This is tragic because it is brought to self-conscious recognition in Tess and Jude, both of whom are alienated from the community. In *Tess of the d'Urbervilles* Hardy examines, in the relation between the physical Tess and the intellectual Angel, the way human relations are limited by the imprisoning ego. However, in *Jude the Obscure* the focus is entirely on the psychological awareness of Jude, who combines in himself the different needs of Tess and Angel: 'His gradual and painful discoveries are those of the wandering ego whose consciousness of its own anchorlessness defines the meaning of *modern*' (Meisel 1972: 139). In this respect, like Gregor (1974), Meisel concludes that Hardy anticipates modern writers such as James Joyce and D.H. Lawrence.

In Meisel's study, Freudian theory is linked with Darwinian theory to provide an intellectual framework. Also tactfully informed by Freudian theory is the work of Frank R. Giordano (1984). Giordano concentrates on suicide, identifying in Hardy a courageous and conscious acknowledgement of the suicidal impulse as an understandable response to the modern condition. But the nature of this self-destructiveness differs. Giordano inclines to the view that Eustacia Vye's death is self-willed. He identifies her and Michael Henchard as 'egotistical suicides', William Boldwood and Jude Fawley as 'anomic suicides', and Giles Winterborne and Tess Durbeyfield as 'altruistic suicides'. Elements of Freudian influence are best seen in the treatment of the repressed personalities of Boldwood and Winterborne. An important corollary of Hardy's concern with his characters' suicidal tendencies, argues Giordano, is his perception of the fundamental human need for love, and his illumination of life as both fragile and precious.

Freud's essay analysing the tendency to split the sensuous and affectionate feelings ('On the Universal Tendency to Debasement in the Sphere of Love', 1912), forms the basis for a stimulating essay by Leon Waldoff (1979). Waldoff begins by reviewing the various forms of determinism in the novel, settling on psychological determinism as the crucial element in Tess's tragedy. In an absorbing discussion of the degree of Tess's moral responsibility, Waldoff concludes that there is a split between the author's insistence on inevitability and his ambiguous presentation of the events in which she is involved: 'Ultimately Tess is a victim of an ambivalent attitude towards woman that is traceable both to Hardy and to the culture in which he lived' (Waldoff 1979: 142).

This ambivalence is split into Alec and Angel, one regarding her as a sexual object and the other as an idealised non-sexual image. But the determining element lies in the character of Angel, whose obsession with sexual purity prevents him from reconciling his image of woman with the reality of Tess. Waldoff sees Angel as a classic Freudian case of a split between affectionate and sexual currents of feeling as a consequence of an unconscious conflict over incest, for when affectionate feelings are too closely associated with a maternal image, a sexual approach to a woman is inhibited. This psychological determinism contributes to the inevitability of the tragedy. And when Tess's experience is viewed in the context of the fates of Hardy's other sexually innocent and experienced women, it is possible, suggests Waldoff, to discern a biographical link between Angel's obsession with purity and 'Hardy's own irrational and unconscious sharing in that obsession in the design of his heroine's fate' (Waldoff 1979: 150).

Psychoanalytic issues raised by Meisel, Waldoff and others are reflected and developed more generally by Rosemary Sumner (1981), whose approach is underpinned by reference to Hardy's *Literary Notebooks* (Björk 1985), which reveals his interest in contemporary psychological theory, particularly the work of Charles Fourier and Auguste Comte. However, Sumner's central argument, which is critically alert to the complexities of Hardy's texts, is that his venturing into taboo areas and his insights into neuroses anticipate the work of later psychologists such as Sigmund Freud, Carl Jung and Alfred Adler.

Sumner's wide-ranging study benefits from her allusion to psychiatric theories, but attends at the same time to broader intellectual and social contexts, and also to matters of narrative form. Sumner begins by looking at Hardy's experiments in *Desperate Remedies* **[94–6]** where he tentatively explores lesbianism in the neurotic character of Miss Aldclyffe. In *A Laodicean* **[105–7]**, Sumner argues, Paula Power's bisexuality is strongly suggested by her ambiguous oscillation between the architect, George Somerset, and her companion, Charlotte De Stancy. Striking parallels are found in *The Well-Beloved* **[110–14]** between Hardy's treatment of the elusive well-beloved and Jung's theory of the anima, as Jocelyn Pierston unconsciously projects his anima upon a series of real women, so that the novel becomes 'very largely, a vehicle for theory' (Sumner 1981: 32).

Hardy's extraordinarily profound understanding of the complexity of sexual repression is revealed in his treatment of William Boldwood in *Far from the Madding Crowd* **[61–6]**, which corresponds to Freud's accounts; while in *The Mayor of Casterbridge*, Hardy's interest is absorbed by the mainly self-destructive psychology of aggression, which anticipates later discoveries by Freud, Adler and others. In Grace Melbury, in *The Woodlanders*, Sumner sees the hidden but violent conflict and ontological insecurity occasioned by her upbringing, which anticipates R. D. Laing's studies, *The Divided Self* (1960) and *Self and Others* (1961).

Rosemary Sumner devotes three chapters to the 'psychological problems of modern man and woman' (Sumner 1981: 99). She argues that in the characterisation of Eustacia Vye Hardy experiments with methods of presenting a neurotic, tortured nature, while in Clym he examines the interrelated psychological problems of a modern, Oedipally fixated intellectual. The problem of the sexually inhibited thinker, first examined in Henry Knight, in *A Pair of Blue Eyes* **[96–8]**, is explored more deeply in Angel Clare, whose dominant superego and repressed emotional conflict are exacerbated by his unconscious projection of his 'anima' onto Tess. In *Jude the Obscure*, in contrast to the well-balanced, resilient Jude, Sue is presented as psychologically complex; a modern woman intellectually interested in sexuality, but repressed in a classically Freudian way, and for much of the time living on the edge of sanity.

More recently, psychoanalytic criticism has drawn on the work of the French psychologist and theorist, Jacques Lacan, who challenges the humanist conception of the integrated subject, and instead postulates the subject as the fragmented product of unconscious desire articulated in language. He suggests that desire, rather than being sexual, as Freud had argued, is directed towards the realisation of unity. This can never be attained because of a psychic split at the 'mirror' stage of development, when the ego misrecognises its image in a mirror as representing its own unity. The 'I' then enters the symbolic order,

CRITICISM

socialised through language, which enacts the repressive system of the father, the realm of law and institution. Unconscious desire, or lack, originates in relation to the absent Other, the locus of signification where identity is established. This may be Woman, who assists in affirming man's selfhood.

Lacanian theory provides part of the framework for T. R. Wright (1989) who examines a range of Hardy's writing. Wright's introduction outlines Freudian theories about human sexuality in the context of the Victorian response to the erotic. What Wright takes from Lacan is primarily the importance of the visual in the construction of identity, since desire, according to Lacan, is established through seeing and subject to continual displacement. Sexuality is thus located in the fantasising associated with voyeurism.

Beginning with the *Life* **[139–41]**, in which Wright discerns a scopophilic, voyeuristic Hardy, he argues that Hardy's game of cat and mouse with literary censorship, which relies on secrecy and engima, is essentially erotic in effect. In the early novels enigmatic heroines such as Cytherea Graye and Elfride Swancourt, are objects for both the male characters and the narrators, and also for the 'implied reader/voyeur' (Wright 1989: 34).

The novels of Hardy's middle period, Wright suggests, from *Far from the Madding Crowd* to *Two on a Tower* **[107–10]**, are concerned with the tension between women as objects and their subjective consciousness. They are interested in women exercising power; in the way Bathsheba Everdene and Ethelberta Petherwin exploit their sexual fascination, or the complexity of Eustacia Vye as a 'product of the tension between her function as an erotic object and her emergence as a subject with disturbing desires of her own' (Wright 1989: 58). There is the perversity of desire in Anne Garland, the teasingly mysterious sexuality of Paula Power, and the secrecy of the meetings between Swithin St Cleeve and Lady Viviette Constantine. However, the erotic remains beyond their control, and ultimately the pleasure of the text is voyeuristic.

Wright argues that *The Mayor of Casterbridge* and *The Woodlanders* **[77–82]** question the nature of 'manliness' and undermine conventional notions of gender roles. Henchard acquires elements of the feminine revealed, accordingly to Wright, in erotic scenes involving Farfrae. The simple moral frame of *The Woodlanders* is disturbed by desire, against which conventional morality and institutional codes such as marriage seem powerless. The major novels are regarded as intensely erotic. Wright draws attention to the voyeuristic narrator in *Tess of the d'Urbervilles* **[83, 178, 184]**, who describes Tess with erotic fascination while attempting to purify her, and to the male characters, who treat her as a sexual object. In *Jude the Obscure*, Hardy explores Sue's inability to evade the woman's status as an erotic object through her role of the New Woman, while *The Well-Beloved* examines the relation between the erotic and artistic creativity, which is driven by desire in endless cycles of pursuit of fulfilment and completion.

The film critic, Kaja Silverman (1984), combines the psychoanalytic theory of Jacques Lacan and Julia Kristeva and the stategies of visual theory in an influential article on *Tess of the d'Urbervilles*. Silverman explores what she terms the novel's 'libidinal economy' (Silverman 1984: 10) in order to show how desire is 'classically organized and sustained through representation' (Silverman 1984: 10). Vision is problematised in the opening chapters by the use of an implied viewer, who is in turn a tourist, a landscape painter, and a passer-by, and also by the foregrounding of Tess against a generalised background, into which she subsequently recedes. Tess is identified as the female object of the male gaze, including the narratological gaze. She is a surface on which pattern is imposed, a pattern which is not only artistic and erotic, but also historical. Drawing on Eric Auerbach's description of a figural view of history, Silverman argues that *Tess of the d'Urbervilles* is caught within this view, but that its ironic final section, entitled 'Fulfillment', lacks the redemptive impulse usually associated with a figural view of history. However, the novel contains so many 'proleptic signifiers' (Silverman 1984:13) that it is 'increasingly difficult to separate the figurative from the figural' (Silverman 1984: 13).

The narrator's erotic and artistic gaze is divided between fetishism and the need for control. Tess is therefore 'figured or dissolved according to the vicissitudes of authorial subjectivity and its ambivalent relation to representation' (Silverman 1984: 27). The two concepts of the feminine proposed by the novel, 'Woman-as-intact-state' and 'Woman-as-figure' (Silverman 1984: 27) represent 'a classic, culturally fostered mechanism for disavowing the male subject's symbolic castration' (Silverman 1984: 27). Silverman concludes that:

> With its insistence upon relational identity and the coercive power of the signifier, figural history in *Tess of the d'Urbervilles* would finally seem to be nothing other than a nightmarish view of the symbolic order – a traumatic apprehension of the central role played in the constitution of the subject by the language and desire of the Other.
> (Silverman 1984:28)

Marjorie Garson (1991) employs a Lacanian approach to a feminist reading of Hardy's major novels in a sophisticated theoretical study.

She reads Hardy's novels as 'fables about the constitution of the self and about its inevitable dissolution' (Garson 1991: 1). Her study is concerned with the oblique expression in Hardy's work of his 'somatic anxiety' (Garson 1991: 1) about wholeness, maleness and women, involving the integrity of the body, class and nature, and how his attempt to create an aesthetic wholeness is mirrored back as dissolution. Nature in Hardy may be present as a fragmented human body, but his concerns may also be reflected in imagery of 'humanoid' figures, such as the gargoyle and the quarter-jack in *Far from the Madding Crowd*, also in imagery of clothing, in plot and in characterisation. In her reading of a 'mythic subtext', which 'may intersect with or turn against the moral fable in interesting and often quite complicated ways' (Garson 1991: 2), Garson finds some of Jacques Lacan's concepts especially helpful, particularly the mirror, the *corps morcelé*, and the constitution of the Woman as Other; though in Hardy, Garson suggests, the Other also always includes the dimension of class, while behind his characters stands Nature the Great Mirror.

Though lucid and written with conviction, Marjorie Garson's book is dense and theoretically complex. She argues that certain of Hardy's texts lend themselves more readily than others to a Lacanian reading:

> *The Woodlanders* is a text in which the *corps morcelé* is not only glimpsed again and again in the landscape but also repeatedly and uncharacteristically literalized in the narrative ... The somatic imagery points to the desire for possession – possession in both the economic and the demonic senses – the analysis of which is one of the novel's central concerns.
>
> (Garson 1991: 81)

An example of Garson's application of Lacanian methodology at the level of scene and incident may be seen in her treatment of *Far from the Madding Crowd*, in which the only integrated character, because he submits to the Other, is Gabriel Oak:

> To see the Great Barn ... as the fortress or stadium which Lacan identifies as often expressing, in dream and fantasy, the illusion of wholeness is not only to clarify the position of Gabriel Oak (who reigns in the Great Barn and who also aligns himself with the Great Mother) but also to relate the barn itself – as an implicitly maternal image, an enduring and capacious female *body* – to other mothers and mother-figures in the novels.
>
> (Garson 1991: 3)

And in the same novel Garson applies Lacan's idea of the mirror-stage to the narcissism of Bathsheba Everdene, as Hardy's way of containing the threat of the independent woman.

Marjorie Garson also links her Lacanian feminist reading with the methodology of the Marxist cultural critic, Fredric Jameson, who regards literary narrative as a socially symbolic act, and as an attempt to resolve contradictions in ideology that generates characters, or groups of characters. She applies this approach in her most challenging analysis of *Tess of the d'Urbervilles*. Garson identifies the novel's shaping character-positions in relation to the concepts of nature and aristocracy. She sees Alec, rather than Angel, as Tess's opposite, and the novel's scapegoat Tess, while associated with the country, must not be associated with its evils. She argues that Hardy is concerned to dehistoricise Tess in order that she should 'serve as a resolution of the tension between nature and aristocracy which I believe underlies the narrative' (Garson 1991: 138).

Garson's analysis reveals Hardy's implication in the objectification of Tess by both Alec and Angel, in the gaps and discontinuities in his treatment of Tess's history and her relation to nature. It emerges most clearly in Garson's Lacanian reading of landscape at Flintcomb-Ash, with its imagery of a fragmented body, and in terms of Tess's anxious dependence on an 'Other which will not look':

> Attempting to constitute a 'real' Tess, a Tess who will exist to herself, Hardy has got her caught in an explicable relation with an Other which mirrors the 'body' which this 'self' represses. 'Nature' reveals the inadequacy of Tess as a figure of unity, and perhaps reflects less the relationship between the main characters than the anxieties and concerns of the author which these characters are invented to resolve.
>
> (Garson 1991: 147)

Hardy is unable to create an aesthetic whole in this novel because, as it endeavours to construct a unified Tess, it reveals:

> ... her genesis in dissolution and fragmentation ... The figures of Tess and of nature, set up to supplement one another, instead subvert one another, and mirror back, to the subject attempting to constitute itself through their reflection, a fragmented body.
>
> (Garson 1991: 150)

(f) MARXIST CRITICISM

Marxist criticism regards bourgeois realist fiction as a source of knowledge about society, for in the novel may be found represented society's structure, inequalities, forces of oppression, and evidence of the class struggle. The author's own understanding of his society is also a source of knowledge, so for the Marxist critic Hardy's fiction is a repository of various kinds of historical information.

An early humanist Marxist critic is Arnold Kettle (1953), whose essay commences: 'The subject of *Tess of the d'Urbervilles* **[82–8]** is stated clearly by Hardy to be the fate of a "pure woman"; in fact it is the destruction of the English peasantry' (Kettle 1953: II, 45). Kettle's critique of mechanical materialism immediately shifts the emphasis from the tragic fate of Tess the individual to that of her class. Her sexual morality and personal actions are secondary to Kettle's interest in the larger historical and economic processes at work in late nineteenth-century Dorset. For Kettle, Hardy's novel has:

> the quality of a social document. ... It is a novel with a thesis – a *roman à thèse* – and the thesis is true. ... The thesis is that in the course of the nineteenth century the disintegration of the peasantry – a process which had its roots deep in the past – had reached its final and tragic stage.
>
> (Kettle 1953: II, 45)

Rejecting the novel as psychological realism, on the grounds of its implausibility, and finding its Aeschylean philosophy 'bogus' (Kettle 1953: II, 52), Kettle subjects the text to a schematic reading, which results in flattening its characterisation, in order to identify its moral fable in its symbolism. This forceful reading of social collapse, however, offers a rather static account of social history, and Kettle later modified his view.

A later historical critic, Raymond Williams (1970), takes issue with Kettle's simplified view. Williams was later to define himself as a Marxist critic, but in the 1960s he was in the main stream of humanist criticism that opposed wholesale industrialisation and urbanisation. He explores Hardy's identity as 'the educated observer and the passionate participant, in a period of general and radical change' (Williams 1970: 106), and what this unique perspective reveals about the history of social class.

Williams tackles head-on the issue of the destruction of the peasantry, finding the term inaccurate, since rural society comprised several occupations:

> The actual country people were landowners, tenant farmers, dealers, craftsmen and labourers, and that social structure – the actual material, in a social sense, of the novels – is radically different, in its variety, its shading, and many of its basic human attitudes from the structure of a peasantry.
>
> (Williams 1970: 100)

Moreover, the pressures of social change come most often not from the invasion of urban aliens, but from within. Williams draws attention to the 'classical experience of mobility' through education that is evident in the lives of Clym Yeobright, Grace Melbury, Tess Durbeyfield, Jude Fawley and Sue Bridehead, and he continues:

> This is not country against town, or even in any simple way custom against conscious intelligence. It is the more complicated and more urgent historical process in which education is tied to social advancement within a class society.
>
> (Williams 1970: 104)

The result is, as Clym's experience as a returning native testifies, that it is difficult 'to hold both to education and to social solidarity' (Williams 1970: 104).

Williams insists on the reflection of historical reality in Hardy's fictional society, in which change had been a constant condition since before Hardy's lifetime. Williams also demonstrates how 'the social forces within his fiction are deeply based in the rural economy itself' (Williams 1970: 113). He effectively deconstructs the sentimental pastoral created by earlier critics: Gabriel Oak experiences the risks of small-capital farming, Henchard is destroyed by his speculation in grain, Melbury's social ambition for his daughter is a corollary of his success as a timber merchant, while Tess is the daughter of a small dealer seduced by the son of a retired manufacturer.

The constantly changing social structure, with its increased social mobility, creates problems in choosing a marriage partner. The choice is not just personal, but economic and class based. It recurs most notably in *Far from the Madding Crowd* [61–6], *The Woodlanders* [77–82] and *Jude the Obscure* [88–94], where social alienation can be destructive. But for Williams, the most significant feature of Hardy's writing is his focus on ordinary lives filled with work, which is both a learning process and a force for human solidarity. Although an educated observer, 'he yet created continually the strength and the warmth of people living together: in work and in love; in the physical reality of a place' (Williams 1970: 116).

Williams's response to the experiential dimension of the ideological dichotomy between custom and education, and the disintegration of the 'knowable community' (Williams 1970: 98–9), is developed further in the work of the materialist critic, George Wotton. Wotton (1985) describes the object of a materialist criticism as 'the relations between history, ideology, writing and criticism', and its aim is 'an understanding of the historical conditions of the production of writing and the ways in which literature operates in the process of reproducing the relations of production of class society' (Wotton 1985: 2). His study takes as its starting-point the centrality of work in Hardy's fiction and develops an argument about the crucial function of his workfolk:

> … their presence is constitutive because all Hardy's characters exist in relation to the experiential knowledge and customary forms of their world. It is in that relation that they achieve their reality as characters. They are also constitutive, however, in the production of contradiction. This is not a matter of the writer's conscious intention. In the conflict which the writing sets up between the customary forms of the workfolk and (bourgeois) civilization, the writing is not simply a representation, a *showing* – of the inevitable clash between town and country, urban and rural manners, folkways and educated society, the effects of 'change' and so on – but a *production*. The presence of the workfolk in Hardy's writing contributes to putting the ideology of the thinking world into contradiction, both by revealing the colonizing nature of bourgeois ideological forms, and by defining the boundaries of bourgeois ideology.
>
> (Wotton 1985: 186–7)

Wotton's book is important, though difficult to follow and in places somewhat repetitive. It is divided into three parts. The first deals with the factors that make up the conditions of production of Hardy's writing. The second employs the concept of the structure of perceptions informing his novels to examine the relations between ideology and writing. The final part concerns the social and ideological function of the production of 'Thomas Hardy' as 'Literature'. Drawing heavily on the writings of Marx, and based on an account of rural economic history, Wotton's deconstructive study is challenging, but delivers less than its theoretical framework promises at the outset. For Wotton, Hardy's writing is rooted in the contradiction of the process of dispossession and proletarianisation of the labour force during the Great Depression of the 1870s and 1880s, existing alongside surviving precapitalist modes of production, represented by the Great Barn in *Far from the Madding Crowd* **[8, 153]**. Beyond that, and also it is argued economic in origin, is the class ideology of the period, which determines Hardy's presentation of Wessex as a collection of individuals, so that, for instance, among the inhabitants of Little Hintock in *The Woodlanders* there are no 'possibilities for working class solidarity, knowledge and action' (Wotton 1985: 52). At the same time Hardy is critical of the way class vision blinds people to the reality of the individual's essential nature, as in Melbury's misreading of Fitzpiers, or the labelling of Tess Durbeyfield as a 'peasant'.

Wotton argues that Hardy wanted to show bourgeois civilisation rapidly destroying local traditions, but that the ideological view produced by his writing was somewhat different. Invoking the Bakhtinian concept of grotesque realism, Wotton suggests that Hardy's workfolk collectively engage in a degradation of the civilised, the ideal and the spiritual through festival, song, dance and ritual – the bonfire in *The Return of the Native* **[66–71]**, the skimmity-ride in *The Mayor of Casterbridge* **[71–6]**, or the dance in *Under the Greenwood Tree* **[58–60]**. Wotton also employs feminist ideology to argue that the reflection in Hardy's writing of the contradictions of its moment of production are also evident in the way he replicates the Victorian sexist ideology of woman as the weaker sex, and as the mysterious Other. At the same time, he puts this ideology into contradiction by the way each of his women is trapped within the male gaze, with resulting complex visions of herself **[83, 171, 184]**.

John Goode (1988) also seeks to understand Hardy's writing both as a product of social factors and as a historical object of production. His primary theoretical influence is the Marxist cultural critic, Fredric Jameson, particularly his book *The Political Unconscious* (1981), which argues that literary narrative is a socially symbolic act requiring interpretation primarily in terms of class structure and its historical context. Driven by theory, Goode's book is illuminating and passionate, though sometimes obtuse. He sees Hardy as an alienated figure, entering culture first through his early poetry, which reveals his rejection of traditional poetic values. In his close study of both Hardy's major and his lesser fiction, Goode argues that he could find no accommodation in his writing with the contemporary cultural intelligentsia. Goode traces the evolution of Hardy's political stance in relation to his narrative methods:

> For Hardy there can be no treaty with the world he addresses through writing. On the contrary the only development for Hardy is from self-conscious appeasement (a scientific game) to open confrontation (the offence he was willing to let 'come out of truth' in the Preface to *Tess of the d'Urbervilles*).
>
> (Goode 1988: 3)

Part of this process is revealed by the feminist strand in Goode's thinking. He discovers a progression from the narrative silencing of Elfride Swancourt's sexuality in *A Pair of Blue Eyes* to the emergence of Tess as 'a woman capable of telling her story in her own voice' (Goode 1988: 129). In the early novels Hardy is seen as playing a 'scientific game', like the game of chess in *A Pair of Blue Eyes* **[96–8]**, 'by which with practice you can learn to give pieces away in order to secure victory' (Goode 1988: 11). Thus the self-conscious pastoral of *Under the Greenwood Tree* manipulates the contemporary reader, but 'what the text does is to subvert the moral prison of Victorian sentimentality by a trace of real earthiness' (Goode 1988: 13). Goode similarly deconstructs the famous timeless image of the barn in *Far from the Madding Crowd*, which is 'violated by the historical actuality of the novel' (Goode 1988: 17–18).

John Goode explains Hardy's production of lesser novels between *The Return of the Native* and *The Mayor of Casterbridge* by the fact that '*The Return of the Native* initiates an ideological break which it cannot complete, but which is never again repaired and which makes Hardy's late novels the radical challenge they continue to be' (Goode 1988: 39). That is, the self can no longer be defined in terms of experience, nor in terms of nature. This is best exemplified in Goode's discussion of *Tess of the d'Urbervilles*, on which he brings feminist ideology to bear. He identifies in this heteroglossic text a discontinuity that is part of its 'polemical design in which the discontinuities are seen as properties of the ideological discourses the text articulates'. These discourses are identified in textual politics as that of an 'ideological hierarchy', centrally the 'correlation of two discourses, that of "nature" and that of "gender"', together with a third, 'that of the "social relations of production"' (Goode 1988: 111). In the course of the novel the discourses of nature and gender are revalued as Tess is increasingly seen as an alienated, working-class woman, and essentially as the representative of a historical process.

Peter Widdowson (1989), in an articulate, provocative work proposes, by analogy with historiography, a 'critiography', which involves a study of the discipline of Literary Studies itself and includes a consciousness of how its material has been constituted. Applied to Hardy, this literary sociology means an investigation of him as:

> a cultural phenomenon defined by its place, function, and parameters of intelligibility within the contemporary social formation. What one should immediately be forced to ask, therefore, is how 'Hardy' got here; which texts constitute 'Hardy'; what 'his' place in the social process may be; how those texts have been, and are, read; what, indeed, 'Hardy' means in our culture.
>
> (Widdowson 1989: 15)

Widdowson argues that the liberal humanist tradition of literary criticism has shaped Hardy the great writer around the development of a canon based on his 'novels of character and environment', to the virtual exclusion of the lesser, flawed novels. The Hardy that has emerged is the nostalgic creator of Wessex, a realistic writer, whose work also reflects a 'Greek' conception of tragedy, includes 'Shakespearean' rustics, and possesses a universal significance. The development of humanist formalist criticism enhanced this process: 'his "improbablism" and anti-realism, his melodramatic, "senseless", and contingent world, in which individual human beings are the victims of social processes they do not control, call the whole humanist myth into question' (Widdowson 1989: 75).

The work of Joe Fisher (1992) is informed by the thinking of the Marxist philosopher Louis Althusser, who emphasises the material determinant in the production of literary texts. He explores the ways in which ideological contradictions may be manifest in fiction through contradictions that are elements of literary production itself. Fisher's project is to reveal these partly hidden patterns in Hardy's fiction. He therefore looks at 'Hardy's trade as a novelist first in terms of his relation to the Victorian fiction market's production process, and secondly in terms of his own manufacturing process in creating an object to be traded in this market' (Fisher 1992: 3).

As a small entrepreneur, Fisher suggests, Hardy produced novels offering, for magazine editors and purchasers for circulating libraries, an acceptable version of Wessex, by editing its 'raw material' and using this as a bid for 'cultural power and its accompanying political platform' (Fisher 1992: 5). However, as part of a deliberate strategy, each text subverts this authority. Conventional attitudes to class and gender are

CRITICISM

undermined by Hardy's exploitation of the 'gap between the trader who sells the story and the narrator who tells it to corrupt the traded object'. This is achieved through the creation of 'hostile and part-visible patterns beneath what might generally be regarded as the "surface" of the text' (Fisher 1992: 7).

What Hardy sells, argues Fisher, is a bourgeois version of Wessex rebuilt for the market, and his qualification for the job of bourgeois novelist is announced in his extensive use of myth and allusion. But his use of allusion in the antithetical counter-text subverts this, for instance in *The Woodlanders*, in which Giles Winterborne appears as a medieval Wild Man and Marty South as a dryad, or in *Tess of the d'Urbervilles* in which Hardy employs the Gaia myth. Discussing this novel, in a chapter entitled 'Götterdämmerung' ('the twilight of the gods'), Joe Fisher offers a strenuous and challenging theoretical approach.

Among the lesser fiction, Fisher sees *Desperate Remedies* **[94–6]** as a mockery of the genre it imitates, creating a 'novel-within-a-novel which makes the whole enterprise of *Desperate Remedies* a Trojan Horse' (Fisher 1992: 21) **[95, 185, 203]**. More obviously political is *The Hand of Ethelberta*, in which Hardy may be seen 'empowering domestic servants in a revolutionary fantasy', while 'The idea of a working-class woman, having rewritten her class, using her sexuality to exploit *haute-bourgeois* and aristocratic men and gain executive control of (their) Structure ... overthrows at least fictionally, a crucial erotic paradigm' (Fisher 1992: 74–5) **[100, 185, 189]**.

Hardy's lesser fiction is the focus of Roger Ebbatson (1993), whose aim is to reclaim some of those works which have been marginalised. The first half of his book, 'Reading Desire', influenced by the theoretical work of Jacques Derrida, J. Hillis Miller and Jacques Lacan, follows a broadly deconstructive approach. *The Trumpet-Major* **[101–4]** reveals its dependence upon absence and deferral of meaning, repression of conflict and effacement of the female; while *Desperate Remedies* explores the relation between unconscious desire, textural structure and language. The lesbian scene 'resonates with unconscious power, exploring as it does the issues of sexuality, gender and class, which entangle both novelist and audience' (Ebbatson 1993: 20). 'Our Exploits at West Poley' is examined through Kristevan linguistics, and the short stories are subjected to a variety of post-structuralist treatments. The second half of the book, 'Speaking Class', the culmination of Ebbatson's argument, offers historicised discussions of 'An Indiscretion in the Life of an Heiress' and 'The Dorsetshire Labourer'. Particularly interesting, though over-reliant on Bakhtin, is Ebbatson's argument that in this well-known essay Hardy effectively silences the labourer by reducing him to an object of contemplation. While Roger Ebbatson's study as a whole is lucid, its flow is impeded by allusions to individual theorists, and by the adoption of several theoretical perspectives.

(g) FEMINIST AND GENDER STUDIES

As feminism has expanded to include gender studies and the investigation of sexuality as a subject in its own right, areas of theory have come increasingly to overlap, cross-fertilise and reinvigorate each other. One of the early major feminist critics of Hardy is Mary Jacobus (1975), who explores the complex psychological presentation of Sue Bridehead and the nature of her emancipation, in *Jude the Obscure* **[88–94]**. Jacobus argues that the integration of the various issues raised by Sue is complicated within the text by the elusive relation that Hardy sets up between her psychology and the ideas she represents. By focussing on Sue's consciousness, Jacobus reveals her process of self-discovery, her refusal to conform to conventional thinking, and the peculiarly modern complexity of her relationship with Jude. However, in the end, suggests Jacobus, Sue is broken by her 'femaleness' after the loss of her unborn child. This is seen as part of Hardy's pattern of contrasts, as her collapse enhances Jude's growing strength and fidelity to his values. Nevertheless, Sue is realised by Hardy as special, as Jacobus concludes:

> The cogency of [Hardy's] general plea combines with his portrayal of Sue's individual 'obscurity'; the realistic sense of the gap between what she thinks and what she does, between belief and behaviour, imparts unique complexity and life to the static contrasts of the novel's original conception.
>
> (Jacobus 1975: 328)

Another Hardy essay by Jacobus (1978) concentrates on the significant changes that Hardy made to *Tess of the d'Urbervilles* **[82–8]** while it was still at the manuscript stage. She argues that Hardy's alterations to the characters of Tess, Alec d'Urberville and Angel Clare were dictated by the need to overcome Victorian censorship, and that Tess's purity is a 'literary construct, "stuck on" in retrospect like the subtitle to meet objections that the novel had encountered even before its publication in 1891' (Jacobus 1978: 78). She concludes that the textual changes which Hardy introduced offer a valuable insight into Victorian society's control of female sexuality.

Elaine Showalter (1979), writing about *The Mayor of Casterbridge* **[71–6]**, explores the effect of patriarchal ideology on the character of Michael Henchard, who in the process of his entry into masculinity, initiated by the selling of his wife and daughter and later confirmed by his success in the male world of the marketplace, loses touch with the feminine side of his personality. However, Showalter argues, the insistent return of the repressed women in his life begins a process of 'unmanning', as Henchard loses the trappings of his patriarchal power as mayor, which reveals precisely the terms of what he has missed. Showalter stresses that Hardy understood the feminine self as 'the estranged and essential complement of the male self' (Showalter 1979: 101). The dichotomy in Henchard that she reveals requires his learning of the feminine attributes of 'observation, attention, sensitivity, and compassion' (Showalter 1979: 114). However, assigning these qualities to women tacitly registers an essentialist view of them. Moreover, in her assumption that the narrator is in fact Hardy, who is daring to 'acknowledge this side of his own art, to pursue the feminine spirit in his man of character' (Showalter 1979: 114), Showalter treats the narrative strategy of the novel as an unproblematic question of intention.

The most influential feminist critic of Hardy has been Penny Boumelha (1982). Her sophisticated post-structuralist study is concerned with the historically conditioned concept of gender. It draws on the work of the Marxist philosopher Louis Althusser, particularly on his theory of social formation that describes the relationship between literature and society. Adopting his method of analysing the presence of ideology in texts, Boumelha uncovers within the body of thought in Hardy's novels, contradictions, distortions and ambiguities. She exposes his refusal to take up a clear position on the issue of gender. She also reveals the fragmentation of the structure and authority of his narratives. Hardy's radicalism in overtly raising the issues of both gender and class is emphasised by Boumelha's New Historicist approach of exploring his writing in the context of scientific, medical and legal discourses, as well as alongside the work of minor writers of fiction on the 'New Woman' question. This interest in the cultural ideologies that produced Hardy's novels is combined with a structuralist reading of the sign 'woman' that the texts create.

Boumelha regards Hardy as a conscious experimenter. She notes his uniquely androgynous voice, which develops with his progressive exploration of the situation of women. In *The Return of the Native* **[66–71]**, which applies the 'fine writing' of tragedy to his sexual realism, the woman's tragedy is conceived of as sexual, while the man's is intellectual, a pattern that Hardy repeats. Eustacia Vye's disruptive sexual longing results in her social marginalisation. The natural law of desire in *The Woodlanders* **[77–82]** produces a 'naturalistic undermining of monogamy' (Boumelha 1982: 110), but for Grace Melbury only marriage can resolve the problem of social class and sexual status.

In Boumelha's most compelling chapter, on *Tess of the d'Urbervilles*, she argues that Hardy attempts to employ an 'androgynous mode of narration, which has as its project to present woman, "pure woman", as known from within and without, explicated and rendered transparent' (Boumelha 1982: 120). However, this breaks down partly because of the narrator's erotic fascination with Tess, but also because she cannot be securely 'placed' **[83, 171, 178]**. By deconstructing the text's gender-based binary oppositions in their historical and social contexts, Boumelha exposes Tess's tragedy as hingeing on the way she is 'constructed as an instance of the natural', structured by the 'ideological elision of woman, sex and nature' (Boumelha 1982: 123). Fundamentally, Boumelha concludes, *Tess of the d'Urbervilles* represents Hardy's recognition of the limits of his project of simultaneously presenting Tess's experiences and gaining an understanding of her female identity.

By contrast, Sue Bridehead is regarded as belonging to the New Woman tradition in fiction, rather than to feminism. What is significant in this novel is the fact that 'Hardy gives for the first time an intellectual component to the tragedy of the woman' (Boumelha 1982: 141). And the tragedy, in this post-Ibsen period, turns on marriage. Boumelha argues that '*Jude the Obscure* is unique in its siting of Jude and Sue at the conjunction of class and sexual oppression' (Boumelha 1982: 137). In Sue, Boumelha sees the operation of the conflict of two contradictory pressures, but she has to learn that the imperative of sexuality 'lies to a large degree outside the control of rationality, will, choice' (Boumelha 1982: 144).

Consciously following in the tracks of Penny Boumelha is Patricia Ingham (1989) who, drawing on Jonathan Culler's *The Pursuit of Signs* (1981), also investigates the sign 'woman', how it was formed by ideology, and in particular how it exists in the narrative language and syntax patterns available to Hardy when he began to write. Her examination of the disjunction in Hardy's novels between his narrative voice and the construction of plots reveals a radical, even subversive writer. Her aim is to examine how the female subject of Hardy's novels is created by the language as the product of ideologies. She discerns in his writing a 'fault-line', which denotes that 'there is in relation to women a subtle subterranean shifting taking place' (Ingham 1989: 6–

7). In Hardy's early novels, she argues, 'in spite of the male narrator's theology of woman, he allows another discourse to emerge which speaks of how a sensitive woman may experience social and individual pressure upon her' (Ingham 1989: 21). Since the narrative syntax of the novels codes much that is not explicitly expressed, conventional readings are undermined; the plot of *Desperate Remedies* **[94–6]** in fact does not enforce patriarchy **[95, 181, 203]**, *Far from the Madding Crowd* **[61–6]** is not a punishment plot designed to bring Bathsheba Everdene to her senses **[62, 186, 188]**, while *The Hand of Ethelberta* **[98–101]** reverses the implications of male hegemony in its title **[100, 181, 189]**. However, in the later novels Ingham sees Hardy endorsing spontaneous female sexuality by evolving a 'new set of feminine signs ... Grace of the womanly, Tess and Arabella of the fallen woman, Sue of the New Woman' (Ingham 1989: 68). Grace Melbury's acceptance of Fitzpiers is prompted by sexual desire, and her love for Giles is also explicitly sexual in origin. Arabella spiritedly refuses to conform to the idea of the guilty fallen woman, while Tess recovers from her 'fall' and the death of her baby. Both Tess and the narrator resist the male characters' attempts to impose on her the categories of signification available to their language. Sue Bridehead, the New Woman, sharing with Jude a self-awareness of oppression, which in her case is sexual, disdains convention by asserting her autonomous sense of identity. All these women create a new meaning for their autonomous selves outside the bounds of male language. The narrative syntax of the novels reinforces this, argues Ingham, for the 'chief syntactic feature of these accounts is a recursiveness of plot that figures an opposition to stability and order' (Ingham 1989: 82).

A stimulating narratological approach to the issue of gender and sexuality is to be found in Rosemarie Morgan (1988). She is interested in the disjunction between the structures of Hardy's narratives and the social ideas that they embody, the presence of multiple voices, and Hardy's deliberate strategy of shifting the identifiable sources of narrative authority.

Morgan's discussion is set in the cultural context within which Hardy was writing, including the responses of contemporary criticism. She argues that Hardy, abhorring the perfect woman in fiction and dissenting from the contemporary feminists' idealisation of marriage, embarked on a lone campaign on behalf of the voluptuous, sexually attractive, intelligent and moral woman, who transgressed the cultural categories of madonna/whore. Morgan asserts: 'Hardy's platform remains consistent and forthright: the world that denies autonomy, identity, purpose and power to women, is to be, on his terms, the loser'

(Morgan 1988: xvi). However, he was writing for a readership situated in a culture for whom female sexuality presented a threat, hence in his early novels he adopted narrative strategies of disguise to allow his voice to get past the censor. In *A Pair of Blue Eyes* **[96–8]**, Elfride Swancourt reverses the traditional female role by being sexually instigative in her relationships with Stephen and Knight. But although Hardy approves of her subversion of cultural codes, he has to pander to Mrs Grundy by counterpointing Elfride's voice throughout with that of a moralising narrator. *Far from the Madding Crowd* marks an advance, for Hardy replaces the proprietory narrator with Gabriel Oak. In his role as observer and censor of Bathsheba's frank sensuality and self-determination, Oak succeeds, by the end of the novel, in crushing her sexual vitality **[62, 185, 188]**.

In *The Return of the Native* a similar kind of policing is imposed on Eustacia Vye, a 'rare, splendid woman' (Morgan 1988: 74), of whose pagan sensuality Hardy approves. Her active policeman is Diggory Venn the reddleman, a 'power-mongering bully and degrader of voluptuous womankind, [who] typifies the punitive male censor of nonconformity' (Morgan 1988: 75). Although in *The Return of the Native*, Eustacia is finally displaced in accordance with Venn's wishes, in the later novels, Morgan argues, Hardy's secure position as a novelist allowed him to be more explicit. In *Tess of the d'Urbervilles* he focuses on the intense life of feminine sensations and employs the language of earthy and physical sexuality to express Tess's mature sexual nature. Tess is presented as a complex and humanly imperfect woman, whose moral, sexual and emotional generosity finally redeems Angel, but who also 'embodies a fierce impulse to self-determination against daunting, and ultimately insurmountable, odds' (Morgan 1988: 89).

By the time of *Jude the Obscure*, Morgan suggests, Hardy felt confident enough to ally himself openly with the voice of Sue Bridehead, although like the other heroines she has only male language to express her right to retain control of her body, and her radical antagonism to marriage. Hardy's strategy of balancing Jude's ascetic view of the 'noble' Sue, culturally determined by male fear, with Arabella's experienced evaluation of Sue's latent sexuality, reveals his tragic misunderstanding and denial of sexual equality. It is in the final novels, argues Morgan, that Hardy abandons narrative subterfuge and permits the emergence of his own 'iconoclastic voice' (Morgan 1988: xvii).

In a more recent essay on Hardy, Penny Boumelha (1999) explores the relative importance of class and gender differences in three pastoral novels, *Under the Greenwood Tree, Far from the Madding Crowd* and *The Woodlanders*. In each of these novels, after an interruption to the courtship pattern, the heroine confirms the rightness of her original choice. Fancy Day returns to Dick Dewy after an interlude of harmless flirtation, Bathsheba Everdene accepts all three suitors, though only Gabriel Oak remains at the end, while Grace's confirmation of the rightness of Giles Winterborne does not interfere with her social elevation and marriage to Edred Fitzpiers. Gender and class are linked in these novels, argues Boumelha, because the social position and economic standing of the heroine's husband determines her social destiny. In Hardy's obsession with love that transgresses class boundaries, it is difference that is eroticised: 'Gender difference and class difference, working in the space between antagonism and desire, are both represented as relations of power, and their intersections can take various forms' (Boumelha 1999: 132–3).

In *Under the Greenwood Tree* Fancy Day is a straightforward representative of female instinct, about which the novel's males are cynical. Her marriage to Dick Dewy is a compromise between the values of communal tradition and modern individualism. The suitability of Bathsheba Everdene and Gabriel Oak is signalled by their shared commitment to work and to economic success. What is involved, argues Boumelha, as well as inequalities of power, is an undermining of the types they start out as (rustic, and woman). Bathsheba becomes more dominant and Oak is transformed by his social elevation. However, her fitness for Oak also involves her humiliation.

The Woodlanders is much more unsettling, Boumelha suggests, because of two particularly disturbing elements, 'the peculiarly unstable character of class and sexuality, and the prevalence of obsession. From the interaction of the two emerges something quite different in the handling of the central plot of marital choice' (Boumelha 1999: 140). In a novel of materialistic determinism, with a 'mobile social environment' (Boumelha 1999: 141) and 'erotic mobility' (Boumelha 1999: 141), Grace Melbury is at the centre of social and marital choice because she is stranded between social classes and between two men. Boumelha concludes that 'In these three pastorally influenced novels of marital choice, then, class difference is as central to the generation of desire and its thwarting or fulfillment as gender difference' (Boumelha 1999: 142).

Kristin Brady (1999) reviews the most significant critical responses to gender in Hardy's novels, arguing that they offer a record, since 1871, of the different ways in which sexuality has been constructed. She points out how in the early years reviewers drew on social and scientific ideas about women and regarded Hardy's representation of female sexual desire as bestial and promiscuous. Indeed, what outraged critics about the heroine of *Tess of the d'Urbervilles* was Hardy's provocative yoking of primitive instinct with moral purity.

After discussing the feminist criticism of the first three-quarters of the twentieth century, Brady correctly locates its transformation in Penny Boumelha's post-structuralist study (1982), which examines Hardy's traditional narrative structures in the light of the Victorians' understanding of women. The relation between femininity and issues of power is seen by materialist critics as being located in Hardy's own class position, while feminist criticism that concentrates on Hardy's employment of the male gaze, culminates in Marjorie Garson's book (1991), in which she shows that Hardy's anxiety went beyond all these issues to the gendering of landscape in his novels.

Brady also draws attention to the growing interest in Hardy's construction of masculinity, as evidenced by Elaine Showalter's essay on *The Mayor of Casterbridge* (1979), and by Elizabeth Langland (1993), who employs feminist theory to argue Hardy's obsessive interest in Jude. There is also the provocative work of James Kincaid (1993), who explores elements of sado-masochism in Hardy's fiction and the implication of the reader in a complex response. Looking to the future, Brady suggests homoeroticism and sadism as potential areas of critical investigation.

Margaret R. Higonnet (1993a) has edited a collection of essays that usefully illustrates the variety of approaches available to feminist and gender studies. Higonnet (1993b) employs *Tess of the d'Urbervilles* to examine the points of intersection between gender and narrative theory, which she locates in the problem of separating the 'voice' of a character from that of the narrator; Elizabeth Langland's (1993) study of gender in *Jude the Obscure* focuses on Jude's ambivalent response to the feminine and to the discourse of masculinity as he strives to define his inner self; while Linda M. Shires (1993) applies a post-structuralist narrative theory to *Far from the Madding Crowd*, to uncover how in paradigmatic incidents Hardy reveals the complexities of the assigned terms of gender **[62, 185, 186]**.

Some of the essays in this volume are indebted to other disciplines: medical history for a study of female hysteria in Hardy's characters (Brady 1993); psychoanalysis to examine how the reader is involved in the gratifications of child-beating, voyeurism and sadomasochism (Kincaid 1993); and film theory about the gaze, using Polanski's film *Tess* (Sadoff 1993). Other essays focus on the related issues of class and gender. Robert Kiely (1993) applies Foucault's theory of discursive power, together with a cinematic theory of alienated representation, to the issue of solitude and narrative representation in *The Woodlanders*; Mary Rimmer (1993) bases her examination of the construction of gender in *A Pair of Blue Eyes* on the socio-economic structures and gender relations found in Hardy's use of the games of chess; and Penny Boumelha (1993) reinstates *The Hand of Ethelberta* as a sophisticated comic subversion of the *Bildungsroman*, for the ideology of female passivity is undermined by the fact that the origin of the bestowal of Ethelberta's hand is her own plot **[100, 181, 185]**.

A rare feminist exploration of Hardy's poetry is U.C. Knoepflmacher's 'Hardy's Ruins: Female Spaces and Male Designs' (1993), which applies a Freudian approach to sexuality, arguing that Hardy wanted to recover the female space that he associated with the houses of his childhood, a process that would permit the annulling of gender without compromising his adult sexuality. Knoepflmacher explores Hardy's increasingly elaborate mother/feminine/house figurations to work out a gender opposition he wished to remove. Such dissolution of binary opposition is possible in 'Domicilium', a poem that empowers the female voice of his grandmother, but only as a memory. The repression of Hardy's own femininity was reversed by the death of Emma, because Hardy was now driven by the desire for fusion. In 'I Found Her out There', Knoepflmacher suggests, Hardy is vicariously liberated with the resurrected Emma into the world of her adolescence, a place devoid of binary opposition, while in 'During Wind and Rain' he inserts himself into a poem based on an account of Emma's earlier separation from her childhood home, as part of his attempt to achieve wholeness and integration.

Knoepflmacher finds significance in the idea that Hardy's emotions on the death of Emma were more appropriate to the death of a mother. His own response to Jemima Hardy's death had been muted, in 'After the Last Breath', but 'The Self-Unseeing', in which the mother is situated like the grandmother in 'One We Knew', suggests that poetry 'for the mature Hardy must repossess and reprocess the child's freedom of movement within a female space' (Knoepflmacher 1993: 123). Knoepflmacher concludes that 'The female shades who stimulated Hardy's imagination were, like the living women in his life, versions of the mother he could not afford directly to impersonate or appropriate' (Knoepflmacher 1993: 124). Hardy's imposition of his mother's home, and the home of his childhood, on his poetic female constructions, is an attempt to repossess a primal, maternal refuge, and Hardy's poetry is revealed as rooted in the elementary emotions of a man who admitted that he never really quite grew up.

(h) POETRY

Hardy summarised his poetic intentions succinctly when he quoted Leslie Stephen: 'The ultimate aim of the poet should be to touch our hearts by showing his own' (Millgate 1984: 131). His success in achieving this aim depends on his poetic awkwardness and incorrectness. As Lytton Strachey noted in his review of *Satires of Circumstance* in the *New Statesman* (1914), Hardy's poetry has 'found out the secret of touching our marrow-bones' (Gibson and Johnson 1979: 64). This apparently artless simplicity made him accessible to a large urban readership composed of ordinary people, but his popularity did not sit comfortably with intellectuals, such as the influential critic, F.R. Leavis (1932) **[120]**, who finds Hardy's 'oddity and idiosyncracy' unsophisticated (Leavis 1932: 53), and marginalises him as 'a naïve poet of simple attitudes and outlook' (Leavis 1932: 52). At the same time Leavis is obviously troubled by Hardy. He tries to relegate him firmly to the past, to the leadership of an older generation of Georgian poets. Nevertheless, he cannot resist according him his due: 'his rank as a major poet rests upon a dozen poems' (Leavis 1932: 56). But even the poems that make up this achievement are not identified

A turning point in the criticism of Hardy's poetry came in his centenary year, in which W.H. Auden (1940) recorded his indebtedness to Hardy for his own education in matters of poetic technique. However, the first thorough-going study did not appear until Samuel Hynes (1961), who tackles the issues that had long baffled critics, his philosophy and his style. Hynes regards Hardy's poetry as essentially static, unable to develop over the length of his poetic career, because even in individual poems he is unable to embody a complete philosophical statement. His poetry is composed instead of impressions. Using terminology from the nineteenth-century thinker, Hegel, with whose work Hardy was familiar, Hynes suggests that a typical Hardy poem develops a thesis and an antithesis, but stops short of providing a synthesis of these attitudes or positions. Hardy offers an impressionist view of modern experience, and he does so, argues Hynes, in a language which ignores convention, which proceeds directly from his way of seeing, from his conviction of the truth and of its availability to the reader.

While Hynes engages with problems of philosophy and style, Philip Larkin (1966) takes up the issue of Hardy's vast oeuvre, and the lack of a Hardy canon **[120, 193]**, in the course of reviewing Carl J. Weber's *Hardy of Wessex* and Roy Morrell's *Thomas Hardy: The Will and the Way*:

To these two gentlemen (and also to Samuel Hynes, author of *The Pattern of Hardy's Poetry*) may I trumpet the assurance that one reader at least would not wish Hardy's *Collected Poems* a single page shorter, and regards it as many times over the best body of poetic work this century so far has to show?

(Larkin 1966: 174)

In a radio interview, Larkin defended his liking for Hardy's temperament and way of seeing life: 'He's not a transcendental writer, he's not a Yeats, he's not an Eliot; his subjects are men, the life of men, time and the passing of time, love and the fading of love' (Larkin 1966: 175).

Larkin freely acknowledges the influence on him of Hardy's verse, which results in his rejection of Yeats as a poetic model:

When I came to Hardy it was with the sense of relief that I didn't have to try and jack myself up to a concept of poetry that lay outside my own life – this is perhaps what I felt Yeats was trying to make me do. One could simply relapse back into one's own life and write from it.

(Larkin 1966: 175)

It is a similar kind of response that gave rise to an important study by Donald Davie (1973). Davie feels that 'in British poetry of the last fifty years (as not in America) the most far-reaching influence, for good or ill, has been not Yeats, still less Eliot or Pound, not Lawrence, but *Hardy*' (Davie 1973: 3), and that this influence has been deleterious **[120]**.

Like other critics, Davie complains about having to cope with nearly one thousand poems, concluding that 'each reader finds in the poems what he brings to them; what he finds there is his own pattern of preoccupations and preferences. If this is true of every poet to some degree, of Hardy it is exceptionally true' (Davie 1973: 29). Davie's own sense of the canonical Hardy is that of a poet of loss, of plangent regret for the passing of time, a poet who dwells on human mortality, an elegiac and philosophical poet, and a poet of rural nostalgia. This is the Hardy that emerges in Davie's first two chapters. Davie then explores how successive poets, particularly Larkin, have fallen under Hardy's spell. Davie contrasts what he identifies as Hardy's scientific humanism and liberalism with the alternative poetic line – Ezra Pound, T.S. Eliot and W.B. Yeats – whose own ideological bases included totalitarianism, Catholicism, Royalism, Nationalism, Classical civilisation and a degree of transcendentalism. Although Davie finds some of Hardy's poems more ambitiously achieved ('After a Journey', 'Wessex Heights', 'During Wind and Rain') for the most part his writing is characterised as a poetry of 'engaging modesty and decent liberalism' (Davie 1973: 40). It is regarded as passively ironic, a poetry of detached observation and withdrawal from the mainstream of cultural life. Hardy's poetry thus represents 'a crucial selling short of the poetic vocation, for himself and his successors' (Davie 1973: 40).

The second area which engages Davie's attention is Hardy's poetic craft. Davie's argument that his poetry is the result of careful, honest engineering rests on the analogy he draws between the technological feats of the Victorians and the early modern age. The poem about *Titanic*, 'The Convergence of the Twain', says Davie, 'itself is an engine, a sleek and powerful machine; its rhythms slide home like pistons inside cylinders, ground exactly to fractions of a millimetre' (Davie 1973:17). Even the irrregularities of a very different poem, 'Overlooking the River Stour', he suggests, are cunningly engineered. However, like Davie's delimitation of the essential Hardy, this idea of the technology of his poetry is narrow. It ignores the visionary quality of many of his poems, marginalises his poems of humanist observation, or mordant wit, and plays down the huge emotional charge that his verse contains. More recently John Powell Ward (1991) has advanced the discussion of Hardy's place in English poetry by looking at the tradition from Wordsworth through John Clare, Hardy and Robert Frost, a line that includes among others Philip Larkin. It is a poetry of the everyday, characterised by 'the verbal reserve and the pragmatic and laconic suspicion of the visionary or the extravagant, for which the English were commonly renowned' (Ward 1991: 7). Ward's study is one of several attempts to assess the influence of major poets on Hardy's poetry. Dennis Taylor (1986) regards Wordsworth as a primary influence, particularly his view of nature as an unfailing source of moral feeling, and his rejection of the artificial poetic language of Augustan poetry for the 'real language of men', as he called it in his Preface to *Lyrical Ballads*. However, it is clear that Hardy turned away from a Wordsworthian view of nature in order to address its defects as the basis of a new aesthetic of 'hitherto unperceived beauty' (Millgate 1984: 118). Similarly, although Hardy's subjects remained close to those of his revered Shelley **[91, 111, 121]**, he resisted Shelley's influence in order to maintain the integrity of his own vision.

James Richardson (1977) explores Hardy's ambivalence towards his Romantic predecessors, arguing that with the vanishing of transcendence Hardy's poetry is concerned with the conflict between necessity and possibility: 'His poetry is an obsessive investigation of desire, and a perpetual elegy on the death of possibility' (Richardson 1975: 15). Especially interesting is a chapter on the similar interest of Hardy and Browning in the theme of self-deception, incorporated into the structure of their verse as a strategy by which Romantic innocence is qualified.

For the present, the question of Hardy's poetic canon seems to have resolved itself **[120, 190–1]**. The materialist critic, Peter Widdowson (1996) has shown that, although successive recent anthologies admit in their introductions the difficulty of selection, when there is no agreement about which are Hardy's best poems, gradually 'by a tacit process of accretion' (Widdowson 1996: 23) a reasonably settled canon of Hardy's achievement has established itself. However, Widdowson warns, the selections of Hardy's poems lack adequate critical justification:

> This means that they carry at once a good deal of evaluative baggage – many assumptions about Hardy, literature, criticism are subliminally inscribed in them – and that these poems tend to exclude, or rank in inferior order, well over three-quarters of Hardy's work.
> (Widdowson 1996: 24).

Widdowson's aim is not an extension of the canon. Rather, his strategy is to test it, by a deliberate counterpointing of pairs of representative canonical poems against neglected ones on similar themes, in order to discern whether one set is intrinsically better than the other. His choices are 'I Found Her out There' and 'Concerning Agnes'; 'Wessex Heights' and 'By Henstridge Cross at the Year's End'; 'The Darkling Thrush' and 'On Stinsford Hill at Midnight'. Widdowson succeeds in making a case for the marginalised poems; for instance he makes the telling point that critics are culturally conditioned to respond to optimism located abstractly in nature, as in 'The Darkling Thrush', because it legitimises their previous pessimism, rather than respond to the humanity of the blithe, anonymous woman in 'On Stinsford Hill at Midnight', whose happiness seems to suggest that pessimism is a matter of choice. In his close readings Widdowson is critically alert to the workings of the poems, though the 'canonical' poems he selects compel critical assent more readily than the neglected ones. 'Concerning Agnes', for instance, is an indulgently nostalgic poem, which is not redeemed, as Widdowson suggests, by the 'controlled classical paean of the last stanza' (Widdowson 1996: 89). But his general strategy is to make a case for the close consideration of poems of humanist social observation, such as 'The Old Workman', as well as the better-known

'No Buyers'; also poems that give a voice to female eroticism, spoken by a woman, such as 'The Dark-eyed Gentleman', 'One Ralph Blossom Soliloquizes', 'In the Days of Crinoline', or 'In a Eweleaze near Weatherbury', about which he is especially illuminating – poems that are strongly aware of female victimisation. As Widdowson points out, even Hardy's remorseful lyrical elegies on Emma depend for their poignancy and meaning on the silencing of her voice. Although Widdowson readily concedes that his endeavour does not radically alter our perception of Hardy's oeuvre, he is surely right in his refreshing conclusion that:

> Overall *this* Hardy is wittier, more humorous, satirical and astringent than is normally perceived in the familiar melancholic or nostalgic quietist; more socially engaged and humanistic than the pessimistic determinist; more erotic and libertarian, more contradictorily positioned ... in relation to female sexuality and male attitudes to it than the fixated, chaste, and remorseful lover of 'Poems of 1912–13' might suggest.
>
> (Widdowson 1996: 83–4)

A comprehensive and systematic study of a large number of poems is a book by Paul Zietlow (1974). Its main argument is that Hardy turned from novels to poetry in order to have greater freedom for self-revelation, and for the recording of intense moments of experience. This study is descriptive rather than evaluative, emphasising Hardy's humanistic values, but primarily attending to his variety of form, tone, thought and voices. Zietlow is particularly perceptive on the dramatic aspects of Hardy's philosophical fantasies. The following year saw the appearance of a stimulating, detailed study by the poet Tom Paulin (1975). Focussing on the importance of sight, and structured by Hardy's aesthetic of perception, Paulin's book, which draws on the intellectual context of Hardy's writing, shows how it is tied to positivism and empiricism. He demonstrates the influence of Auguste Comte's view that all real knowledge is based on observed facts, and the philosopher, David Hume's replacement of the perceiving self by a mind that is the sum of what it perceives. Hardy's insistence in his work on what is authentically visible is matched by his sensibility to sound, to the cadences of actual speech. Among Paulin's numerous excellent close readings, his analysis of 'My Spirit will not Haunt the Mound' reveals its precision, but also its spoken quality that produces a sense of Emma actually talking to Hardy. In spite of Hardy's allegiance to the impressions of the senses, he can occasionally contradict his pessimism. For Paulin, 'there are times when [Hardy] breaks out of Hume's imaginative universe and achieves a visionary freedom' (Paulin 1975: 211). 'During Wind and Rain' is such a poem, which, like 'Old Furniture' and many others, receives an illuminating reading.

John Lucas (1986), whose criticism is informed explicitly by socialism, also points to Hardy's variety and to his optimism. He emphasises that Hardy can be funny, in 'The Ruined Maid' or 'The Levelled Churchyard', can offer a positive response to love in 'A Church Romance', and even to death in 'The Last Signal'; and in a poem such as 'Old Furniture' can communicate a reverence for the homely things through which generations of ordinary people give meaning to their lives. At the same time, in 'The Convergence of the Twain', Hardy condemns the debased materialism of the age.

Hardy's poetry emerges strongly from Lucas's essay as a poetry of social engagement, belief in human solidarity, and celebration of the bonds of community. Lucas asserts that 'Hardy is the natural poet of a community whose natural modes of utterance are song and dance' (Lucas 1986: 28), and he emphasises the importance of music and laughter in Hardy's verse, particularly in poems that dramatise its voices including, in 'Friends Beyond', the voices of the dead.

However, for Lucas, Hardy's evocation of the community is most often located in a past recalled by memory, which is seen as partly a response to inhabiting a world of dizzying change. The past, in which the stable community shared a solidarity and common views, is beguiling. Like his voices and visions, it was real for Hardy, but in Lucas's view, as for Donald Davie, this quietism detracts from his greatness because 'his persistent locating of vision of community in the past can come perilously close to a disabling nostalgia or to a merely enervate sadness' (Lucas 1986: 48). Nevertheless, some of Hardy's poems are acknowledged as being among the greatest in the language; 'The Voice', 'After a Journey', and 'At Castle Boterel' are simply 'beyond criticism' (Lucas 1986: 39).

Dennis Taylor (1999) assesses Hardy as a poet of the nineteenth century, when poetry was still regarded as the superior genre, and he offers some illuminating close readings. Taylor notes Hardy's ambition to be a famous poet, Horace Moule's important gift to him of *The Golden Treasury*, his reading in poetry and his diligent note-taking from the work of earlier poets. He began writing in the 1860s when 'the era of Tennyson, Browning, and Arnold was slowly changing into the era of Swinburne, Hopkins, and Hardy' (Taylor 1999: 183). Hardy's early idol was Swinburne, whose *Poems and Ballads* appeared in 1866, and whose radical development encouraged Hardy's own experiments with poetic form, particularly in the 1860s, which Dennis Taylor suggests was a significant decade for nineteenth-century poetry: 'Important developments were taking place in sonnets, ballads, hymns, classical imitations, romance imitations' (Taylor 1999: 186). 'The Impercipient', as Taylor points out, ironically adopts the hymn form to express loss of faith. Most of the poetic forms Hardy uses before 1900 are conservative, and include mimicry of old songs, other poets, and traditional verse forms. While his poetry reflects the powerful influence of his early life in Dorset, it also draws on his experience of the world of the intellect. Disparate poems such as the comic dialect poem, 'The Ruined Maid' (1866), and 'Neutral Tones'(1867) raise those major questions about the nature and meaning of experience that preoccupied the Victorians. About fifty of Hardy's poems written between 1870 and the close of his novel-writing career were published, including a number of narratives in ballad form. The best of these balladic narratives Taylor identifies as 'The Dance at the Phoenix', completed around 1878, in which Hardy successfully employs the ballad stanza form to achieve a dance rhythm. Some of these narrative poems were concerned with the Napoleonic period and anticipate *The Dynasts*.

Taylor suggests that when Hardy took up poetry again in the 1890s, critics did not respond positively because he returned to themes that had interested him in the 1860s, and worked to enhance them in new poems. However, his trip to Italy in 1887 inspired the remarkable 'Shelley's Skylark', and he produced what Taylor describes as a most significant poem, 'Nature's Questioning', a poem of personal and philosophical meditation, most likely written in the early 1890s. The Boer War gave rise to a group of poems, foremost among which is 'Drummer Hodge', which is distinctly modern in its imagistic linking of the universal with the particular. In one sense, as Taylor claims, Hardy is an academic poet who steeped himself in his 'history-soaked language' (Taylor 1999: 196), which he recognises explicitly in his poem, 'On an Invitation to the United States'. For Taylor one of Hardy's finest meditative poems is the brooding 'The Souls of the Slain', while the climax of his output as a lyric poet, suggests Taylor, came with 'The Darkling Thrush', which closes the century by drawing on the Romantic tradition of the forlorn bird. And he also strives to achieve in *The Dynasts* an epic comparable with Spenser, Milton and Wordsworth, which, like Tennyson's *Idylls of the King* and Browning's *The Ring and the Book*, incorporates post-Romantic disillusion.

John Paul Riquelme (1999) examines the modernity of Hardy's poetry. Although, unlike T.S. Eliot and W.B. Yeats, Hardy avoids the spiritual, focussing instead on a human world, his modernist tendencies may be seen in several ways. There is his challenge to the Romantic poets, evident in his subversion of the lyric, which often presents a voice falling silent. Riquelme offers a detailed study of 'Nature's Questioning' as typical of Hardy's modern imagination. He examines its ambiguous use of language, its negation, its qualification of the use of personification, and its concluding silence. A typically modernist acceptance of the diminution of consciousness is found in 'The Impercipient', while the wind in 'During Wind and Rain', unlike Shelley's wind in 'Ode to the West Wind' is uncompromisingly literal. In this poem, as in 'Rain on a Grave', what is underscored is the permanence of loss.

Hardy's war poems reveal 'self-reflective doublings' (Riquelme 1999: 210). Riquelme draws attention particularly to 'Drummer Hodge', 'In Time of "The Breaking of Nations" ', and ' "Men Who March Away" '. The ambiguous nature of the double self is also explored in 'Wessex Heights', a poem that raises questions about the integrity and conti- nuity of identity. In Hardy's late poems, Riquelme argues, Hardy became concerned with presenting multiple views, selves and voices, as he does in 'Voices from Things Growing in a Churchyard', in which he is seen as employing an anti-self, or mask. But perhaps Hardy is most strikingly modern in his anticipation of that tendency towards silence evident in the much later work of Samuel Beckett, in a poem such as 'Surview', and most notably in his final poem, 'He Resolves to Say No More', in which the silence he chooses is both unquiet and beyond his control.

(i) OTHER TOPICS AND ISSUES

Michael Millgate (1999) offers an illuminating commentary on the sources used by Hardy's biographers, by which their versions of his life may be evaluated. Millgate reviews the creation of Florence Hardy's *Life*, noting its selectivity, as well as Florence's alterations and deletions. The principle behind his own book, *The Life and Work of Thomas Hardy*, is 'to reconstruct the text as Hardy left it at the time of his death' (Millgate 1999: 3). Millgate's use of surviving typescripts and his employment of other sources, such as various notebooks, manuscripts of novels and verse, together with Hardy's correspondence, shed light on his early years, particularly the importance to him of the life of a rural community and the Church's presence within it.

While Hardy's *Architectural Notebook* and letters reveal something of his years in London, there is little documentary information about the women in his life at this period, nor about his friendship with

Horace Moule. Similarly, no proper understanding may be gained of the failure of his marriage. Moreover, in the absence of evidence, Millgate counsels against speculating about Hardy's relationship with Tryphena Sparks, or indeed about the early stages of his friendship with Florence Dugdale.

Hardy's notebooks are recognised as valuable sources for biographers. *Thomas Hardy's 'Studies, Specimens etc.'*, *The Personal Notebooks of Thomas Hardy* and *The Literary Notebooks of Thomas Hardy* contain his poetic exercises, his accumulation of material about the Napoleonic period, and his 'philosophy'. Millgate's own study (1984), *The Life and Work of Thomas Hardy* adds a good deal of information about the scope of Hardy's social life in London at the peak of his literary career. Millgate concludes his review with the suggestion that 'the challenge, biographically speaking, is somehow to come to terms with what is truly distinctive about Hardy's final years, his extraordinarily, even uniquely, sustained productivity as a poet' (Millgate 1999: 15).

Hardy revised his work obsessively. Revisions to the fiction were made during the writing of the manuscripts, during the preparation of the serials, and also during the production of the first volume editions. Further revisions took place in 1895–6 and in 1912, when collected editions of Hardy's work appeared. In some cases the extensive nature of the revisions has cast doubt on whether the different texts are in fact the same novels.

Genetic criticism, the study of the evolution of texts, was first applied to Hardy by Mary Ellen Chase (1927). Although she focuses only on three novels, she brings to light the changes Hardy had to make to get his novels published in contemporary magazines, and his consequent habit of rewriting. John Paterson (1960) traces the development of the text of *The Return of the Native* **[66–71]** from manuscript to its final book form. J.T. Laird's study (1975) is essential for the reader interested in the changes that Hardy made to his characterisation in *Tess of the d'Urbervilles* **[82–8]**, and especially the alterations he made to Tess's violation. Mary Jacobus (1976) offers a feminist perspective of *Tess of the d'Urbervilles*. Her argument, based on a scholarly investigation of Hardy's revisions to the main characters in the manuscript, is that his purification of Tess was made in order to evade Victorian censorship.

Other useful studies include Patricia Ingham (1976) on *Jude the Obscure* **[88–94]**, and an essay on *Far from the Madding Crowd* **[61–6]** by Simon Gatrell (1979), who has also produced the foremost book in the field of textual studies (Gatrell 1988). This work initiated a new critical methodology, tracing the processes that characterise the evolution of Hardy's writings from the manuscript stage to the collected edition of 1912. At the same time Gatrell's book illuminates Hardy's working life as a writer. Textual study of Hardy's short stories is represented by Martin Ray (1997).

Robert Schweik (1999), while asserting Hardy's intellectual independence, acknowledges a variety of influences on his writing, particularly in the areas of science, philosophy and religion. Although Hardy lost his faith and became an agnostic, Christianity remained a strong influence. He took issue with its doctrines, but did not suggest any substitute for faith, and retained a profound nostalgia for the Christian tradition. Several of Hardy's poems regret the impossibility of faith, and offer secularised versions of Christian stories, while the novels and *The Dynasts* represent Christianity as simply one creed among many, and its God as imperfect.

Hardy's scientific interests were wide. He researched astronomy and physics in order to make science the vehicle for romance in *Two on a Tower*, a novel that includes a vision of a dying universe; and his later familiarity with Einstein's theory of relativity is evident in his poem 'The Absolute Explains'. Hardy's interest in archaeology is apparent in his concern with preserving Stonehenge, in the narrative context provided for *A Group of Noble Dames*, and in the story 'A Tryst at an Ancient Earthwork'. Most frequently, archaeology is used in the novels to introduce temporal perspective to the vicissitudes of contemporary human life. As Robert Schweik argues, Hardy was influenced by the evolutionary theories of Darwin; for instance in the significance of heredity in *The Well-Beloved*, in Stephen Knight's dizzying view of evolutionary time in *A Pair of Blue Eyes*, and in the Darwinian woodland of *The Woodlanders*. Hardy portrays man inhabiting a universe oblivious to humanity, alienated in *The Return of the Native*, and in *Tess of the d'Urbervilles* and *Jude the Obscure* subject to the law of the survival of the fittest. Hardy's other debts are perhaps more obvious; Feuerbach's concept of God as a human invention, Comte's religion of humanity (though a little too optimistic for Hardy), Schopenhauer's idea of will, and von Hartmann's notion of the Immanent Will as Unconscious, which in *The Dynasts* Hardy seeks to make more purposive.

Another fruitful area of study has been the visual arts, particularly painting **[14, 58, 80]**. Several critics have been drawn to the aesthetic, visual quality of Hardy's writing, including Penelope Vigar (1974), who focuses on the narrative pictures and visual impressions that assist in the development of character. Joan Grundy (1979) also discusses Hardy's painterly, impressionistic techniques, but spreads her interest to include sculpture, the theatre, music and dance, and pays critical attention to *The Dynasts* **[136–9]**. A fine analysis of Hardy's references to photography is developed by Arlene M. Jackson (1984). She explores Hardy's deliberate preoccupation with point of view, framing, and selection of shots. David Lodge (1977) argues that in Hardy's novels his imagination produces a visual rather than a purely verbal medium, which anticipates some of the visual effects of film and creates a world at once real and more dramatically intense.

However, the major work is by J.B. Bullen (1986), which explores a creative process that gives visual embodiment to Hardy's religious and ethical ideas. Reading Hardy within his artistic milieu, Bullen demonstrates how his visual sensibility structures his novels in a series of images. He uncovers connections between the conscious and the unconscious in Hardy's fiction that relate psychology and mythology. In particular, Bullen gives a detailed account of Hardy's knowledge of J.M.W. Turner's painting, and his understanding of how expressionism creates a deeper reality. This concern with Hardy's connection with Turner, John Ruskin and the general climate of art in the period is developed by Annie Escuret (1989).

In a perceptive essay, Norman Page (1999) reflects on Hardy's art and aesthetics. He argues that Hardy's autodidacticism had nurtured an independence of mind and an openness to ideas that instinctively resisted the authority of hierarchies and canons of taste. Page notes that Hardy rejects 'representation or "realism" in favour of a highly, even eccentrically personal vision' (Page 1999: 38). His fiction includes elements of surrealism, and he pursues beauty in the ordinary and even in the ugly, regarding it idiosyncratically as a cultural and even an individual construct, rather than as an absolute.

Page observes that 'Hardy's ideas concerning literature and literary style, as well as his more general notions of art, were ... profoundly influenced by his experience of nonliterary arts' (Page 1999: 49). His devotion to painting, music and architecture, Hardy's sense of what he called 'the solidarity of all the arts' (*LW*, 321), produced an ecclecticism that was also subject to an imagination that blurred distinctions between literary forms and produced narrative poems and poetic fictions. Moreover, in spite of Hardy's determined provincialism and individualism, Page suggests, his consistent seeking after fugitive impressions is a concern he shares with the aesthetic movement.

Like Norman Page, Linda M. Shires (1999) regards Hardy's aesthetic as fundamentally anti-realistic, but rather than associating him with the aesthetic movement, she sees him as a proto-modernist. His 'disproportioning' and 'impressions', his use of multiplicity, and his production of incongruity, all question traditional representation. This is signalled in the title of *Tess of the d'Urbervilles*, the subject of Shires's essay. The novel's title is seen as a challenge to conventional presentation, 'but is faithful, instead, to an authorial aesthetic of incongruity' (Shires 1999: 149).

Shires proceeds to demonstrate that in *Tess of the d'Urbervilles* Hardy parodies traditional narrative conventions, complicating the time scheme, overwriting Tess's fate, observing her 'rape', and refusing to stereotype character (even that of Alec). The reader sees characters, particularly Tess, through the multiple perspectives of point of view and of different genres. There is also the double view of Tess as virgin and woman, advanced by a narrator who is mocked and undermined by the implied author for wanting to possess Tess's femininity. And as the novel progresses, Tess becomes less and less individualised. Shires summarises: 'Through his handling of Tess and her three suitors, Hardy challenges the foundations of realist character-drawing and perspective' (Shires 1999: 156).

Beyond these radical methods, argues Shires, Hardy mixes genres that confront each other, he offers contradictory philosophies of life, he includes startling intertextual references, and concludes the novel with a lame re-writing of *Paradise Lost*. This radical aesthetic, suggests Shires, is part of this novel's Victorian context, which includes the writings of Carlyle, Ruskin and Browning, but particularly those of Ruskin, who addresses most directly the aesthetic of the alienated consciousness. In this fractured, disunified text, Shires concludes, as indeed in his last three novels, 'it is possible to see Hardy as a proto-modernist' (Shires 1999: 161).

A wider range of other concerns are reflected in Hardy criticism, too many to discuss here. A book which has stood the test of time is a study by Harvey Curtis Webster (1947). Focussing mainly on the novels, but culminating in a discussion of *The Dynasts*, Webster's study of the development of Hardy's philosophy locates the origins of his pessimism in his encounter with Darwin and scientific rationalism [12, 77, 81, 121]. It traces the evolution of Hardy's thought from determinism to a concern with social issues in *The Woodlanders*, *Tess of the d'Urbervilles* and *Jude the Obscure*. Hardy's sense of the possibilities for change and improvement correspond with his anticipation of the removal of determinism with the coming to consciousness of the Immanent Will. Roger Ebbatson (1982) returns to Darwin in a study which argues that Hardy, from *The Woodlanders* onwards, presents the forces of social change more trenchantly than in an early novel, such as *Far from the Madding Crowd* [61–6]. Gillian Beer (1983) draws a parallel between Hardy's tragic plots and the determinism of Darwin's process of natural selection, since only one possibility among many is selected. Hardy's difficulty in finding a place for humanity in the deterministic natural order is also examined. Deborah L. Collins (1990) reviews the influences on Hardy of Positivism, Darwinism and Schopenhauer, finding in his fiction despair at the impossibility of understanding the nature of God coupled with a profound humanistic quest for meaning; while Timothy Hands (1989) sees Hardy as 'an author whose complex religious biography becomes subsumed in his writing career' (Hands 1989: 126). This is traced in Hardy's language, his creation of characters, and his ideas.

A different philosophical approach is to be found in Bruce Johnson (1983). Drawing on Husserl, he argues for a phenomenological dimension of Hardy's imagination, which is concerned with the significance of the non-human in the human. His characters divide between those who represent continuity between the natural world and humanity (Gabriel Oak, Giles Winterborne, Tess Durbeyfield) and those intellectuals and isolated figures (Sergeant Troy, Angel Clare, and Sue Bridehead). Contact with inner primal energy is modified or frustrated in various ways, yet survives in the consciousnesses of the characters. F. R. Southerington (1971) works outwards from a consideration of Hardy's frame of mind to his beliefs. On this basis his novels divide into the personal and the ideological. The best section of this book is a sustained discussion of the ideas that inform the structure of *The Dynasts*, which is regarded as both a historical drama and a philosophical poem, in which the paradoxical state of the Will as both unconscious and conscious is transformed by its gradual awakening to consciousness.

Dale Kramer's essay on *Jude the Obscure* (1999b) is concerned with the response of its reader. He argues that Hardy endeavours to affect the intuitive reading process by a structural manipulation of the text, and cumulatively to secure a shift in the reader's response to the struggle of Jude and Sue. Kramer begins by summarising the contemporary reception of *Jude the Obscure*, both as a serial and as a single-volume novel, which was published just as the traditional three-volume form of the Victorian novel was in a state of transition. It is a very personal novel, conveying Hardy's anger at moribund social conventions. It also raises a number of questions of central importance to late nineteenth century culture. However, argues Kramer, it is exploratory rather than didactic. Moreover, its precise historical period remains unfixed and a case may be made for seeing it as being set either in the 1860s or the 1890s.

Kramer is primarily concerned to explore a division among readers as to whether Jude or Sue is the proper focus of the novel. He notes that Jude is presented from the inside, while Sue has to be understood from evidence adduced from a number of conflicting perspectives. Sue thus becomes the focus of particular reading strategies, such as feminism, or psychoanalysis. However, Sue is at the centre of Hardy's structural manipulation of the reader as a means of encouraging analysis of the protagonists' struggle and understanding of its true nature. The opposition that Jude and Sue initially encounter is composed of elements such as class, income, social attitudes, contemporary thinking and religion; but halfway through the narrative the essential opposition is revealed to be the inner workings of Sue's personality.

Kramer locates this narrative shift at the point when Sue marries Phillotson. Jude's idealisation of Sue is ironically matched by her sexual interest in him, which the reader intuits from her physical revulsion from Phillotson. Their reluctance to pursue Jude's divorce is thus seen as preventing what would have been a 'normal' marriage. Kramer notes: 'It is remarkable how different are the tones of the novel previous to, and following, Sue's marriage. The emphasis shifts almost entirely from the damage caused by social convention and philosophical unconventionality to damage caused nearly purely on psychological grounds.' (Kramer 1999b: 178). In spite of most critics' assertions to the contrary, there is evidence in the text for a developing inside view of Sue, argues Kramer, and for seeing the novel's unhappiness as being placed 'resoundingly within personality' (Kramer 1999b: 179).

An important, though somewhat eccentric, book that ignores scholarly conventions, is an essay on Hardy by John Bayley (1978). Bayley finds in the instability of Hardy's writing a division and contrast in his consciousness between his physical perceptions and his ideas. Bayley concentrates on the lesser novels, particularly *Desperate Remedies* [95, 181, 185], which is highly regarded, and seeks to revalue the position of the major novels in Hardy's oeuvre, finding *Tess of the d'Urbervilles* and *Jude the Obscure* uncharacteristic. Division and disunity are concepts marshalled against the conventional critical pursuit of artistic coherence. The pleasure of reading Hardy depends on abandoning this pursuit. For Bayley, Hardy's strength lies in his poetry, and in parts of the minor novels, such as *A Pair of Blue Eyes* [96–8], *Two on a Tower* [107–10], and *The Hand of Ethelberta* [98–101]. The essay is an illuminating attempt to encourage the reader's engagement with the whole of Hardy's writing, but it is limited by a curiously old-fashioned reliance on authorial intention.

Hardy's language has long been a preoccupation of criticism. David Lodge (1966) is concerned to reveal in the scene in the garden at Talbothays in *Tess of the d'Urbervilles*, the different narrative voices Hardy employs. The breadth of Hardy's use of language is addressed by Norman Page (1980). And there are two wide-ranging studies of Hardy's language by Ralph W.V. Elliott (1984) and Raymond Chapman (1990). However, the major book on this subject is by Dennis Taylor (1993). His compelling study looks at Hardy's supposed stylistic awkwardness within the context of mid-Victorian philology and reveals with startling clarity that he was very consciously employing the whole spread of language from old words that were still extant to those recently entered into currency, in order to challenge contemporary language.

Peter Widdowson (1999) discusses the relation between Hardy's literary oeuvre and modern critical theory. His essay commences by identifying as problematic the tension between Hardy's adherence to realism ('Novels of Character and Environment') and his opposition to naturalism (his idea of art as a 'disproportioning' of reality).

Widdowson offers a useful review of the development of Hardy criticism, of both fiction and poetry, before going on to give a synopsis of the way theory has been applied to Hardy's work as a way of evaluating theoretical models. For Widdowson, what materialist, feminist, and post-structuralist approaches have in common is 'a cultural politics which seeks to subvert the orthodox "Hardy" and to (re) mobilize the "disproportioning" dimension of his work' (Widdowson 1999: 80). Hardy becomes, suggests Widdowson, 'a terrain of riven textuality whose major landmarks are faultlines which expose the substrata of cultural politics, class, sexuality, and gender, themselves striated by the unstable language of which they are composed' (Widdowson 1999: 87–8).

Widdowson argues that the focus on class has shifted attention from Hardy the countryman to Hardy the successful bourgeois 'metropolitan man-of-letters' (Widdowson 1999: 88), obsessed with issues of social mobility. Widdowson also suggests that the theoretical interest in sexuality and gender has initiated a debate polarising Hardy as either proto-feminist or misogynist. A fundamental question that Widdowson raises is the extent to which Hardy is consciously in control of his texts. The conclusion of his essay leads into speculation about the future direction of Hardy criticism. He points out that there is no 'post-colonialist' criticism looking at Hardy's place in the construction of 'Englishness' and 'English Literature'. In spite of the interest of the texts in homoeroticism and problems of gender, there is still no gay, lesbian or 'queer' criticism. Perhaps the most interesting challenge for Hardy criticism that Widdowson identifies is that resulting from the increasingly frequent representation of his fiction on film and television, since the relation between the written text and its visual production clearly raises issues of response and interpretation that have yet to be subjected to serious critical study

CHRONOLOGY

1840	2 June: Thomas Hardy born, first child of Thomas Hardy, a builder, and Jemima Hardy (*née* Hand), who had been married five and a half months. Later siblings were Mary, Kate and Henry.
1848	Enters the new National School in Stinsford.
1850	Removed by his mother to a Nonconformist school in Dorchester, run by Isaac Last.
1853	Follows Last when he sets up his own independent 'commercial academy' in Dorchester, where he receives a sound education.
1856	July: articled to John Hicks, a Dorchester architect. Commences friendship with Henry Bastow and also Horace Moule, who becomes his mentor.
1860	Employed by Hicks as an assistant.
1862	April: seeks work in London. Finds a position as a draughtsman with the architect, Arthur Blomfield. November: elected to the Architectural Association.
1863	Awarded architectural prizes; but considers writing as a possible career. It is likely that he became engaged to Eliza Nicholls.
1867	Returns to Dorset and works for Hicks on church restoration. Begins work on his first novel.
1868	Completes *The Poor Man and the Lady*, which was rejected for publication. It remains unpublished. Receives advice from George Meredith.
1869	Works on church restoration in Weymouth for the architect G.M. Crickmay. Commences writing *Desperate Remedies*.
1870	On a professional visit to St Juliot, near Boscastle in Cornwall, meets his first wife, Emma Gifford.
1871	*Desperate Remedies* published.
1872	*Under the Greenwood Tree* published. Moves to London to work on school plans for the architect T. Roger Smith. *A Pair of Blue Eyes* begins to appear as a serial in *Tinsleys' Magazine*. Decides to give up architecture for a career as a writer. Leslie Stephen asks for a serial for the *Cornhill Magazine*.
1873	*A Pair of Blue Eyes* published in three volumes. Horace Moule commits suicide in his rooms in Cambridge.

1874   *Far from the Madding Crowd* begins serialisation in the *Cornhill Magazine*, and is published in two volumes later in the year. 17 September: Hardy marries Emma Gifford in London, to which they return after their honeymoon in Paris.

1875   The Hardys return to Dorset and settle in Swanage. *The Hand of Ethelberta* serialised in the *Cornhill Magazine*.

1876   They move again first to Yeovil and then to Sturminster Newton in Dorset, where Hardy commences writing *The Return of the Native*. *The Hand of Ethelberta* published in two volumes.

1878   The Hardys return to London and find a house in Tooting. *The Return of the Native* serialised in *Belgravia*, and later published in three volumes. Researches background material for *The Trumpet-Major* in the British Museum.

1879   Begins to publish short stories, commencing with 'The Distracted Preacher', in *New Quarterly Magazine*.

1880   *The Trumpet-Major* serialised in *Good Words*, and published in three volumes. In October falls seriously ill with a prolonged, mysterious ailment. *A Laodicean*, written during this illness, appears in *Harper's New Monthly Magazine*.

1881   *A Laodicean* published in three volumes. The Hardys return to Dorset, settling in Wimborne Minster.

1882   *Two on a Tower* serialised in the *Atlantic Monthly*, later published in three volumes.

1883   The Hardys move from Wimborne to Dorchester where they await the completion outside the town of a new house, Max Gate, designed by Hardy and built by his brother.

1884   Begins writing *The Mayor of Casterbridge*. Made a Justice of the Peace and enters local society.

1885   The Hardys move into Max Gate, where Hardy is to remain for the rest of his life.

1886   *The Mayor of Casterbridge* appears in the *Graphic* and is published in two volumes. *The Woodlanders* commences serialisation in *Macmillan's Magazine*. Hardy's friend the poet William Barnes dies.

1887   *The Woodlanders* published in three volumes. The Hardys holiday in Italy and France.

1888   *Wessex Tales*, Hardy's first book of short stories, published in two volumes.

1889   At work on *Tess of the d'Urbervilles*.

1890   *A Group of Noble Dames*, a series of short stories, appears in the *Graphic*. Hardy's experience with editors over *Tess of the d'Urbervilles* gives rise to his essay, 'Candour in English Fiction'.

1891   *Tess of the d'Urbervilles* serialised in the *Graphic* and published in three volumes. *A Group of Noble Dames* published in one volume.

1892   20 July: his father, Thomas, dies. *The Pursuit of the Well-Beloved* serialised in the *Illustrated London News*. Marital difficulties become increasingly evident.

1893   Meets Mrs Florence Henniker, one of several artistic society women with whom he had close friendships, and begins an intense romantic attachment, the subject of several poems. Commences writing *Jude the Obscure*.

1894   *Life's Little Ironies*, Hardy's third volume of short stories published. December: *Jude the Obscure* begins serialisation in *Harper's New Monthly Magazine*.

1895   *Jude the Obscure* published in volume form as part of Osgood, McIlvaine's first collected edition of Hardy's Wessex Novels. Its reception is a factor in Hardy's decision to give up fiction.

1896   Hardy writes a number of major poems.

1897   *The Well-Beloved* (substantially rewritten) added to the Wessex Novels. Visits Switzerland.

1898   *Wessex Poems*, Hardy's first volume of poetry, published.

1899   Beginning of the Boer War, which occasioned the first of Hardy's series of war poems. Growing estrangement from Emma, although they both still lived at Max Gate.

1901   *Poems of the Past and the Present* published.

1902   Macmillan become his publishers.

1904   3 April: death of his mother, Jemima. Appearance of Part First of *The Dynasts*, his epic-drama in verse on the Napoleonic wars.

1905   Meets Florence Dugdale who soon became his secretary. Receives honorary degree from Aberdeen University.

1906   Part Second of *The Dynasts* published.

1908   Part Third of *The Dynasts* published, completing a comprehensive account of his thought. Publishes a memorial edition of *Select Poems of William Barnes*.

1909   *Time's Laughingstocks*, Hardy's third collection of poems published. Developing relationship with Florence Dugdale.

1910   Awarded Order of Merit, having previously declined a knighthood. Receives the freedom of Dorchester.

1912   Publication begins of the Wessex Edition of Hardy's collected works. Awarded Gold Medal of the Royal Society of

Literature. 27 November: Emma Hardy dies. Hardy is prompted to commence writing 'Poems of 1912–13'.

1913   *A Changed Man and other Tales*, his final book of short stories published. Makes a pilgrimage to Cornwall in pursuit of the past. Receives honorary degree at Cambridge and becomes an Honorary Fellow of Magdalene College.

1914   10 February: marries Florence Dugdale. *Satires of Circumstance*, his fourth collection of verse, published. Beginning of the First World War has a profound effect on Hardy's view of humanity's future.

1915   His cousin and heir, Frank is killed at Gallipoli. 24 November: Hardy's sister Mary dies.

1916   *Selected Poems of Thomas Hardy* published.

1917   *Moments of Vision*, Hardy's fifth volume of poetry published. He and Florence begin work on *The Life of Thomas Hardy*.

1919–20 The de-luxe Mellstock Edition of Hardy's work published.

1922   *Late Lyrics and Earlier* published, with its substantial and important 'Apology'.

1923   *The Famous Tragedy of the Queen of Cornwall* published. Florence Henniker dies. Visit of the Prince of Wales to Max Gate. Friendship established with T.E. Lawrence, who was living locally.

1924   Dramatisation of *Tess* performed at Dorchester, with Gertrude Bugler, a local girl, for whom Hardy feels an attraction, in the title role.

1925   *Human Shows, Far Phantasies, Songs and Trifles*, Hardy's seventh volume of verse, published.

1928   11 January: Hardy dies. His heart is buried in Emma's grave at Stinsford, his ashes in Westminster Abbey. *Winter Words*, his final collection of poems, published posthumously.

BIBLIOGRAPHY

Armstrong, Isobel (1993): *Victorian Poetry: Poetry, Poetics and Politics* (London and New York: Routledge).

Auden, W.H. (1940): 'A Literary Transference', *Southern Review*, 6: 78–86.

Bayley, John (1978): *An Essay on Hardy* (Cambridge: Cambridge University Press).

Bayley, John (1982): 'The Love Story in *Two on a Tower*', in *Thomas Hardy Annual*, 1, (ed.) Norman Page (London: Macmillan), 60–70.

Beer, Gillian (1983): 'Finding a Scale for the Human: Plot and Writing in Hardy's Novels', in *Darwin's Plots: Evolutionary Narrative in Darwin, George Eliot and Nineteenth Century Fiction* (London: Routledge and Kegan Paul), 236–58.

Berger, Sheila (1990): *Thomas Hardy and Visual Structures* (New York and London: New York University Press).

Björk, Lennart A. (ed.) (1985): *The Literary Notebooks of Thomas Hardy*, 2 vols (London: Macmillan).

Boumelha, Penny (1982): *Thomas Hardy and Women: Sexual Ideology and Narrative Form* (Brighton: Harvester Wheatsheaf).

Boumelha, Penny (1993): ' "A Complicated Position for a Woman": *The Hand of Ethelberta*', in Margaret R. Higonnet (ed.) (1993a) *The Sense of Sex: Feminist Perspectives on Hardy* (Urbana and Chicago: University of Illinois Press), 242–59.

Boumelha, Penny (1999a): 'Introduction', in Thomas Hardy, *The Return of the Native*, in A.M. Slade (ed.) (1999) (London: Penguin), xix–xxxvi.

Boumelha, Penny (1999b): 'The Patriarchy of Class: *Under the Greenwood Tree, Far from the Madding Crowd, The Woodlanders*', in Dale Kramer (ed.) (1999a) *The Cambridge Companion to Thomas Hardy* (Cambridge: Cambridge University Press), 130–44.

Brady, Kristin (1982): *The Short Stories of Thomas Hardy* (London: Macmillan).

Brady, Kristin (1993): 'Textual Hysteria: Hardy's Narrator on Women', in Margaret R. Higonnet (1993a) *The Sense of Sex: Feminist Perspectives on Hardy* (Urbana and Chicago: University of Illinois Press), 87–106.

Brady, Kristin (1999): 'Thomas Hardy and Matters of Gender', in Dale Kramer (ed.) (1999a) *The Cambridge Companion to Thomas Hardy* (Cambridge: Cambridge University Press), 93–111.

Brooks, Jean R. (1971): *Thomas Hardy: The Poetic Structure* (London: Elek Books).

Brown, Douglas (1954): *Thomas Hardy* (London: Longman's, Green and Co.).

Buckler, William E. (1980): 'Thomas Hardy's Sense of Self: The Poet Behind the Autobiographer in *The Life of Thomas Hardy*', *Prose Studies* 1: 69–86.

Buckler, William E. (1983): *The Poetry of Thomas Hardy: A Study in Art and Ideas* (New York: New York University Press).

Bullen, J.B. (1986): *The Expressive Eye: Fiction and Perception in the Work of Thomas Hardy* (Oxford: Clarendon Press).

Butler, Lance St John (ed.) (1977): *Thomas Hardy After Fifty Years* (London: Macmillan).

Butler, Lance St John (ed.) (1989): *Alternative Hardy* (Basingstoke: Macmillan).

Casagrande, Peter J. (1982): *Unity in Hardy's Novels: 'Repetitive Symmetries'* (London: Macmillan).

Cecil, Lord David (1943): *Hardy the Novelist: An Essay in Criticism* (London: Constable).

Chapman, Raymond (1990): *The Language of Thomas Hardy* (Basingstoke: Macmillan).

Chapple, J.A.V. (1970): *Documentary and Imaginative Literature 1880–1920* (London: Blandford Press).

Chase, Mary Ellen (1927): *Thomas Hardy: From Serial to Novel* (Minneapolis: University of Minnesota Press).

Collins, Deborah L. (1990): *Thomas Hardy and his God: A Litany of Unbelief* (Basingstoke: Macmillan).

Cunningham, Valentine (1975): *Everywhere Spoken Against: Dissent in the Victorian Novel* (Oxford: Clarendon Press).

Danby, John F. (1959): *'Under the Greenwood Tree'*, *Critical Quarterly*, 1: 5–13; reprinted in R.P. Draper (ed.) (1987) *Thomas Hardy: Three Pastoral Novels: A Casebook* (London: Macmillan), 89–97.

Davie, Donald (1973): *Thomas Hardy and British Poetry* (London: Routledge and Kegan Paul).

Davies, Sarah (1993): *'The Hand of Ethelberta*: De-Mythologising "Woman" '*, *Critical Survey*, 5: 123–30.

Deacon, Louis and Coleman, Terry (1966): *Providence and Mr Hardy* (London: Hutchinson & Co).

Dean, Susan (1977): *Hardy's Poetic Vision in* The Dynasts*: The Diorama of a Dream* (Princeton, NJ: Princeton University Press).

De Laura, David J. (1967): ' "The Ache of Modernism" in Hardy's Later Novels', *Journal of English Literary History*, 34: 380–99.

Dolin, Tim (ed.) (1997): Thomas Hardy, *The Hand of Ethelberta* (London: Penguin).

Dolin, Tim (ed.) (1998): Thomas Hardy, *Tess of the d'Urbervilles* (London: Penguin).

Draffan, Robert A. (1973): 'Hardy's *Under the Greenwood Tree*', *English*, 22: 55–60.

Draper, R.P. (ed.) (1975): *Hardy: The Tragic Novels: A Casebook* (London: Macmillan).

Draper, R.P. (1985): 'Hardy and the Question of Regionalism', *Thomas Hardy Journal*, 1: 28–40.

Draper, R.P. (ed.) (1987): *Thomas Hardy: Three Pastoral Novels: A Casebook* (London: Macmillan).

Ebbatson, Roger (1982): *The Evolutionary Self: Hardy, Forster, Lawrence* (Brighton: Harvester Press).

Ebbatson, Roger (1993): *Hardy: The Margin of the Unexpressed* (Sheffield: Sheffield Academic Press).

Elliott, Ralph W.V. (1984): *Thomas Hardy's English* (Oxford: Basil Blackwell).

Escuret, Annie (1989): 'Thomas Hardy and J.M.W. Turner' in Lance St John Butler (ed.) *Alternative Hardy* (Basingstoke: Macmillan), 205–25.

Falck-Yi, Suzanne B. (ed.) (1993): Thomas Hardy, *Far from the Madding Crowd* (Oxford: Oxford University Press).

Feltes, N.N. (1986): *Modes of Production of Victorian Novels* (Chicago and London: University of Chicago Press).

Fisher, Joe (1992): *The Hidden Hardy* (Basingstoke: Macmillan).

Ford, Boris (ed.) (1958): *From Dickens to Hardy*; revised 1982 (London: Penguin Books).

Garson, Marjorie (1991): *Hardy's Fables of Integrity: Woman, Body, Text* (Oxford: Clarendon Press).

Gatrell, Simon (1979): 'Hardy the Creator: *Far from the Madding Crowd*', in Dale Kramer (ed.) (1979) *Critical Approaches to the Fiction of Thomas Hardy* (London: Macmillan), 74–98.

Gatrell, Simon (1988): *Hardy the Creator: A Textual Biography* (Oxford: Clarendon Press).

Gattrell, Simon (1993): 'Introduction', in Thomas Hardy, *Far from the Madding Crowd*, (ed.) Suzanne B. Falck-Yi (1993) (Oxford: Oxford University Press), xiii–xxviii.

Gatrell, Simon (1999): 'Wessex', in Dale Kramer (ed.) (1999a) *The Cambridge Companion to Thomas Hardy* (Cambridge: Cambridge University Press), 19–37.

Gibson, James (1996): *Thomas Hardy* (Basingstoke: Macmillan).

Gibson, James and Johnson, Trevor (eds) (1979): *Thomas Hardy's Poems: A Casebook* (London: Macmillan).

Giordano, Frank R. (1984): *'I'd Have My Life Unbe': Thomas Hardy's Self-Destructive Characters* (Alabama: University of Alabama Press).

Gittings, Robert (1975): *Young Thomas Hardy* (London: Heinemann Educational).

Gittings, Robert (1978): *The Older Hardy* (London: Heinemann Educational).

Goode, John (1979): 'Sue Bridehead and the New Woman', in Mary Jacobus (ed.) (1979) *Women Writing and Writing about Women* (London: Croom Helm), 100–13.

Goode, John (1988): *Thomas Hardy: The Offensive Truth* (Oxford: Basil Blackwell).

Gregor, Ian (1966): 'What Kind of Fiction Did Hardy Write?', *Essays in Criticism*, 16: 290–308.

Gregor, Ian (1974): *The Great Web: The Form of Hardy's Major Fiction* (London: Faber & Faber).

Gregor, Ian and Irwin, Michael (1984): 'Your Story or Your Life?: Reflections on Thomas Hardy's Autobiography', in *Thomas Hardy Annual*, 2, (ed.) Norman Page (London: Macmillan), 157–70.

Gribble, Jennifer (1996): 'The Quiet Women of Egdon Heath', *Essays in Criticism*, 46: 234–57.

Grundy, Joan (1979): *Hardy and the Sister Arts* (London: Macmillan).

Guerard, Albert J. (1949): *Thomas Hardy: The Novels and Stories* (Cambridge, MA: Harvard University Press); revised 1964 (London: New Directions).

Hands, Timothy (1989): *Thomas Hardy: Distracted Preacher?* (Basingstoke: Macmillan).

Hands, Timothy (1995): *Thomas Hardy* (Basingstoke: Macmillan).

Hardy, Evelyn and Gittings, Robert (eds) (1979): *Some Recollections*, by Emma Hardy (Oxford: Oxford University Press).

Hardy, Florence Emily (1933): *The Life of Thomas Hardy* (London: Macmillan).

Harvey, Geoffrey (1995): 'Thomas Hardy: Moments of Vision', in Harold Orel (ed.) *Critical Essays on Thomas Hardy's Poetry* (New York: G.K. Hall & Co.), 35–46. Reprinted from *The Romantic Tradition in Modern English Poetry* (London: Macmillan, 1986).

Hetherington, Tom (ed.) (1986): Thomas Hardy: *The Well-Beloved* (London: Oxford University Press).

Higonnet, Margaret R. (ed.) (1993a): *The Sense of Sex: Feminist Perspectives on Hardy* (Urbana and Chicago: University of Illinois Press).

Higonnet, Margaret R. (1993b): 'A Woman's Story: Tess and the Problem of Voice', in Margaret R. Higonnet (ed.) (1993a) *The Sense of Sex: Feminist Perspectives on Hardy* (Urbana and Chicago: University of Illinois Press), 14–31.

Higonnet, Margaret R. (1998): 'Introduction' in Thomas Hardy, *Tess of the d'Urbervilles*, (ed.) Tim Dolin (London: Penguin), xix–xli.

Holloway, John (1953): *The Victorian Sage* (London: Macmillan).

Howard, Jeanne (1977): 'Thomas Hardy's "Mellstock" and the Registrar General's Stinsford', *Literature and History*, 6: 179–200.

Howe, Irving (1968): *Thomas Hardy* (London: Macmillan).

Hyde, William J. (1958): 'Hardy's View of Realism: A Key to the Rustic Characters', *Victorian Studies*, 2: 451–9.

Hynes, Samuel (1961): *The Pattern of Hardy's Poetry* (London: Oxford University Press).

Ingham, Patricia (1976): 'The Evolution of *Jude the Obscure*', *Review of English Studies*, 27: 27–37, 159–69.

Ingham, Patricia (1989): *Thomas Hardy: A Feminist Reading* (Hemel Hempstead: Harvester Wheatsheaf).

Ingham, Patricia (ed.) (1997): Thomas Hardy: *The Pursuit of the Well-Beloved* and *The Well-Beloved* (London: Penguin).

Ingham, Patricia (ed.) (1998): Thomas Hardy: *The Woodlanders* (London: Penguin).

Jackson, Arlene M. (1984): 'Photography as Style and Metaphor in the Art of Thomas Hardy', in *Thomas Hardy Annual*, 2, (ed.) Norman Page (London: Macmillan), 91–109.

Jacobus, Mary (1975): 'Sue the Obscure', *Essays in Criticism*, 25: 304–29.

Jacobus, Mary (1976): 'Tess's Purity', *Essays in Criticism*, 26: 318–38; reprinted with alterations as 'Tess: The Making of a Pure Woman', in Susan Lipshitz (ed.) (1978) *Tearing the Veil: Essays in Femininity* (London: Routledge and Kegan Paul), 77–92.

Jacobus, Mary (ed.) (1979): *Women Writing and Writing about Women* (London: Croom Helm).

Jacobus, Mary (1982): 'Hardy's Magian Retrospect', *Essays in Criticism*, 32: 258–79.

Johnson, Bruce (1983): *True Correspondence: A Phenomenology of Thomas Hardy's Novels* (Tallahassee: Florida State University Press).

Johnson, Lionel (1894): *The Art of Thomas Hardy* (London: Mathews & Lane); revised edition, 1922.

Keith, W. J. (1988): *Regions of the Imagination: The Development of British Rural Fiction* (Toronto: University of Toronto Press).

Kettle, Arnold (1953): *'Tess of the d'Urbervilles'*, in *An Introduction to the English Novel*, Vol. 2 (London: Hutchinson University Library), 45–56.

Kiely, Robert (1993): 'The Menace of Solitude: The Politics and Aesthetics of Exclusion in *The Woodlanders*', in Margaret R. Higonnet (ed.) (1993a) *The Sense of Sex: Feminist Perspectives on Hardy* (Urbana and Chicago: University of Illinois Press), 188–202.

Kincaid, James R. (1993): 'Girl-watching, Child-beating, and Other Exercises for Readers of *Jude the Obscure*', in Margaret R. Higonnet (ed.) (1993a) *The Sense of Sex: Feminist Perspectives on Hardy* (Urbana and Chicago: University of Illinois Press), 132–48.

King, Jeannette (1978): 'Thomas Hardy: tragedy ancient and modern', in *Tragedy in the Victorian Novel* (Cambridge: Cambridge University Press), 97–126.

King, Jeannette (1992): *'The Mayor of Casterbridge*: Talking about Character', *Thomas Hardy Journal*, 8: 42–6.

Knoepflmacher, U.C. (1993): 'Hardy Ruins: Female Spaces and Male Designs', in Margaret R. Higonnet (ed.) (1993a) *The Sense of Sex: Feminist Perspectives on Hardy* (Urbana and Chicago: University of Illinois Press), 107–31.

Kramer, Dale (1975): *Thomas Hardy: The Forms of Tragedy* (London: Macmillan).

Kramer, Dale (ed.) (1979): *Critical Approaches to the Fiction of Thomas Hardy* (London: Macmillan).

Kramer, Dale (ed.) (1999a): *The Cambridge Companion to Thomas Hardy* (Cambridge: Cambridge University Press).

Kramer, Dale (1999b): 'Hardy and Readers: *Jude the Obscure*', in Dale Kramer (ed.) (1999a) *The Cambridge Companion to Thomas Hardy* (Cambridge: Cambridge University Press), 164–82.

Laird, J.T. (1975): *The Shaping of* Tess of the d'Urbervilles (Oxford: Clarendon Press).

Langbaum, Robert (1995): *Thomas Hardy in Our Time* (Basingstoke: Macmillan).

Langland, Elizabeth (1993): 'Becoming a Man in *Jude the Obscure*', in Margaret R. Higonnet (ed.) (1993a) *The Sense of Sex: Feminist Perspectives on Hardy* (Urbana and Chicago: University of Illinois Press), 32–48.

Larkin, Philip (1966): 'Wanted: Good Hardy Critic', *Critical Quarterly*, 6: 174–9; reprinted (1983) in *Required Writing* (London: Faber & Faber), 168–74.

Lawrence, D.H. (1936) 'Study of Thomas Hardy', in *Phoenix: The Posthumous Papers of D.H. Lawrence*, 398–516; extracts printed in R.P. Draper (ed.) (1975) *Hardy: The Tragic Novels: A Casebook* (London: Macmillan), 64–72.

Leavis, F.R. (1932): *New Bearings in English Poetry* (London: Chatto & Windus), 52–62.

Leavis, F.R. (1948): *The Great Tradition* (London: Chatto & Windus).

Lerner, Laurence (1975): *Thomas Hardy's* The Mayor of Casterbridge: *Tragedy or Social History?* (London: Chatto & Windus for Sussex University Press).

Lodge, David (1966), 'Tess, Nature, and the Voices of Hardy', in *Language of Fiction* (London: Routledge and Kegan Paul), 164–88.

Lodge, David (1977): 'Thomas Hardy as a Cinematic Novelist', in Lance St John Butler (ed.) (1977) *Thomas Hardy After Fifty Years* (London: Macmillan), 78–89.

Lucas, John (1977): *The Literature of Change: Studies in the Nineteenth-Century Provincial Novel* (Brighton: Harvester Press).

Lucas, John (1986): *Modern English Poetry from Hardy to Hughes* (London: Batsford).

Marsden, Kenneth (1969): *The Poems of Thomas Hardy: A Critical Introduction* (London: Athlone Press).

Meisel, Perry (1972): *Thomas Hardy: The Return of the Repressed* (New Haven and London: Yale University Press).

Miller, J. Hillis (1968): ' "Wessex Heights": The Persistence of the Past in Hardy's Poetry', *Critical Quarterly*, 10: 339–59.

Miller, J. Hillis (1970): *Thomas Hardy: Distance and Desire* (Cambridge, MA: Harvard University Press).

Miller, J. Hillis (1975): Introduction to New Wessex Edition of *The Well-Beloved* (London: Macmillan).

Miller, J. Hillis (1982): *Fiction and Repetition: Seven English Novels* (Oxford: Basil Blackwell).

Millgate, Michael (1971): *Thomas Hardy: His Career as a Novelist* (London: The Bodley Head).

Millgate, Michael (1982): *Thomas Hardy: A Biography* (London: Oxford University Press).

Millgate, Michael (ed.) (1984): *The Life and Work of Thomas Hardy*, by Thomas Hardy (London: Macmillan).

Millgate, Michael (1987): 'Unreal Estate: Reflections on Wessex and Yoknapatawpha', in R.P. Draper (ed.) (1987) *Thomas Hardy: Three Pastoral Novels: A Casebook* (London: Macmillan), 61–80.

Millgate, Michael (1999): 'Thomas Hardy: The Biographical Sources', in Dale Kramer (ed.) (1999a) *The Cambridge Companion to Thomas Hardy* (Cambridge: Cambridge University Press), 1–18.

Morgan, Rosemarie (1988): *Women and Sexuality in the Novels of Thomas Hardy* (London: Routledge).

Morrell, Roy (1965): *Thomas Hardy: The Will and the Way* (Kuala Lumpur: University of Malaya Press).

Orel, Harold (1963): *Thomas Hardy's Epic Drama: A Study of* The Dynasts (Lawrence: University of Kansas Press).

Orel, Harold (1979): 'What *The Dynasts* Meant to Hardy', *Victorian Poetry* 17: 109–23.

Page, Norman (1975): 'Hardy's Dutch Painting: *Under the Greenwood Tree*', *Thomas Hardy Year Book*, 5: 39–42; reprinted in R.P. Draper (ed.) (1987) *Thomas Hardy: Three Pastoral Novels: A Casebook* (London: Macmillan), 106–11.

Page, Norman (ed.) (1980a): *Thomas Hardy: The Writer and His Background* (London: Bell & Hyman).

Page, Norman (1980b): 'Hardy and the English Language', in Norman Page (ed.) (1980a) *Thomas Hardy: The Writer and His Background* (London: Bell & Hyman), 151–72.

Page, Norman (1999): 'Art and Aesthetics', in Dale Kramer (ed.) (1999a) *The Cambridge Companion to Thomas Hardy* (Cambridge: Cambridge University Press), 38–53.

Paterson, John (1960): *The Making of* The Return of the Native (Berkeley and Los Angeles: University of California Press).

Paulin, Tom (1975): *Thomas Hardy: The Poetry of Perception* (London: Macmillan).

Pettit, Charles P.C. (ed.) (1994): *New Perspectives on Thomas Hardy* (London: Macmillan).

Pinion, Frank B. (1977): *Thomas Hardy: Art and Thought* (London: Macmillan).

Pinion, Frank B. (1992): *Thomas Hardy: His Life and Friends* (Basingstoke: Macmillan).

Purdy, R.L. and Millgate, M. (1978–88): *The Collected Letters of Thomas Hardy*, 7 Vols (Oxford: Clarendon Press).

Quinn, Maire A. (1976): 'Wessex and the World', *Thomas Hardy Year Book*, 5: 70–5.

Ray, Martin (1997): *Thomas Hardy: A Textual Study of the Short Stories* (Aldershot: Ashgate).

Richardson, James (1977): *Thomas Hardy: The Poetry of Necessity* (Chicago and London: University of Chicago Press).

Rimmer, Mary (1993): 'Club Laws: Chess and the Construction of Gender in *A Pair of Blue Eyes*', in Margaret R. Higonnet (ed.) (1993a) *The Sense of Sex: Feminist Perspectives on Hardy* (Urbana and Chicago: University of Illinois Press), 203–20.

Riquelme, John Paul (1999): 'The Modernity of Thomas Hardy's Poetry', in Dale Kramer (ed.) (1999a) *The Cambridge Companion to Thomas Hardy* (Cambridge: Cambridge University Press), 204–23.

Rutland, William R. (1938): *Thomas Hardy: A Study of His Writings and Their Background* (Oxford: Basil Blackwell).

Ryan, Michael (1979): 'One Name of Many Shapes: *The Well-Beloved*', in Dale Kramer (ed.) (1979) *Critical Approaches to the Fiction of Thomas Hardy* (London: Macmillan), 172–92.

Sadoff, Dianne Fallon (1993): 'Looking at Tess: The Female Figure in Two Narrative Media', in Margaret R. Higonnet (ed.) (1993a) *The Sense of Sex: Feminist Perspectives on Hardy* (Urbana and Chicago: University of Illinois Press), 149–71.

Schweik, Robert (1999): 'The Influence of Religion, Science, and Philosophy on Hardy's Writings', in Dale Kramer (ed.) (1999a) *The Cambridge Companion to Thomas Hardy* (Cambridge: Cambridge University Press), 54–72.

Seymour-Smith, Martin (1994): *Hardy* (London: Bloomsbury Publishing).

Shires, Linda M. (1993): 'Narrative, Gender and Power in *Far from the Madding Crowd*', in Margaret R. Higonnet (ed.) (1993a) *The Sense of Sex: Feminist Perspectives on Hardy* (Urbana and Chicago: University of Illinois Press), 49–65.

Shires, Linda M. (ed.) (1997): Thomas Hardy, *The Trumpet-Major* (London: Penguin).

Shires, Linda M. (1999): 'The Radical Aesthetic of *Tess of the d'Urbervilles*', in Dale Kramer (ed.) (1999a) *The Cambridge Companion to Thomas Hardy* (Cambridge: Cambridge University Press), 145–63.

Showalter, Elaine (1979): 'The Unmanning of the Mayor of Casterbridge', in Dale Kramer (ed.) (1979) *Critical Approaches to the Fiction of Thomas Hardy* (London: Macmillan), 99–115.

Shuttleworth, Sally (ed.) (1999): Thomas Hardy, *Two on a Tower* (London: Penguin).

Silverman, Kaja (1984): 'History, Figuration and Female Subjectivity in *Tess of the d'Urbervilles*', *Novel* 18: 5–28.

Slade, Tony (ed.) (1999), Thomas Hardy, *The Return of the Native* (London: Penguin).

Southerington, F.R. (1971): *Hardy's Vision of Man* (London: Chatto & Windus).

Springer, Marlene (1983): *Hardy's Use of Allusion* (London: Macmillan).

Sumner, Rosemary (1981): *Thomas Hardy: Psychological Novelist* (London: Macmillan).

Sutherland, J.A. (1976): *Victorian Novelists and Publishers* (London: Athlone Press).

Tanner, Tony (1968): 'Colour and Movement in Hardy's *Tess of the d'Urbervilles*', *Critical Quarterly*, 10: 219–39; reprinted in R.P. Draper (ed.) (1975) *Hardy: The Tragic Novels: A Casebook* (London: Macmillan), 182–208.

Taylor, Dennis (1981): *Hardy's Poetry, 1860–1928* (London: Macmillan).

Taylor, Dennis (1986): 'Hardy and Wordsworth', *Victorian Poetry*, 24: 441–54.

Taylor, Dennis (1988): *Hardy's Metres and Victorian Prosody* (Oxford: Clarendon Press).

Taylor, Dennis (1993): *Hardy's Literary Language and Victorian Philology*. (Oxford: Clarendon Press).

Taylor, Dennis (ed.) (1998): Thomas Hardy, *Jude the Obscure* (London: Penguin).

Taylor, Dennis (1999): 'Hardy as a Nineteenth-Century Poet', in Dale Kramer (ed.) (1999a) *The Cambridge Companion to Thomas Hardy* (Cambridge: Cambridge University Press), 183–203.

Taylor, Richard H. (ed.) (1978): *The Personal Notebooks of Thomas Hardy* (London: Macmillan).

Taylor, Richard H. (1982): *The Neglected Hardy: Thomas Hardy's Lesser Novels* (London: Macmillan).

Thomson, George H. (1962): 'The *Trumpet-Major* Chronicle', *Nineteenth-Century Fiction*, 17: 45–56.

Toliver, Harold E. (1962) 'The Dance under the Greenwood Tree: Hardy's Bucolics', *Nineteenth-Century Fiction*, 17: 57–68.

Turner, Paul (1998): *The Life of Thomas Hardy: A Critical Biography* (Oxford: Blackwell).

Van Ghent, Dorothy (1953): *The English Novel: Form and Function* (New York: Holt Rinehart & Winstan); reprinted 1961 (New York: Harper).

Vigar, Penelope (1974): *The Novels of Thomas Hardy: Illusion and Reality* (London: Athlone Press).

Waldoff, Leon (1979): 'Psychological Determinism in *Tess of the d'Urbervilles*', in Dale Kramer (ed.) (1979) *Critical Approaches to the Fiction of Thomas Hardy* (London: Macmillan), 135–54.

Ward, John Powell (1991): *The English Line: Poetry of the Unpoetic from Wordsworth to Larkin* (Basingstoke: Macmillan).

Weber, Carl J. (1940): *Hardy of Wessex: His Life and Literary Career* (New York: Columbia University Press).

Webster, Harvey Curtis (1947): *On a Darkling Plain: The Art and Thought of Thomas Hardy* (Chicago and Cambridge: University of Chicago Press).

Widdowson, Peter (1989): *Hardy in History: A Study in Literary Sociology* (London: Routledge).

Widdowson, Peter (1996): *Thomas Hardy* (Plymouth: Northcote House in association with the British Council).

Widdowson, Peter (1999): 'Hardy and Critical Theory', in Dale Kramer (ed.) (1999a) *The Cambridge Companion to Thomas Hardy* (Cambridge: Cambridge University Press), 73–92.

Williams, Merryn (1972): *Thomas Hardy and Rural England* (London: Macmillan).

Williams, Raymond (1970): 'Thomas Hardy', in *The English Novel from Dickens to Lawrence* (London: Chatto & Windus); reprinted 1984 (London: Hogarth Press), 95–118.

Williams, Raymond (1973): 'Wessex and the Border', in *The Country and the City* (London: Chatto & Windus), 197–214.

Wing, George (1976): 'Middle-class Outcasts in Hardy's *A Laodicean*', *Humanities Association Review*, 27: 229–38.

Wing, George (1980): 'Hardy and Regionalism', in Norman Page (ed.) (1980a) *Thomas Hardy: The Writer and His Background* (London: Bell & Hyman), 76–101.

Woolf, Virginia (1932): 'The Novels of Thomas Hardy', in *The Common Reader: Second Series* (London: Hogarth Press); re-issued (1986), 245–57.

Wotton, George (1985): *Thomas Hardy: Towards a Materialist Criticism* (Goldenbridge: Gill & Macmillan).

Wright, Walter F. (1967): *The Shaping of* The Dynasts: *A Study in Thomas Hardy* (Lincoln: University of Nebraska Press).

Wright, T.R. (1989): *Hardy and the Erotic* (Basingstoke: Macmillan).

Zabel, Morton Dauwen (1940): 'Hardy in Defence of his Art: The Aesthetic of Incongruity', *Southern Review*, 6: 125–49.

Zietlow, Paul (1974): *Moments of Vision: The Poetry of Thomas Hardy* (Cambridge, MA: Harvard University Press).

FURTHER RESOURCES

Web site: The Thomas Hardy Association and The Thomas Hardy Society: http://www.yale.edu/hardysoc/SOCIETY%20UK/HardySoc.htm.

Victoria Research Web site: http://www.indiana.edu/~victoria/.

INDEX

Abercorn, Duchess of 36
absurdist form 75, 76, 100, 149
Academy 33, 42
Adler, Alfred 169
Aeneid 11
Aeschylus 146, 147, 150
agricultural decline 8, 30, 87,
    153–4, 156
agricultural labourer 7–8, 30,
    152–3
allusion, use of 96, 181
Althusser, Louis 146, 180, 183
American readers 28, 114
Antell, John (uncle) 39
archaeology 199
Archer, William 42
Architectural Association 13
architecture, influence on fiction
    13, 28–9, 105–7
Arch, Joseph 30
Aristotle 71, 76, 150–1
Armstrong, Isobel 139
Arnold, Matthew 32, 85, 121, 159,
    195; 'Pagan and Medieval
    Religious Sentiment' 28, 106;
    'The Scholar Gypsy' 89
astronomy 107–8, 199
Athenaeum 20, 36, 42
Athenaeum Club 37
Atlantic Monthly 29, 30
Auden, W.H. 145, 190
Augustan poetry 192

Bakhtin, Mikhail 181
Baldwin, Stanley 5, 53
ballad form: fiction 64, 65, 117,
    161; poetry 124–5
Barnes, William 9–10, 33, 44
Barrie, Sir James 52–3, 140
Bastow, Henry 10
Bayley, John 95, 203
Beckett, Samuel 197
Beeny Cliff 18, 46
Beer, Gillian 201

Belgravia 26
Bennett, Arnold 48
Berger, Sheila 71
biblical imagery 68
Bishop, Elizabeth 10
Björk, Lennart, *The Literary
    Notebooks of Thomas Hardy*
    25–6
Blomfield, Arthur 13, 16
Bockhampton *see* Higher
    Bockhampton
Boer War 41, 42, 128–9, 196
Boscastle 46
Boumelha, Penny 71, 82, 88, 93,
    183–4, 186–7, 188, 189
Bournemouth 25
Braddon, Mary Elizabeth 94
Brady, Kristin 119, 187–8
British Museum Library 28, 41
Brooks, Jean R. 76, 87, 149–50, 163
Brown, Douglas 70, 76, 82, 87,
    153–4, 156
Browne, Martha 10–11, 35
Browning, Elizabeth 41
Browning, Robert 15, 41, 135, 195,
    201; *The Ring and the Book* 196
Buckler, William E. 135, 141
Bugler, Gertrude 51
Bullen, J.B. 200
Byron, Lord 33, 120

Carlyle, Thomas 159, 201
Casagrande, Peter J. 66
Cecil, Lord David 153, 156
censorship 5, 22, 34, 35–6, 182
Chambers's Journal 15
Chambers, Robert, *Vestiges of the
    Natural History of Creation* 12
change, theme of 66–7, 73, 76,
    105, 106, 151, 154–5, 176, 201
Chapman & Hall 17
Chapman, Raymond 204
Chapple, J.A.V. 54
Chase, Mary Ellen 198

Chesterton, G.K. 48
Church, the 8, 197; attack on 85–6, 88–9, 91, 109, 110; influence on education 8–9 *see also* religious faith, loss of; science, debate between religion and
Clare, John 136, 192
classical imagery 61, 68, 69, 85–6, 91, 149 *see also* Aeschylus; Aristotle; Sophocles
Clodd, Edward 41, 44
Cockerell, Sir Sydney 52
Collins, Deborah L. 202
Collins, Wilkie 16, 19, 94
colour imagery 161
comedy 60, 71, 100, 101, 119; bathos 81; irony 74, 91, 103–4, 108–10, 112, 113, 115, 128, 156; poetry 124, 128, 195; satire 97, 99, 101, 109, 110, 112, 146; tragi-comedy 76, 79 108, 112, 146, 149
Comte, Auguste 14–15, 16, 23, 27, 67–8, 69, 108, 121, 169, 194, 199, 202; *A General View of Positivism* 14
Conrad, Joseph 44
continuity 59, 62, 64, 103–4, 122; influence of outsiders on 77–9, 102 *see also* change; urban life
Copyright Association 25
copyright laws 20, 25
Cornhill 21, 22, 24–5, 101
Cornwall 18, 20, 157
Crickmay, G.R. 16, 17
Crimean War 10
Culler, Jonathan, *The Pursuit of Signs* 184
Cunningham, Valentine 107
cycling 41, 43

Daily Telegraph 52
Danby, John F. 60
Darwin, Charles 11–12, 16, 168, 199, 201–2; *On the Origin of Species* 12; theme in fiction 77, 81; theme in poetry 121
Darwin, Erasmus, *Zoonomia* 12
Davie, Donald 135–6, 191–2, 195

Davies, Sarah 101
Dean, Susan 139
deconstruction 87, 166–7
De Laura, David J. 93
Derrida, Jacques 145, 166, 181
Dickens, Charles 13, 16, 20; *Hard Times* 9
Disraeli, Benjamin 25, 159
Dolin, Tim 101
Dorchester 8, 9, 10–11, 13, 22, 29, 30–4, 141, 152
Dorset 5, 27, 29, 30, 152, 158
Dorset County Chronicle 24, 31–2
Doyle, Arthur Conan 48
Draffan, Robert A. 60
Draper, R.P. 156
Dryden, John, *Works of Virgil* 6
Dugdale, Florence *see* Hardy, Florence

Ebbatson, Roger 96, 104, 119, 181–2, 201
education as theme in fiction 9, 34, 78, 88
Edward VII, King 42
Eliot, George 16, 23–4, 36, 122, 150, 159; *Adam Bede* 24
Eliot, T.S. 191
Elliott, Ralph W.V. 204
Ellis, Havelock 29, 30
English Review 45, 125
Escuret, Annie 200
Essays and Reviews (1860) 12

fatalism 6, 12, 27, 72, 83, 87, 92–3, 147, 149, 150, 161, 162
Faulkner, William 156
Feltes, N.N. 54
feminist criticism 65, 70, 71, 76, 82, 83, 88, 93, 96, 98, 100, 101, 145, 172–4, 179, 182–9, 203, 204
Feuerbach, L.A. 199
First World War 5, 48–9, 128, 129–30
Fisher, Joe 96, 180–1
folk tales 22, 161
Ford, Boris 54
Fordington 11
Fortnightly Review 36, 47–8, 49

Foucault, Michel 188
Fourier, Charles 82, 169
Freud, Sigmund 26, 65, 88, 93, 167–71
Frost, Robert 192

Galsworthy, John 48, 53
Garson, Marjorie 65, 70, 81–2, 88, 172–4, 188
Gatrell, Simon 66, 157–8, 198–9
gender issues 34, 88, 93, 96, 98, 182–9, 204
The Gentleman's Magazine 25
Georgian poets 190
Gibson, James 29, 46, 50, 53–4
Gifford, Edwin Hamilton 24
Gifford, Emma *see* Hardy, Emma
Gifford, John 21
Gifford, Lilian 47
Giordano, Frank R. 76, 168–9
Gissing, George 32
Gittings, Robert 6, 17, 46, 50, 53
Gladstone, William 32
The Golden Treasury, Palgrave 195
Goldsmith, Oliver, *The Vicar of Wakefield* 66
Goode, John 60, 66, 87, 93, 98, 104, 178–9
Good Words 27–8
Gosse, Edmund 33, 53, 89, 108
Grahame, Elspeth 41
Granville Barker, Harley 48, 52
Graphic 20, 30, 32, 34, 35–6
Graves, Robert 51
Gray, Thomas 5; 'Elegy Written in a Country Churchyard' 61
Great Chain of Being, concept of 11–12
Gregor, Ian 76, 81, 93–4, 141, 163–4
Gribble, Jennifer 70
Grove, Agnes 40, 52
Grundy, Joan 199–200
Grundyism 5, 35
Guerard, Albert J. 145

Haggard, H., Rider, *King Solomon's Mines* 8
Hand, Jemima *see* Hardy, Jemima
Hands, Timothy 135, 202

hanging 10–11, 115
Harding, Louisa 10, 140
Hardy, Emma (1st wife) 29, 40, 42, 49, 50, 96, 122, 140; courtship 18, 21, 22, 23; death 46, 51, 131–3, 189, 194; marriage 24–5, 37, 41, 44, 141; *Some Recollections* 18, 46
Hardy, Florence Emily (2nd wife) 43–4, 45, 46, 197; *The Early Life of Thomas Hardy*, *The Later Years of Thomas Hardy* 49–50, 53, 139, 140; marriage 47, 51
Hardy, Frank George (cousin) 49
Hardy, Henry (brother) 6, 7, 29, 31, 46, 47
Hardy, Jemima (mother) 6–7, 8, 9, 10, 25, 27, 31, 37, 126, 189; death 43, 45
Hardy, Katherine (Kate, sister) 6, 25, 37, 38–9, 47
Hardy, Mary (grandmother) 7, 45, 126, 189
Hardy, Mary (sister) 6, 25, 37, 38, 40, 49
Hardy Players 44, 51
Hardy, Thomas (father) 6–7, 8, 31, 51, 58, 126
Hardy, Thomas (grandfather) 8, 58
Hardy, Thomas (writer), non-fiction: *Architectural Notebook* 197; 'Candour in English Fiction' 35; 'The Dorsetshire Labourer' 30, 153, 181; *Life and Work of Thomas Hardy (Life)* 7, 11, 18, 32, 33, 35, 37, 44, 49–50, 53, 82, 107, 125, 135, 139–41, 146–7, 171, 197, 198; *Literary Notebooks* 25–6, 169, 198; 'On the Application of Coloured Bricks and Terra Cotta to Modern Architecture' 13; *Personal Notebooks* 198; Preface to *Select Poems of William Barnes* 44; 'The Profitable Reading of Fiction' 32; *Studies, Specimens etc.* 15, 198; 'The Trumpet Major Notebook' 28
Hardy, Thomas (writer), novels: *Desperate Remedies* 17, 19, 20,

10

57, 94–6, 140, 169–70, 181, 185, 203; *Far from the Madding Crowd* 8, 10, 21–4, 48, 57, 61–6, 152, 158, 159, 162, 164, 170, 171, 173, 176, 179, 185, 186–7, 188, 198, 201; *The Hand of Ethelberta* 25, 26, 57, 98–101, 158, 181, 185, 189, 203; *Jude the Obscure* 9, 38–40, 57, 88–94, 140, 148, 149, 150, 151–2, 156, 159, 164, 168, 170, 172, 176, 181, 182, 184, 186, 188; 198, 199, 201, 202–3; *A Laodicean* 13, 28–9, 57, 105–7, 158, 170; *The Mayor of Casterbridge* 8, 10, 31–4, 57, 71–6, 147, 149, 150–1, 153, 158, 159, 164, 168, 170, 171, 179, 183, 188; *A Pair of Blue Eyes* 13, 17, 18, 20–1, 57, 96–8, 140, 157, 159, 170, 179, 186, 189, 199; *The Poor Man and the Lady* 7, 16, 19, 20–1, 29, 94, 97; *The Return of the Native* 26–7, 57, 66–71, 146–7, 148, 150–1, 153, 158, 159, 164, 179, 183–4, 186, 198, 199; *Tess of the d'Urbervilles* 8, 11, 13, 14, 16, 20, 25, 26, 34–7, 40, 57, 82–8, 147–8, 150, 151, 153–4, 155–6, 158, 159, 160, 161, 162, 164, 166–7, 168–9, 171–2, 174, 175, 179, 181, 182, 184, 185, 186, 188, 198, 199, 200, 201, 203; *The Trumpet Major* 27–8, 44, 57, 101–4, 158; *Two on a Tower* 29–30, 57, 107–10, 158, 171, 199, 203; *Under the Greenwood Tree* 8, 17, 19–20, 57, 58–60, 128, 157, 158, 179, 181, 186–7; *The Well-Beloved* 10, 37–8, 40, 57, 110–14, 165, 170, 172, 199; *The Woodlanders* 33, 57, 77–82; 147, 149–50, 151, 158, 159, 164, 170, 171, 173, 176, 181, 184, 186–7, 189, 199, 201

Hardy, Thomas (writer), play: *The Famous Tragedy of the Queen of Cornwall* 51

Hardy, Thomas (writer), poems: 'After a Journey' 46, 192, 195;

'Afternoon Service at Mellstock' 8, 49; 'After the Last Breath' 43, 45, 189; 'After the Visit' 44; 'Afterwards' 125–6; 'Ah, are you Digging on my Grave' 48, 124; 'An Ancient to Ancients' 124, 134; 'At an Inn' 38, 40; 'At a Seaside Town in 1869' 17; 'At Castle Boterel' 131–2, 195; 'At Middle-Field Gate in February' 126; 'At the Railway Station, Upway' 122; 'At the Word "Farewell"' 18; 'An August Midnight' 126; 'Beeny Cliff' 46; 'Beyond the Last Lamp' 48; 'A Broken Appointment' 38, 42, 126–7; 'By Henstridge Cross at the Year's End' 193; 'Channel Firing' 47–8, 129; 'The Chapel-Organist' 130; 'Childhood among the Ferns' 52; 'A Choirmaster's Burial' 8; 'Christmas in the Elgin Room' 52; 'A Church Romance' 6, 45, 126, 195; *Collected Poems* 50, 119–20, 191; 'Coming up Oxford Street; Evening' 133; 'Concerning Agnes' 52, 193; 'The Convergence of the Twain' 47, 48, 126, 192, 195; 'The Coquette, and After' 130; 'The Dance at the Phoenix' 196; 'The Dark-eyed Gentleman' 194; 'The Darkling Thrush' 42, 123, 193, 196; 'The Division' 38, 45; 'Domicilium' 7, 120, 189; 'Dream of the City Shopwoman' 133; 'Drinking Song' 52; 'Drummer Hodge' 41, 128–9, 196, 197; 'During Wind and Rain' 49, 122–3, 189, 192, 195, 197; *The Dynasts* 41, 42–3, 44, 48, 50, 99, 120, 136–9, 162, 165, 196, 199, 201, 202; 'Family Portraits' 52; 'The Fire at Tranter Sweatley's' 25, 40–1; 'Former Beauties' 130; 'Friends Beyond' 40, 128, 195; 'God's Education' 45; 'God's Funeral'

48, 121; 'The Going of the Battery' 41; 'He Never Expected Much' 52; 'Heredity' 49, 122; 'He Resolves to Say No More' 52, 197; *Human Shows, Far Phantasies, Songs and Trifles* 51–2; 'I Found Her out There' 193; 'I Looked Up from My Writing' 49; 'I Look into My Glass' 40; 'Immanent Will' 126; 'The Impercipient' 40, 196, 197; 'In a Eweleaze near Weatherbury' 130–1, 194; 'In Death Divided' 38, 127; 'In Tenebris I' 42, 124, 134; 'In Tenebris III' 7; 'In the Days of Crinoline' 194; 'In the Servants' Quarters' 48; 'In Time of "The Breaking of Nations"' 48, 49, 122, 130, 197; 'I Watched a Blackbird' 52; 'The Last Signal' 33, 195; 'Last Words to a Dumb Friend' 51; *Late Lyrics and Earlier* 50–1, 121–2; 'The Levelled Churchyard' 195; 'Logs on the Hearth' 49, 128; 'Lyrics and Reveries' 47; 'The Man he Killed' 129; '"Men who March Away"' 48, 197; 'Middle-Age Enthusiasms' 40; 'Midnight on the Great Western' 134; 'Miscellaneous Poems' 42, 48; *Moments of Vision* 49, 120; 'My Spirit will not Haunt the Mound' 194; 'Nature's Questioning' 125, 196, 197; 'Neutral Tones' 15, 40, 124, 196; 'The New Dawn's Business' 52; 'No Buyers' 133, 194; 'Old Furniture' 49, 122, 195; 'The Old Workman' 133, 193; 'On an Invitation to the United States' 196; 'One Ralph Blossom Soliloquizes' 194; 'One We Knew' 7, 45, 126, 189; 'On One Who Lived and Died Where He Was Born' 51; 'On Stinsford Hill at Midnight' 193; 'On the Departure Platform'

45, 133; 'On the Esplanade' 17; 'The Opportunity' 51; 'Overlooking the River Stour' 26, 126, 192; 'The Oxen' 8, 49, 126; 'Panthera' 45; 'The Phantom Horsewoman' 46, 132–3; 'The Pity of It' 49; 'Poems of 1912–13' 18, 46, 120, 131; 'Poems of Pilgrimage' 42; *Poems of the Past and the Present* 42; 'A Poor Man and a Lady' 17; 'Proud Songsters' 52; 'Rain on a Grave' 197; 'The Ruined Maid' 42, 124, 130, 195, 196; *Satires of Circumstance* 44, 45, 46–8, 120; 'The Self-Unseeing' 6, 42, 123–4, 189; 'She, to Him' 15; 'A Sheep Fair' 51; 'Shelley's Skylark' 42, 121, 196; 'Shut out that Moon' 121, 134; 'A Singer Asleep' 45, 48, 134; 'Snow in the Suburbs' 24, 51, 133; 'Something Tapped' 127; 'The Souls of the Slain' 41, 129, 196; 'Standing by the Mantelpiece' 23, 52; 'The Strange House' 51; 'A Sunday Morning Tragedy' 45, 125; 'Surview' 197; 'Tess's Lament' 42; 'Thoughts of Phena, at News of her Death' 17, 37, 40, 126; 'A Thunderstorm in Town' 38; *Time's Laughingstocks* 43, 45; 'To an Unborn Pauper Child' 42; 'To Lizbie Browne' 10, 127; 'To Louisa in the Lane' 10, 52; 'A Trampwoman's Tragedy' 45, 125, 130; 'Two-Years Idyll' 26; 'The Voice' 46, 131, 195; 'Voices from Things Growing in a Churchyard' 51, 128, 197; 'Waiting Both' 51; 'The Walk' 46, 131; 'War Poems' 42; 'A Wasted Illness' 29; 'We Field-Women' 133; 'The Well-Beloved' 112, 113; 'We Sat at the Window' 25; 'Wessex Heights' 38, 127, 158, 165–6, 192, 193, 197; *Wessex Poems* 15, 40–1; 'When I Set Out for

Lyonnesse' 18; 'Who's in the Next Room?' 128; 'Why Do I?' 52; *Winter Words* 23, 52, 124; 'A Wish for Unconsciousness' 52, 124
Hardy, Thomas (writer), short stories: *A Changed Man and Other Tales* 47, 57, 115; 'The Distracted Preacher' 28, 34, 119, 158; 'Fellow-Townsmen' 28, 34, 119; 'The Fiddler of the Reels' 38; 'The First Countess of Wessex' 119; *A Group of Noble Dames* 34, 57, 114, 199; 'How I Built Myself a House' 15; 'An Imaginative Woman' 38, 115, 118; *An Indiscretion in the Life of an Heiress* 17, 119, 181; 'Interlopers at the Knap' 6, 34, 119; *Life's Little Ironies* 38, 57, 114–15, 116; 'The Melancholy Hussar of the German Legion' 38, 116; 'On the Western Circuit' 38, 117–18; 'Our Exploits at West Poley' 119; 'The Romantic Adventures of a Milkmaid' 30, 115, 118–19; 'The Three Strangers' 30, 34, 115, 158; 'A Tradition of Eighteen Hundred and Four' 38, 115–16; *Wessex Tales* 34, 57, 114, 115, 158; 'The Withered Arm' 11, 34, 116–17
Harper & Brothers 39, 40, 42
Harper's New Monthly Magazine 28, 29, 39, 48
Hartmann, Edward von, *Philosophy of the Unconscious* 137, 199
Harvey, Geoffrey 136
Head, Mary (grandmother) 39
Hegel, G.W.F. 190
Henniker, Florence 38, 40, 45, 127, 141
Hetherington, Tom 114
Hicks, John 9, 10, 16
Higher Bockhampton 6–8, 13, 16–17, 19, 22, 37, 141
Higonnet, Margaret R. 88, 188
historical perspective 22, 60, 66, 73, 87, 101–3 104, 137, 153,

155, 156–7, 172, 175–9; New Historicism 183
Hoare, Lady 47
Hogg, Jabez, *Elements of Experimental and Natural Philosophy* 12
Holder, Revd Caddell 18, 21
Holloway, John 87
Hopkins, Gerard Manley 195
Housman, A.E. 53
How, W.W. 39
Howard, Jeanne 60
Howe, Irving 93, 95, 153, 156
humanist criticism 70–1, 76, 81, 93–4, 146, 156, 158–64, 175, 180; existential 65, 87, 139, 149–50, 162; Marxist 87, 175; New Criticism 87, 145, 159, 162
Hume, David 194
Husserl, E.G.A. 202
Hutchins, John, *History and Antiquities of the County of Dorset* 28, 114
Hutton, Richard Holt 27, 32, 33, 36
Huxley, T.H. 11–12
Hyde, William J. 154
Hynes, Samuel 135, 190; *The Pattern of Hardy's Poetry* 191

Ibsen, Henrik 114
Iliad 11
Illustrated London News 36, 37
Immanent Will 27, 43, 121, 126, 138, 162, 199, 201, 202
Ingham, Patricia 96, 98, 114, 184–5, 198
Irwin, Michael 141
Italy, trip to 33, 196

Jackson, Arlene M. 200
Jacobus, Mary 88, 93, 98, 182
James, Henry 32, 150
Jameson, Fredric 146, 174; *The Political Unconscious* 178
Jefferies, Richard 156
Jeune, Lady Mary 36, 39, 40
Johnson, Bruce 202
Johnson, Lionel 70, 76, 147–8, 153

Johnson, Samuel, *Rasselas* 6
Joyce, James 168
Jung, Carl 88, 169

Kean, Charles 14
Keats, John 33, 120; 'Ode to a
    Nightingale' 123
Kegan Paul, Charles 28
Keith, W.J. 155–6
Kettle, Arnold 87, 175
Kiely, Robert 82, 188–9
Kimmeridge 15
Kincaid, James R. 94
King, Jeannette 76, 150
Kingston Maurward 7
Kipling, Rudyard 48, 53
Knoepflmacher, U.C., 'Hardy's
    Ruins: Female Spaces and Male
    Designs' 189
Kramer, Dale 66, 70, 76, 81, 93,
    150–2, 202–3
Kristeva, Julia 172

Lacan, Jacques 65, 70, 81–2, 88,
    104, 146, 167, 170–4, 181
Laird, J.T. 198
Laing, R.D., *The Divided Self* 170;
    Self and Others 170
Langbaum, Robert 70
Langland, Elizabeth 93, 188
language 133–5, 196, 203–4
Larkin, Philip 134, 135, 136, 190–1,
    192
Last, Isaac 9
Lawrence, D.H. 65, 86, 87, 93, 145,
    148, 168
Lawrence, T.E. 51
Leavis, F.R. 190
Lerner, Laurence 76
Lewis, Cecil Day 134
Locker, Arthur 35
Lodge, David 161, 200, 203
London 13–16, 20, 24, 27–9, 32–3,
    37, 99, 112, 113, 140
London Mercury 51
Longman's Magazine 30
loss, sense of 58, 60, 75, 126–7,
    127–8
Lucas, John 98, 136, 195
Lyceum Club 44

Lyell, Sir Charles 16; *Principles of
    Geology* 12

MacDonald, Ramsay 53
Macmillan, Alexander 16, 19, 27;
    Wessex Edition 45–6
Macmillan, Sir Frederick 43, 45
Macmillan Pocket Edition 44
Macmillan's Magazine 20, 33, 35
Mantell, Gideon Algernon, *The
    Wonders of Geology* 12
market for fiction 20, 32, 35, 101,
    180–1
marriage, theme of 34, 92, 95, 109,
    117–18, 119; adultery and
    divorce 39, 79, 88
Marsden, Kenneth 135
Martineau, Harriet 34
Martin, Julia Augusta 7, 140
Marxist criticism 60, 65–6, 71, 82,
    87, 93, 96, 100, 101, 104, 119,
    145, 146, 156–7, 174, 175–82,
    183, 204; poetry 136, 193–4
materialist criticism *see* Marxist
    criticism
Max Gate 31–4, 44, 46, 47, 48, 49,
    51, 107
M'Culloch, J.M.R., *Principles of
    Political Economy* 14
medieval, interest in the 28, 105–7
Meisel, Perry 76, 93, 168
Melbury Osmond 6, 33
melodrama 64, 65, 75, 86, 94–5,
    100, 107, 109, 110
Meredith, George 17, 19, 32, 45
Miller, J. Hillis 87, 94, 110, 113,
    139, 164–7, 181
Mill, John Stuart 16, 34, 85, 90,
    121; *On Liberty* 14;
    Utilitarianism 14
Millgate, Michael 15, 17, 18,
    26–7, 41, 53, 71, 81, 95, 98,
    101, 107, 110, 113, 140, 141,
    156, 197–8
Milton, John 196; *Lycidas* 61;
    Paradise Lost 201
modernism 145, 196–7, 200
Morgan, Rosemarie 65, 71, 88, 93,
    141, 185–6
Morley, John 16

Morrell, Roy 65, 87, 95–6, 139, 162; *Thomas Hardy: The Will and the Way* 190
Morris, Mowbray 36
Morton, Thomas, *Speed the Plough* 5
Moule, Henry 43
Moule, Revd Henry 11, 13
Moule, Horace 11–13, 14, 21, 23, 35, 52, 96, 195; reviews 19, 20
Murray's Magazine 35
music 6, 8, 14, 19, 50, 58, 59, 195, 196, 199
mutability 15, 123

Napoleonic era 7, 25, 28, 33, 43, 101, 102–3, 104, 114 136–7, 196
National Observer 36
nature 6, 7, 52, 58, 123, 124, 125–6; Wordsworth's view of 14, 120–1, 153, 156, 192; symbolism of 60, 66–7, 70, 77, 79, 86, 112, 113
nature, organic unity of 159
Nelson, Horatio 43
Newbold, Henry 46
Newman, John Henry 159; *Apologia pro Vita Sua* 14
New Quarterly Magazine 28
New Review 35
New Statesman 190
New Woman 34, 39, 88, 93, 105–6
Nicholls, Eliza Bright 15, 16, 40, 47
Nicholls, Mary Jane 15, 17
North American Review 45
Novalis 72
'Novels of Character and Environment' 57, 58, 60, 114, 180, 204
'Novels of Ingenuity' 57, 98, 105

oral tradition 84, 115, 116
Orel, Harold 139
Osgood, McIlvaine & Co. 34, 36, 38, 39
Owen, Wilfred 48, 129
Oxford 11
Oxford Movement 14

paganism, conflict with Christianity 28, 68, 85–6, 90, 106
Page, Norman 60, 200, 203
Pall Mall Magazine 38, 39, 52
Pater, Walter 32
Paterson, Helen 22, 23, 51
Paterson, John 198
Patmore, Coventry 33; *The Angel in the House* 34
Paulin, Tom 136, 194–5
pessimism 6, 42, 51, 60, 124, 201
Petrarch 127
Pinion, F.B. 53, 95
Polanski, Roman, *Tess* (film) 188
Pole, Catherine (Cassie) 17
politics 32; radical 5, 16
Pope, Alexander, *An Essay on Man* 12
Portsmouth, Lady 33
post-structuralism 145, 146, 166, 183, 188, 204
Pound, Ezra 134, 191
Providence and Mr Hardy, Deacon, Louis and Coleman, Terry 17
psychological viewpoint: in fiction 26, 32, 62, 65, 66, 72, 79, 83–4, 95, 96, 98, 111, 118, 154–5; psychoanalytic theorists 65, 70, 76, 83, 87–8, 94, 113–14, 119, 146, 148, 167–74, 188–9, 203
Puddletown 7, 10, 17, 22, 158

Quarterly Review 36
Quinn, Maire A. 154

Ransom, John Crowe, *The New Criticism* 145
Ray, Martin 119, 199
realism 57, 58, 59–60, 65, 71, 73–4, 80, 84–5, 100, 101, 105, 109–10, 117, 152–3, 154, 156–7, 160–1, 204; anti-realism 26, 57, 88,145, 200
regionalism 154–6
religious faith, loss of 5, 10, 12, 15, 16, 23, 121–2, 196, 199, 202
revision of work 140, 198
Richardson, James 135, 192–3
Rimmer, Mary 98, 189

Riquelme, John Paul 196–7
'Romances and Fantasies' 57, 96, 107, 113, 114
Romantics, the 15, 42, 120–1, 123, 134, 135, 192–3
Royal Observatory 29
Royal Society of Literature 46
Ruskin, John 14, 107, 200, 201
Rutland, William R. 95, 162
Ryan, Michael 114

Sadoff, Dianne Fallon 188
Saint-Pierre, Bernardin de, *Paul et Virginie* 6
Samson Low 29, 30
Sassoon, Siegfried 48, 50
Saturday Review 11, 19, 20, 30, 33, 36, 39, 42, 45, 48
Savile Club 27
Schlesinger, John, *Far from the Madding Crowd* (film) 66
Schopenhauer, Arthur, *The World as Will and Idea* 27, 43, 121, 126, 137–8, 199, 202
Schweik, Robert 199
science: developments in 5, 12, 16; debate between religion and 11–12, 14–15; theme in fiction 78, 107–8, 110, 199
Seale, James 11
seasonal rhythm 19, 59, 62, 66, 77, 86, 126
sensation fiction 94, 95–6
serial form 20, 27, 32, 33, 69, 82, 198
sexuality, theme of: fiction 62, 63, 65, 66, 70, 71, 79–80, 82–3, 88, 90–1, 96, 97, 101, 107, 110, 111, 113–14, 115, 148, 149, 169–72, 182–9; poetry 130–1
Seymour-Smith, Martin 53
Shakespeare, William 14, 148, 149, 156; *As You Like It* 58
Sharpe, John (uncle) 8
Sharpe, Martha (aunt) 8
Shaw, George Bernard 44
Shelley, Percy Bysshe 33, 90–1, 121, 192; 'Epipsychidion' 37–8, 91, 111; 'Ode to the West Wind' 197; 'To a Skylark' 123

Shires, Linda M. 104, 200–1
Shirley, Revd Arthur 6, 8, 9
Showalter, Elaine 76, 183, 188
Shuttleworth, Sally 110
Silverman, Kaja 172
Smith, Elder & Co. 23, 25, 26, 28, 32
Smith, T. Roger 20, 21
social class 5, 7, 9; theme in fiction 25, 34, 60, 67, 78–9, 81, 86, 90, 95, 96, 97, 98, 99, 109, 110, 115, 119 *see also* Marxist criticism
sociological viewpoint: fiction 26, 76, 87, 152–3, 154–5, 157, 180; poetry 133
Sophocles 81, 146, 148, 150, 151, 161
Southerington, F.R. 138–9, 202
Southern Review 145
Sparks, Martha (cousin) 10
Sparks, Tryphena (cousin) 17, 37, 40, 126, 131
Spectator 19, 21, 23, 27, 32, 33, 36, 44, 140
Spenser, Edmund 196
Springer, Marlene 96
Star 36
Stephen, Leslie 21–3, 24, 26, 43, 190; *An Agnostic's Apology* 23
Stevenson, Robert Louis 33
Stinsford choir 8, 19, 58
Stinsford Church 6, 9, 53
St James's Gazette 30, 33
St Juliot 18–19, 20, 46
Strachey, Lytton 190
Strauss, David Friedrich, *Der Leben Jesu* 122
structuralism 94, 110, 139, 145, 164–7
Sturminster Newton 26, 27, 35
Sumner, Rosemary 65, 70, 76, 88, 93, 96, 98, 107, 110, 113–14, 169–70
Sutherland, J.A. 54
Swanage 25
Swetman, Betty (grandmother) 33
Swinburne, Algernon Charles 45, 134: *Poems and Ballads* 15, 195

Tanner, Tony 67, 161

Taylor, Dennis 94, 98, 101, 104, 107, 110, 113, 135, 192, 195–6, 204
Tennyson, Alfred 15, 27, 96, 134; *Idylls of the King* 196; *In Memoriam* 23
text, evolution of 198–9
Thomson, George H. 104
The Thoughts of the Emperor M. Aurelius Antoninus 23
Tillotson, W.F. 35, 37
time, passage of (poetry) 125–7
Times 48, 49, 52
Tinsley Brothers 17, 19
Tinsleys' Magazine 20
Titanic 47, 126
Toliver, Harold E. 60
Tolstoy, Leo 148
tragedy 70, 71, 74, 81, 87, 91–3, 100, 101, 146–52, 160
Trollope, Anthony 16, 20
Turner, J.M.W. 14, 200
Turner, Paul 53

urban life 70–1, 89, 115, 118–19, 153–5, 177
Utilitarian Society 14

Van Ghent, Dorothy 87, 160–1
Victoria, Queen 5, 10, 33
Vigar, Penelope 199
Virgil, *Georgics* 61
visual aspects of work 14, 58, 60, 63, 64–5, 80, 133, 161, 199–200

Waldoff, Leon 88, 169
War Propaganda Bureau 48
Ward, John Powell 136, 192

Way, Augusta 35, 51
Weber, Carl J., *Hardy of Wessex* 190
Webster, Harvey Curtis 162, 201
Wells, H.G. 44, 48
Wessex 5, 22, 25, 26, 29, 31, 33, 45, 65, 145, 146, 152–8, 180–1
Westminster Review 23–4, 29, 30, 36
Weymouth 16, 17, 19, 28
Wheel of Fortune 74–5
Widdowson, Peter 101, 136, 156, 180, 193–4, 204
Wilberforce, Bishop 11–12
Wilde, Oscar, *The Picture of Dorian Gray* 114
Williams, Merryn 87, 156–7
Williams, Raymond 65–6, 154–5, 175–7
Wimborne, Lord and Lady 29
Wimborne Minster 29–30
Wing, George 107, 154
women, status of 5, 9, 34; in poetry 130–1 *see also* feminist criticism; New Woman
Woolcombe 35
Woolf, Virginia 48, 145
Wordsworth, William 5, 14, 120–1, 136, 153; *Lyrical Ballads* 133, 192
The World 40
Wotton, George 60, 66, 71, 177
Wright, T.R. 65, 93, 110, 113, 171–2
Wright, Walter F. 139

Yeats, W.B. 46, 135, 191
Yeovil 25

Zabel, Morton Dauwen 145
Zietlow, Paul 136, 194